Shadows on the Past

Studies in the Historical Fiction Film

IN THE SERIES *Culture and the Moving Image*

EDITED BY ROBERT SKLAR

Shadows on the Past

Studies in the Historical Fiction Film

LEGER GRINDON

Temple University Press
Philadelphia

Temple University Press, Philadelphia 19122
Copyright © 1994 by Temple University. All rights reserved
Published in 1994
Printed in the United States of America

The paper used in this publication meets the minimum requirements
of American National Standard for Information Sciences—
Permanence of Paper for Printed Library Materials
ANSI Z39.48-1984 ∞

Library of Congress Cataloging-in-Publication Data

Grindon, Leger, 1949–
    Shadows on the past : Studies in the historical fiction film / Leger Grindon.
        p.   cm.—(Culture and the moving image)
    Includes bibliographical references and index.
    ISBN 1–56639–181–4 (alk. paper)—ISBN 1–56639–182–2 (pbk.)
    1. Historical films—History and criticism.   2. Motion pictures—Political
aspects.   I. Title.   II. Series.
PN1995.9.H5G75   1994
791.43'658—dc20   93–33042

]]]]]] *To my sisters and brother, Angel, Julie, and Michael*

Contents

Illustrations

Acknowledgments

Throughout this project I have sought recommendations for improvements. My friends and colleagues have responded with generosity. Their assistance has contributed grace and reason to the manuscript and rendered the shortcomings that remain much less conspicuous.

Parts of this book have appeared as essays in journals including *Persistence of Vision*, the *Velvet Light Trap*, *Film and History*, and *Film History*, and in the critical anthology *Resisting Images: Essays on Cinema and History*, edited by Robert Sklar and Charles Musser (Philadelphia: Temple University Press, 1990). Thanks to each of these publications for encouraging my work and extending rights to include the essays in my book.

Robert Sklar has helped me to think through problems with precision and added clarity and balance to my writing. The broad range of his interests and the sense of social engagement he brings to scholarship have been an inspiration for my work. At points of crisis, his constancy and support have enabled me to move forward.

Many others have offered invaluable help as this manuscript took shape. Noel Carroll initially encouraged me to work on the subject, and William Simon supplied support and advice that kept me going. Jonathan Buchsbaum and Evelyn Ehrlich responded to my treatment of French cinema during the 1930s. Susan Ryan, Graham Bruce, Lucille Chia, and Joel Kanoff shared their thoughts on Visconti. Guiliana Bruno and Gloria Monti helped me with Italian translations and their special knowledge of the culture. Matthew Bernstein was generous in sharing his research and writing on Walter Wanger. Robert Rosenstone applied the wisdom of a historian to a lavish Hollywood production. The patience and encouragement of Janet Francendese of Temple University Press helped bring this work to completion. And finally I am grateful for the steadfast support and affection of my wife Sharon. I thank all these as well as the wider community of friends and associates who contributed to my work.

Shadows on the Past

Studies in the Historical Fiction Film

Chapter 1

Analyzing the Historical Fiction Film

From the earliest days of their artistic practice, filmmakers have engaged in the centuries-old tradition of grappling with the present by writing about the past. "This time-honored disguise and this borrowed language"[1] noted by Marx is a means by which the cinema associates past events with contemporary issues that it seeks to explain, justify, or exalt. Examples abound. While his compatriots contested Nazi foreign policy, Sergei Eisenstein filmed *Alexander Nevsky* (1938), in which Nevsky battles the Teutonic Knights. The victory at Agincourt in Laurence Olivier's *Henry V* (1945) echoed the Normandy landing that brought British troops to the Continent in World War II. Spike Lee's *Malcolm X* (1992) linked contemporary issues of racial justice and African American identity to its portrait of Black life in the decades following World War II.

Pierre Sorlin accepts as a fundamental principle that history as used in film "is a mere framework, serving as a basis or a counterpoint for a political thesis. History is no more than a useful device to speak of the present time."[2] The historical film indulges its contact with the immediate and generally refuses the past its distinct and foreign character. As a result, history in the cinema is seldom disinterested, but rather constitutes an address to the present. This address speaks of a displacement, an attempt to reinforce or disguise the meaning of the fiction, which causes some observers to view the historical film as distinct from social engagement. For example, Siegfried Kracauer writes of such films that "the world they show is an artificial creation radically shut off from the space-time continuum of the living, a closed cosmos that does not admit of extension."[3] Such a limited view allows the ideological underpinnings of these films to pass unquestioned into popular culture. The central project of this book is to argue for a wider view; in it I want to reveal the historical film's political aspirations—political in the sense that these works promote an understanding of the past that responds to social conflicts and assumes, as Thomas Elsaesser writes, "a self-consciously civic mode of address."[4]

This study examines the aims and conventions that shape historical fiction on the screen and probes into the nature of its influence on Western culture. I concentrate on those fiction films that have a meaningful relationship to historical events, setting aside both the documentary or nonfiction film and the costume picture that adopts a period setting but fails to engage historical issues. That is, I am interested in films that make claims to a persuasive representation of the past, that arise out of historical scholarship but do not partake in the discipline of history. Distinct from historical learning, these films are nevertheless related to it. Historical fiction films interpret and comment on significant past events, as do historians; this interpretive role places historical films in a context of historiography and enables them to have an impact on the public that often exceeds that of scholarship in range and influence. In the course of this book, I explore the motives behind the turn to history, focusing on the relationship between past and present as well as on the use of generic conventions to shape historical data into a narrative. The remainder of this introductory chapter provides a framework for analysis and discusses the historical fiction film as a genre.

| Behind the Turn to History

Some of the keys to the meaning latent in the historical film can be found by looking at the motives behind the displacement of the present to the past: an appeal to authority, a veiling of intention, an escape into nostalgia, and a search for origins. The appeal to authority is reinforced by embellishing the historical film with scholarly references, period detail, or antiquated manners. Such rhetorical gestures often present history as an avenue to the truth and serve to verify the meaning of the text. This approach is evident in *The Birth of a Nation* (1915), which quotes a historical work by Woodrow Wilson and duplicates famous Civil War photographs in its compositions. History as a veil hides controversial positions and defuses audience resistance or political censorship. Ernst Lubitsch used a historical camouflage in his post–World War I German productions *Madame Dubarry* (1919) and *Anna Boleyn* (1920). Drawing from the history of France and England allowed Lubitsch to snipe at the recent enemy and protected him from German censors who might otherwise have objected to the films' cynical view of patriotic duty and social hierarchies. The escape into nostalgia seeks a "golden age," a "paradise lost." Motivated by a regressive impulse to return to the past, such a history implicitly criticizes the present as deficient in the values and energy that fortify culture. The picnic at Tara that opens *Gone With the Wind* (1939) presents a bucolic age before the outbreak of the Civil War. More recently, *JFK* (1991) alludes to an age of innocence and integrity before the political shocks of the 1960s transformed the nation. The search for origins seeks to discover the foundation of a civilization's achievement and calls for a reaffirmation of the strengths of its forebears (as in *Young Mr. Lincoln*, 1939). The search may also take a critical view, attempting to uncover the source of a current malaise or a discomforting dilemma, such as the anxieties over colonialism, "the third world," and the post–World War II Western hegemony apparent in *Lawrence of Arabia* (1962).

From the Standard of Authenticity
to the Variables of Interpretation

Both filmmakers and commentators regularly invoke authenticity as a standard for evaluating historical films. For years directors heralded their works as precise recreations of events. D. W. Griffith defended *The Birth of a Nation* by speaking of the medium in utopian terms and proclaiming that "the time will come in less than ten years . . . where the children in public schools will be taught practically everything in moving pictures. Certainly they will never be obliged to read history again."[5] Decades later, Roberto Rossellini claimed of his *The Rise to Power of Louis XIV* (1966), "It is all in the documents, nothing is invented."[6]

The function of authenticity in historical fiction films is generally misunderstood as a disinterested reproduction of the past. The chapters that follow redirect analysis toward the more central relationship between politics and historiography. Whether a fictional narrative, a film, or a discursive essay, history bases its interpretation on a body of data and testimony and is governed by variable standards of evidence, description, and argument. When artists join history and fiction, the play of interpretation becomes more expansive and explicit. The very process of cinematic interpretation was opened to inquiry by a landmark critique published shortly after 1968.

In response to a growing concern over ideology and the cinema, film commentators turned in the late 1960s from questions of authenticity to textual politics. This approach received a stimulus from the collective analysis of *Young Mr. Lincoln* by the editors of *Cahiers du Cinéma*. Their article sought to reveal a subtext in the film by probing the motives of studio management, the "fissures" in the style of John Ford, and the representation of Abraham Lincoln in American folklore. Though the social investigation was diverted into a Lacanian reading of psychosexual themes, the essay prepared the ground for future inquiry.[7]

In "Historical Fiction: A Body Too Much," Jean-Louis Comolli measures the historical subject as a means of dismantling the illusion of cinema. Comolli argues that the multiple interpretations clinging to any historical episode (the personalities, legends, iconography, and so forth) give the viewer a reference that undermines any implicit claim to verisimilitude. Kracauer attacked the historical film because its "irrevocable staginess" made the audience aware of the artificial construct, but for Comolli the artifice is a benefit. The historical fiction, he writes, makes "the coded more visible, the supposedly known more awkward, the belief more problematic: there is more to denigrate, a body and a knowledge too much."[8] Emphasizing the range of historical interpretation, the play of formal options, and the awareness of the spectator, Comolli finds the historical film to be a genre that exposes the mechanics of fiction and the play of ideology.

The mere selection of a historical episode carries latent associations or even explicit political allegiances. Joan of Arc tells a tale of France different from Marie Antoinette's; St. Francis speaks of Christianity in a softer tone than Martin Luther. Interpretation takes this process a step farther. The portrayal of the French Revolution through events ranging from the fall of the Bastille to the rise of Napoleon has been a conspicuous example of the politics underlying historical interpretation. Though the revolutionary period spans a decade, it is the crisis of 1793 that holds the popular imagination. From Griffith's *Orphans of the Storm* (1921) to *Danton* (1982), filmmakers have condensed the screen Revolution into a rivalry between Robespierre and Danton, an iconography of the guillotine, and a "Reign of Terror." The transformation of revolutionary leaders into bloodthirsty monsters that pervades popular culture is a triumph for conservative ideologues. Some schools of interpretation so dominate public consciousness that their view becomes an uncontested "truth." For example, the interpretation of "Reconstruction" in which white southern gentry overcome northern "carpetbaggers" and ignorant blacks to restore justice to the American South became the basis for two of Hollywood's most popular films, *The Birth of a Nation* and *Gone With the Wind*.

What is left out of a historical fiction can suggest almost as much about its politics as what is emphasized. In his 1927 wide-screen epic, Abel Gance portrayed Napoleon as a revolutionary hero who liberated Italy, eliding the Russian view of the aggressive tyrant who put Moscow to the torch.

The Representation of Historical Cause

Central to interpretation in history is a concept of historical cause—the representation of the significant forces producing social change. Discursive argument can present demographic data, economic graphs, or the ebb and flow of disease as causal agents. Matching extrapersonal factors with individual experience, the historian can integrate a range of elements in charting the evolution of society. Screen fiction employs different means for expressing causation: It bases its histories upon dramatic and visual signs; it presents a comprehensive field rather than a sequential argument. Yet, explicitly or implicitly, each historical film expresses notions about the causal forces operating in history. It represents those forces through dramatic elements, such as characterization and plot, and spectacle elements, such as the historical setting and the handling of mass action.

The dramatic elements integrate personal and social factors in portraying historical cause. If the story fails to attain a sufficient level of generalization, a bias toward the heroic individual and psychological motivation marks the interpretation. For example, the film may reduce the break between the pope and the Church of England to a mere consequence of Henry VIII's lust for women and authority. On the other hand, the film may fashion characters into quintessential representatives of their class, nation, or culture. Romance may reflect the political conflicts of an era, as in the relationships of the evolving heroine in the Cuban production *Lucia* (1968). For historical fiction Georg Lukacs prescribes a "typical" character who embodies the complexity of individual experience and, at the same time, acts as a microcosm of social forces:

> What matters therefore in the historical novel is not the re-
> telling of great historical events, but the poetic awakening
> of the people who figured in those events. What matters
> is that we should re-experience the social and human mo-
> tives which led men to think, feel and act just as they did in
> historical reality.[9]

The historical film strives to expand its characters into a portrait of a people to synthesize the individual and collective causes operating in history.

The spectacle elements tend toward a generalized, extrapersonal perspective in portraying historical cause (illustration 1). Trading verbal precision for a visual panorama, the historical spectacle presents the impact of the natural terrain, the urban environment, or the social manners of the period. Filming famine, plague, or an ocean voyage creates a landscape invested with

1 | *Orphans of the Storm* (1921), production still. The spectacle tends toward a generalized, extrapersonal perspective. Courtesy Museum of Modern Art/Film Stills Archive

meaning; the image of a peasant's hut, a merchant's caravan, or an aristocrat's library carries penetrating social observations. Scale and visual perspective also provide accents. The closeup probing of a troubled face for psychological insight promotes a more personal view than a panorama of fleeing refugees or a crane shot expanding upon the splendors of a royal palace. The film expresses historical cause in the comprehensive gestalt of the screen spectacle as well as in the characters and incidents of the plot.

A repertory of dramatic and visual signs shape the causal explanations underlying the historical film. The oppositions below counterpoint a series of options that a filmmaker can employ.

The Representation of Causal Forces

Personal Elements	Extrapersonal Elements
Plot	Historical setting
Individual	Society
Distinct personality	Group profile
Personal psychology	Collective action
Intimate scene	Public ritual
Characterization	Spectacle

Rather than marking off strict boundaries, these qualities indicate variable signs and relational concepts—affinities and contrasts—that allow a film to produce meaning. The critic, however, must analyze the particular details of a film before coming to a conclusion about its representation of historical cause.

| Principles of Genre Criticism and the Historical Film

Although critics seldom study the historical film as a category, films of this kind have the familiar themes and patterns that distinguish a genre.[10] Without the fixed archetypes, recurring plots, and traditional iconography of genres like the Western or the horror film, most filmed historical fiction does, nevertheless, conform to a set body of expectations. Let us consider some relevant principles of genre criticism before approaching the historical film and its generic elements.

In their *Theory of Literature*, René Welleck and Austin Warren explain that "theory of genres is a principle of order: it classifies literature and literary history not by time and place (period or national language) but by specifically literary types of organization and structure." Furthermore, they note that modern genre study gives priority to description and analysis rather than setting a normative standard. That is, the contemporary analyst reveals and reflects upon meaningful elements that link a series of works.[11]

The writing of Claude Lévi-Strauss, particularly his comparative analysis of myth, has influenced the past generation of genre study. Lévi-Strauss examines myths as well-known tales that a culture repeats and changes over time in response to social dilemmas or conflicts. His method seeks to identify recurring elements and their shifting relations as a means of studying how the society thinks about these problems.[12]

The fact that both myths and genres repeat and transform familiar stories led critics to apply three principles adopted from Lévi-Strauss to genre study: First, patterns and relationships between recurring formal elements in the stories hold meaning; second, the repetition and transformation of tales address open or submerged social tensions; third, tales attempt to reconcile or overcome these tensions or conflicts within the culture. Thomas Schatz, a leading exponent of Lévi-Strauss's structural method in the study of film genres, writes:

> Considering the genre film as a popular folk tale assigns to it a mythic function which generates its unique structure, whose function is the ritualization of collective ideals, the celebration of temporarily resolved social and cultural conflicts, and the concealment of disturbing cultural conflicts behind the guise of entertainment.[13]

The recurring elements of a genre do not constitute a stable constellation. For the genre itself has a history that reflects the changing conditions acting upon it.

Genre study frames a field of works around common properties that, to use Hans Robert Jauss's term, create a "horizon of expectations." This "horizon" evolves as new works enrich and transform the genre.[14] As the history of the genre responds to the formal influences of the art world and the sociopolitical forces active in the culture, the challenge for the commentator is to chart the genre's trajectory and explain the interaction between the evolution of the form and its meaning in the social context.

Three goals are vital for genre study: identification of central themes that express cultural conflicts; definition of recurring elements and their relationships, which constitute the genre's conceptual structure; and investigation of the genre's response to social conditions, which guides its evolution and gives meaning to its forms.

The relationship of the individual to society is the central theme—the animating conflict—of the historical fiction film. A tension exists between the personal needs of the individual and the needs of the community for cooperative action and mutual responsibility; at the same time, the individual and society are bound in permanent union. This tension between the intimacies of private life and the field of public action is dramatized in the historical film, as, for example, in the story of Julius Caesar and Marc Antony, men caught between their passion for Cleopatra and the command of the empire. The historical film wrestles with the countervailing relations between the individual and society, the private and the public, the citizen and the state. The genre strives to incorporate and supersede personal experience in its account of the evolution of society by portraying the personal and extrapersonal forces propelling historical change.

The recurring generic figures of the historical fiction film are the romance and the spectacle—the one emphasizing personal experience; the other, public life. Each film negotiates the relations between the individual and society and expresses the balance between personal and the extrapersonal forces through its treatment of the two generic elements. In addressing these issues every film draws upon contemporary social conditions and, in portraying history, depicts the historical circumstances from which the film arises.

Vital meaning in a text can be revealed through an understanding of generic conventions. As Rick Altman explains:

> The fundamental principle justifying genre study is this: the single text is no more interpretable by itself than an ancient document representing the sole surviving text in its language. Only in relation to other texts does any text deliver up meaning. The categories operative in a given text can be made visible only by the conflation of numerous films of the same genre.[15]

With this in mind, a brief sketch of the central generic elements and their relationship is in order.

| The Function of Romance in the Historical Film

The chief archetypes of the historical romance are the lovers and the great leader, and marriage is its chief goal. The fate of the lovers points to the historical attitude of the film, happy marriage signifying the alliance of social groups or the reconciliation of conflicting forces—as in *The Birth of a Nation*, where children of the North and South are bound, or *The House of Rothschild* (1934), in which Jew and gentile wed. An ominous union might indicate an unresolvable tension between the private and public life: examples include the political compact between the aristocracy and the bourgeoisie in the marriage of Angelica and Tancredi at the conclusion of Luchino Visconti's Italian production of *Il Gattopardo* (*The Leopard*, 1963), or the failed or thwarted romances in *Intolerance* (1916), *Madame Dubarry*, *The Private Life of Henry VIII* (1934), and *Gone With the Wind*. Even the absence of romance is used to raise the question of suppression; in *Lawrence of Arabia*, for example, sexual turmoil characterizes the hero as alienated, and the lack of romance comes to signify the barren politics of cultural difference and Western colonialism.

The great leader archetype represents the interests of a class or group, the code of the community, and the conscience of society. As a model of self-sacrifice and courage, the great leader often opposes the romance. In attempting to persuade the lovers to restrain their passion and serve the wider, public cause, the leader plays out the role of the father–superego of the Oedipal relation. Although the great leader serves a crucial function in the historical film, the role may be minor. In many instances the leader is separated from the lovers, as in *The Life of Émile Zola* (1937), in which Zola acts as the father–protector for the persecuted Captain Alfred Dreyfus and his wife. In others, the leader must resolve a conflict between love and duty, as in *Mary of Scotland*, (1936), in which the heroine's romance undermines her political goals, and she is overcome by her rival, Elizabeth, who is free of romantic entanglements. Though serving as a central ideal, the leader may be a nearly absent figure, such as the off-screen Christ in many biblical films or Garibaldi in the Italian production *1860* (1933).

Two major Hollywood productions from 1939, *Juarez* and *Gone With the Wind*, demonstrate the complex ways in which the great leader and the lovers provide the dramatic conflicts animating the representation of history in the romance.

In *Juarez*, the lovers and the great leader are presented as warring forces, and the romance embodies the division between intimate life and social duty prevalent in the historical film. The story sets in opposition the revolutionary Benito Juarez, crusading for social justice in Mexico, and the tragic lovers Maximilian and Carlota, the Hapsburg monarchs imposed on that country by Napoleon III. Undermining the film's strained allegiance to the Mexican Revolution, Maximilian and Carlota emerge as a devoted couple thwarted by the schemes of the French. Naive, uncomprehending monarchs, the tragic lovers are unable to quiet the native upheaval or recognize the injustice of colonialism. Finally they are destroyed by the forces of Juarez, played as a petrified deity by Paul Muni (illustration 2). Avoiding any dramatic confrontation between the revolutionary leader and the royal lovers, the film shifts constantly from domestic romance to armed struggle, splitting into two separate stories with alien sympathies and creating an unbridgeable gap between intimate feelings and social action.

The film's confused sensibility reflects its development as a Hollywood product rooted in pre–World War II political maneuvers.[16] The United States Department of State, fearing initiatives from Italy and Germany in Latin America, hoped to promote resistance within the hemisphere by dramatizing the colonial designs of Napoleon III in a motion picture. Jack Warner responded to the call of the Roosevelt administration by directing his writers to develop *Juarez* as a clash between totalitarian intervention and native democracy. In spite of its concrete political aims, a lavish production, and numerous rewrites, the film never brings to life its sympathy for Mexican independence; instead, it appears to be about the contending claims of the United States and Europe for dominance over Latin America. Not only is the emotional currency of the drama invested in the European royal couple, but Juarez himself is explicitly modeled on Abraham Lincoln, his American contemporary. The film establishes a bogus correspondence between them, places pictures of Lincoln in the hero's chambers, and dresses Juarez in the stovepipe hat and dark suit of the legendary American president instead of the Indian clothing of his native land. The parallel may have appealed to viewers north of the Rio Grande, but Mexican critics saw through the charade (one comparing Warner's Juarez to Frankenstein's monster).

2 | *Juarez* (1939), production still. The great leader—here, Benito Juarez (Paul Muni)—represents the interests of a class or group, the code of the community, and the conscience of society. Courtesy Museum of Modern Art/Film Stills Archive

Rather than portraying a positive love between a Mexican couple engaged in revolutionary action, the film centers on European royalty victimized by politics through the agency of Juarez, a national savior, but also a stern, superhuman figure who destroys romance. Muni's revolutionary, dressed in the cultural myths and animated by the international goals of the United States, puts an end to social turmoil but destroys the emotional center of the narrative.

Gone With the Wind is marked with a similar romantic–historical fatalism. Caught between the outmoded values of a "golden age" and debilitating contemporary conditions, the lovers fail to resolve the break between the past and the present (illustration 3).

3 | *Gone With the Wind* (1939), production still. The romantic couple—Rhett Butler (Clark Gable) and Scarlett O'Hara (Vivien Leigh)—fail to resolve the break between the past and the present. Courtesy Museum of Modern Art/Film Stills Archive

Ashley Wilkes embodies the antebellum ideals of the plantation gentry, but, crippled by a nostalgia for a lost world, he is incapable of dealing with the postwar crisis. As the shrewd, cynical, pragmatic counterpoint to Wilkes, Rhett Butler embraces trade and the ascendant code of commerce, not the rural ethos of the plantation. He profits from the lost "cause," and the surrender ensures his spiraling prosperity. He fails only in his love for Scarlett O'Hara.

Scarlett personifies the conflict between Ashley's romantic idealism and Rhett's realpolitik. She insists on the wealth and security that can be gained only by ruthless maneuvering, but refuses to shed the pretense of antebellum grace. Scarlett becomes a hypocritical confection who brutally engineers her success yet cannot face the personal consequences and emotional turmoil that result. The romance expresses this division as she marries Rhett but persists in her girlish infatuation with Ashley. Unable to resolve the conflict within herself, Scarlett becomes incapable of feeling for others, and both men reject her.

The absence of the great leader from this film is noteworthy. No one appears to reconcile social value with harsh circumstance. With the death of Ashley's wife, Melanie, a figure representing endurance and morality, comes the grim resolution. Dazed and abandoned, Scarlett can speak only of returning to the plantation to rebuild her plans on the bedrock of tradition. *Gone With the Wind* offers no mediation between the embattled individual, collective experience, and the harsh struggle for survival. This bleak historical fiction presents no union that carries society from past to present; no marriage joining the romantic couple; no leadership harmonizing personal desires with public responsibility and community spirit.

The emphasis on characterization in the romance tends to promote personal motives and individual action as the driving forces behind history. Although lovers and the great leader can signify the typical behavior of a group or the aspirations of a movement, the intimate scenes invited by the romance limit the expression of extrapersonal forces. For this kind of film, the problem of representing history is one of integrating the romance with the social setting in such a way as to balance the personal and extrapersonal forces moving civilization. The romance finds its counterpoint in the spectacle.

| The Function of Spectacle in the Historical Film

The spectacle emphasizes the extrapersonal forces (social, economic, geographic, and so forth) bearing on the historical drama. The spectacle's relation to the romance expresses the links between the individual, nature, and society, and serves as a vehicle for historical explanation. In contrast to the romance, which is shaped by the plot and characters, the features of the spectacle are period setting—architecture, as in the temple of Moloch in

Cabiria (1914) and the gladiator school in *Spartacus* (1960), mass action (conquering armies, coronations, striking workers), and the broad visual landscape or "nature," represented by the plague in *Monsieur Vincent* (1947), the sea and the shore in *The Vikings* (1958), and the desert in *Lawrence of Arabia*, and representing the protagonist's adversary in *Suez* (1938) or his ally in *Alexander Nevsky*.

Whereas mass conflict animates the clash of forces, the public ceremony dramatizes peaceful social change. Each kind of screen spectacle serves as a counterweight between tumultuous upheaval and stable continuity as well as a means of integrating the individual into the community. That is, the conflict can unify characters into an army, political party, or religious sect on the basis of a shared ideal or common struggle, and ceremonies, such as the ball and the wedding, act as social rituals bridging the gap between the privacy of romance and the display of public approval. The films of D. W. Griffith and Sergei Eisenstein illustrate the development and function of these forms.

Griffith

Griffith's films combine intimate personal tales with historical vision by integrating the romantic drama and the social spectacle. The movement of camera perspective from distant shot to medium and close range in a flexible and easy-to-follow cutting pattern provided an avenue from the most private reaction to a vista of immense scale. Griffith's analytical editing system developed particular modes that embellished characterization and performance style. These now familiar conventions, such as the point-of-view shot, the 180-degree rule, shot–countershot, and so forth, largely benefited the personal drama, but also served as vehicles for transition and integration.

Equally important, but not so widely recognized, was Griffith's command of the grand spectacle, which relied on parallel editing, location shooting, and care in composition. Parallel editing gave him a means to link different spatial and temporal elements and to develop conceptual contrast and comparison through juxtaposition. Exploring this mode in such Biograph films as *A Corner in Wheat* (1909), Griffith expanded it to grandiose dimensions in *Intolerance.* Shooting *The Birth of a Nation* outside a studio allowed an escape from the proscenium arch to a natural historical landscape, where Griffith's camera could open the frame to an enormous range, both laterally and in depth. The wide scope of the full-scale shots of the Battle of Petersburg is remarkable even by contemporary standards. Setting battles, chases, and even intimate scenes in natural countryside locations unchanged by modern times reinforces the verisimilitude of the historical period. The multiple elements of the spectacle required Griffith to plan a careful and complex ordering of composition. In *The Birth of a Nation*, he achieved an extraordinary sensitivity in directing performance in intimate scenes with effective composing of mass action. Impressive examples are the departure of the troops from Piedmont, the guerrilla raid, and the rescue by the Klan.

Matching the tight scale of analytical editing with expansive exterior compositions, Griffith inflated the personal drama while condensing the historical spectacle. Consider the merging of personal feeling and collective action in the departure from Piedmont and the Battle of Petersburg. Griffith celebrates the dispatch of Piedmont's soldiers with street bonfires, an all-night ball, and finally a parade of the troops from the town. The director balances the scale of these social ceremonies with Ben's goodbye to his little sister, Flora. The cutting from the mass scenes to the intimate encounter maintains an emotional association between the collective experience and the private farewell. The same principle organizes Griffith's battle. Long shots from the commanding general's point of view lay out the field of opposing armies on a grand scale. Then the camera moves to Colonel Ben Cameron with his comrades in the trenches. Before the attack begins, Ben moves from his position to aid a wounded enemy soldier and receives a cheering ovation from the Yankees across the field. Only after marking the underlying brotherhood uniting the nation does Griffith move from the personal incident to the clash of the armies. The sequence ends with compositions of mangled bodies littering the field, and a title, "War's Peace," indicating the terrible common suffering.

Even as he reduces the four years of combat into one battle at Petersburg, Griffith embellishes the emotional encounter until it

4 | *The Birth of a Nation* (1915). As Ben Cameron (Henry Walthall) embraces his sister, Flora (Mae Marsh), intimate emotions radiate toward a collective recognition. Leger Grindon collection

achieves the scope of spectacle. A famous example is the homecoming scene. After the Confederate surrender, Ben takes the long walk south to Piedmont. There he looks upon his home, now neglected and battered, and, speechless, greets Flora (illustration 4). Touching her, Ben feels the suffering his family has endured during the years of war. Finally the arms of his mother reach from the threshold, and her embrace pulls him back into the home and the family. The encounter generates its powerful tension through lingering gesture, silent recognition, and composition that reaches into the off-screen space. The homecoming of the defeated, the plight of war-ravaged civilians, and the regenerative bond of family feeling expand into an emotional spectacle that radiates outward toward a collective recognition.

Another means of integration is the comparison of personal details from the fiction with the historical generalizations in the spectacle—for example, the association of the guerrilla raid on

Piedmont with the presentation of "Sherman's March." In the raid, a lawless band of Yankee irregulars attacks the Carolina town, and the episode details the assault on the Cameron home. The harrowing experience of the Camerons establishes a textual reference that Griffith draws on later in the vivid condensation of the Sherman campaign. Introducing the image with the title "Sherman's March to the Sea," Griffith pans from a tight composition of a mother and children huddled on a hill to a long shot of the valley below, where the Union Army pillages the countryside. Nature shelters the civilians while the troops destroy a solitary house—an emblem of the shattered family. The single image alludes to the earlier raid, and the experience of the Camerons becomes generalized in the historical spectacle to embrace the vast population of the South. The single image condenses an enormous chapter from the war and conveys an electrifying emotional charge.

Griffith developed these cinematic forms in the parallel stories of *Intolerance*. From the spectacle in the battle for Babylon to the personal intensity of the modern murder trial, the director demonstrated remarkable agility in combining intimate experience with collective activity, but Griffith proved unable to transcend personal experience and portray the complex causal forces moving history. As Sergei Eisenstein noted:

> It is not that representation cannot be raised with correct presentation and treatment of the structure of metaphor, simile, image. Nor is it that Griffith here altered his method, or his professional craftmanship. But that he made no attempt at a genuinely thoughtful abstraction of phenomena— at an *extraction of generalized conclusions* on historical phenomena from a wide variety of historical data: that is the core of the fault.[17]

Eisenstein himself grappled with "generalized historical phenomena" in a remarkable series of films.

Eisenstein

Transforming the spectacle of landscape, conflict, and ceremony into a representation of extrapersonal forces, Eisenstein moved the historical film on to a more conceptual plane. Eisenstein molded landscapes into expressive terrain; the factory in *Strike* (1924), the vessel in *The Battleship Potemkin* (1925), and the city of Petersburg in *October* (1928) represented institutional forces within the culture and became moving parts in the machinery of history. Eisenstein shaped characters into conflicting social groups: the workers against the owners in *Strike,* the sailors against the officers in *Potemkin,* the Bolsheviks against the Provisional Government in *October.* The films transform ceremonies, such as the funeral of Vakulenchuk in *Potemkin* or the dance of Kornilov's troops in *October,* into spectacles of solidarity that have emotional power and narrative significance without the need for character development or dramatic intimacy.

In these early films, Eisenstein omitted the romantic drama and reduced characterization in favor of archetypes and the collective hero:

> We brought collective and mass action onto the screen, in contrast to the individualism and the "triangle" drama of the bourgeois cinema. Discarding the individualist conception of the bourgeois hero, our films of this period made an abrupt deviation—insisting on an understanding of the mass as hero.[18]

Even in drawing these archetypal characters, Eisenstein depends on evocative imagery rather than the intimate episode or psychological nuance. In *Strike* he uses visual metaphors, comparing the police spies to a fox, a bear, an owl. He carries the fable-like spectacle to a climax with the magnified slaughter of a bull intercut with the massacre of the workers. In these films the collective hero embodies class as a historical force that supersedes individual action.

Eisenstein created editing formats with a structure that expressed extrapersonal significance as well as generating emotion. With intellectual montage—such as the celebrated "For God and Country" sequence from *October*—Eisenstein joined the image chain through logical connections that offer a model of visual reasoning. Unfortunately, the fame of intellectual montage seems to have overshadowed the remarkable array of forms that Eisenstein deployed. Take, for example, his use of rhythm and line to build an emotional response. *Potemkin* exhibits the effect in two contrasting sequences. In the foggy harbor interlude midway through the film, a lingering pace and a graphic diffusion of the landscape engender anticipation and an almost melancholy temper; later, as the battleship races to confront the fleet, accelerating montage and a sharp linear composition build excitement in a climax evocative of Griffith.

In Eisenstein there are no central characters to provoke associations or distract from the momentum of the images. Growth from microcosm to macrocosm animated editing chains such as the "Proletariats, Learn to Bear Arms" montage from *October*, which begins with the assembling of the parts of a rifle and continues until an entire unit of Bolsheviks are recruited and battle-ready. While Griffith's conceptual imagery, such as his "cradle endlessly rocking," lacked the complexity necessary to evoke a comprehensive historical vision, Eisenstein's editing produced a remarkable range and clarity in causal chains that incorporated a dialectical progression into the editing process. One of the most successful examples comes early in *October*, beginning with the title "Long Live the Provisional Government." In the opening image priests pay homage to the new government with incense, followed by gentlemen in formal attire savoring mutual congratulation. Russian and German infantrymen fraternizing at the front match the celebration, but a closeup of a bowing diplomat and the title "Obligations to the Allies Must Be Honored" interrupt the new friendship. Shelling resumes, and the soldiers are driven back to their trenches. The sequence continues with beleaguered workers lowering an artillery piece, intercut with soldiers under fire who seem to be crushed by the weight of the cannon. The oppression of the workers and infantry is followed by breadlines, immobile in the snow, as titles announce the declining ration for the populace. The editing conveys the shift from celebration to disillusionment, and, more important, lays out the political relations between army, proletariat, and consumer that will result in a new uprising. The sequence comes to a close with cheering crowds at the Finland Station greeting Lenin's arrival and joining his cry for "Peace, Bread, Land." Without resorting to the detailed experience of any single individual, the editing analyzes the failures of the Provisional Government and the need for Bolshevik action. Eisenstein summarized his contribution:

For us this *quantitative accumulation* even in such "multiply-ing" situations was not enough: we sought for and found in juxtapositions was more than that—a *qualitative leap.*

The leap proved beyond the *limits of the possibilities* of the stage—a leap beyond the *limits of situation:* a leap into the field of montage *image*, montage *understanding*, montage as a means before all else of revealing the *ideological conception.*[19]

The combined achievement of Griffith and Eisenstein brought to the screen an encyclopedia of visual forms to express historical meaning in the cinematic spectacle. The advent of sound would bring a shift away from the visual spectacle.

| The Biographical Film

For the historical film the new sound technology constrained location shooting and directed attention to dialogue, character-ization, and the heroic personality; the biographical film soon dominated the genre. In 1941 Joseph Freeman noted that "in the past seven years Hollywood has produced more than forty films which are biographical in the strict sense of the word."[20] *The Private Life of Henry VIII* led to *The Private Lives of Elizabeth and Essex* (1939); national heroes abounded, from *Disraeli* (1929) to *Juarez;* Garbo and Dietrich starred as *Queen Christina* (1933) and *The Scarlett Empress* (1934). The Soviet industry exhibited a similar tendency with pictures that included *Chapayev* (1934), *The Childhood of Maxim Gorky* (1938), and a two-part film on *Peter the First* (1937–39).

A central feature in the biography films of the 1930s is the portrayal of the individual as the catalyst for historical change. The hero's personal power and high moral standards separate him or her from the common experience and established institutions; yet, paradoxically, the leader becomes the agent for social trans-formation. The emphasis on the unique personality or political genius as the key to history complements a tendency apparent in the Hollywood filmmaking of the period. In describing the "clas-sical Hollywood cinema," David Bordwell and Kristin Thompson write that its conception of narrative depends on the assumption that the action will spring primarily from *individual characters as causal agents*. Natural causes (floods, earthquakes) or societal causes (institutions, wars, economic depressions) may serve as catalysts or preconditions for the action, but the narrative invariably centers on personal, psychological causes: decisions, choices, and traits of character.[21]

Such economic factors as the star system promoted this concept. So did the analytical editing style, in which the force of performance and modes of personal interaction (e.g., the shot–countershot, point-of-view formats, and responsive close-ups) served to narrow the focus from the expansive *mise-en-scène* of the spectacle to the nuances of character. The spectacle as an indicator of extrapersonal historical forces declined further as the studios restricted location shooting, and panoramas were condensed into inserted montage sequences, such as the Napoleonic wars in *The House of Rothschild* or the battles between the armies of Antony and Octavius in *Cleopatra* (1934). These montage interludes became standard in the historical film genre and appeared formally divorced from the intimate scenes that dominated these pictures.

Later in the decade Eisenstein's historical biographies fashioned a striking revision of spectacle elements. In contrast to the earlier mass hero, Eisenstein centralized character; at the same time, he drew his protagonist in stunning visual strokes that fused personality and spectacle. In *Alexander Nevsky* Eisenstein had used visual typage to invest the Teutonic Knights with a menacing character through their strong visual presence. That film was a prelude to the achievement of *Ivan the Terrible* (1944–46), in which meaning grows from the fusion of character and spectacle.

Ivan the Terrible constructs its meaning through gesture, costume, and composition, giving prominence to the spectacle over the spoken word. In part one, for example, Prince Kurbsky broods over Ivan's glory in a palace corridor as, behind him, an icon of Christ looks down, bearing witness to his betrayal. The character of the czar is constructed through magnified shadows, piercing glances, and the gestures of Ivan's curving, increasingly grotesque body. Nikolai Cherkasov, who played Ivan, complained of the impossible contortions required to realize Eisenstein's visual ideas. The visual spectacle portrays the mood of the characters and develops the plot independent of words or action.

Exhibiting decidedly different elements of spectacle from the Soviet master's silent work, the film's landscape shifts from expansive location shooting to the architectonic enclosures of the studio, from exterior to interior. *Ivan the Terrible* expresses psychological torment and moral clash in low archways, the flickering play of candlelight and torches, and chambers that combine the grandeur of a palace and the constriction of a prison yard.

In *Ivan the Terrible*, Eisenstein exchanges the dynamic rhythm of *Strike* and *October* for a drawn and majestic pace. These shots also are short, but the images within a scene move in small compositional shifts between nearly contiguous spaces. The scene at Anastasia's bier serves as an example. Ivan kneels at the base of the casket as the archbishop chants a prayer of remorse. The grief-stricken monarch is flanked by his boyar enemies as well as his trustworthy servants. At the news of Kurbsky's betrayal, Ivan regains his strength, hurls aside two giant candlesticks, and drives the archbishop from the church. As his spirits revive, Ivan's body ascends, until—looming above the casket, arms raised and surrounded by a corps of torchbearing lieutenants—he shouts his commands. The body movements of the czar, the shifting gazes of his entourage, and the cadence of speech and song express the introspection and conflict in the spectacle.

In a major change from Eisenstein's work in the 1920s, the film bases its episodes, not upon massed conflict, but in ominous ceremony. From the coronation in part one to the mock crowning and procession ending part two, ceremony, legitimate and disguised, acts as the framework for the history. The structure seems appropriate because *Ivan the Terrible* endorses the continuity of government and reinforces the authority of the leader rather than promoting collective revolutionary action. The result of Eisenstein's direction is a virtuoso integration of a drama of character with a historical spectacle.[22]

| Form and Meaning in the Representation of History

The formal qualities of romance and spectacle develop the tension between the individual and the community and can function on numerous levels in a particular film or, as a trend, within the historical film genre. Both qualities can emphasize integration, synthesis, and union; or stress rupture, fragmentation, and an irreconcilable conflict between the individual and the community. The romance generally favors intimate scenes and psychological motivation. The tighter the shots and the more individuated the lovers, the less likely the romantic couple are to carry implications for social groups. As a result, one finds a tension in the romance between the highly specified details of realism and the more general qualities of allegory. A pronounced focus on character promotes a view in which personal motives and individual acts are the primary causal force behind historical change.

The spectacle, on the other hand, gravitates toward the typical character, the grand scale, and the broad perspective. The large groups that constitute the spectacle resist complex psychology, tending toward simplified archetypes. The editing strives for the generalization, synthesis, and ability to convey a concept that one finds in the comparative parallel motifs of Griffith, the intellectual juxtapositions of early Eisenstein, or the elliptical condensations of 1930s Hollywood montage inserts. The drive to express the extrapersonal forces in history pushes the spectacle away from the intimacy of romance and solicits a different repertory of cinematic forms. The romance and spectacle, key elements in the historical genre, give form to the film's underlying assumptions about the causal forces motivating historical change.

To portray the complex interaction between text and context, each of the following chapters will be devoted to a close reading of one film: *La Marseillaise* (1938), *Reign of Terror* (1949), *Senso* (1954), *The Rise to Power of Louis XIV* (1966), and *Reds* (1981). In each of these films the interaction of past and present, politics and history, romance and spectacle, establishes contending discourses, but also a continuity, making each film part of an evolving tradition of the historical fiction film. These films were chosen to represent a wide range of practice in Europe and Hollywood, from lavish film spectacles to modest television productions. Analysis will show how circumstances motivate the choice of subject, how various historical episodes position the work within distinct fields of interpretation, and how plots rearrange common elements. To be sure, other historical films could serve my purposes, but these productions seem to me to offer especially apt examples of influential practices and representative trends. Close attention to a limited number of works restricts, but does not eliminate, prospects for generalization, while contributing to a nuanced understanding of significant productions. This study does not pretend to be a comprehensive generic profile; instead, it offers a flexible method for understanding the role of history in the cinema.

Chapter 2

The Politics of History: *La Marseillaise*

*Renoir is above the struggle; he observes. La Marseillaise
has more than anything the look of newsreels.*
—FRANÇOIS TRUFFAUT, 1971

*We wanted to put ourselves in the place of the people that
we have chosen. I would lie in saying that I am impartial.
No, I am not, and with all our heart we march with the
Marseillaise to Paris with a determined goal.*
—JEAN RENOIR, 1937

La Marseillaise was a product of France in 1937, Depression
France, France of the Popular Front. This chronicle of the French
Revolution is enmeshed in its political milieu, and only distance
from the circumstances of the production can sustain François
Truffaut's view of the film as detached and nonpartisan. A return
to contemporary reports places the film firmly amid the struggles
of its time, and one sees not the objective account, but the
disjointed polemic.

|　The Political Circumstances

News of *La Marseillaise* began to appear in the press early in
1937. On February 11 *Paris-Soir* announced, "For the first time
in France there is going to be a production of a major film by
national subscription. Officially sponsored by the government,
supported by the Confédération Générale du Travail (C.G.T.),[1]
directed by Jean Renoir, the film will have for its subject the
French Revolution and will probably be titled *La Marseillaise*." [2]
The picture was planned on an ambitious scale, with a projected
budget of three million francs.[3] A massive subscription drive was
initiated in an attempt to finance the picture outside normal chan-

nels. A subscription would entitle the holder to a reduction at the box office when the film opened. Posters announced a

> film for the people, made by the people. It will be the film of the French nation against a minority of exploiters, the film of the rights of man and of the citizen. For the first time the people itself will produce it, by means of a vast public subscription. Two francs from each producer. Two francs for each subscription. Two francs that will be subtracted from the price of the seat in the cinema when the film is shown. Subscribe![4]

Publicity described an all-star cast portraying the fabled men of 1792. Louis Jouvet was to portray Robespierre, and Pierre Renoir would play the revolutionary journalist Brissot. Erich von Stroheim was to lead the Prussians at Valmy, Jean Gabin to march with the workers through the Paris streets, and Maurice Chevalier to sing the "Marseillaise" in chorus with the patriotic crowd. The renowned scriptwriters Charles Spaak, Henri Jeanson, Marcel Achard, and Marcel Pagnol planned to combine their talents on the scenario.

An impressive array of organizations and individuals initiated the production. On March 12, 1937, a mass meeting to promote the film at the Salle Huyghens drew an audience of more than five thousand, including Jean Zay, Minister of Education and Fine Arts; Leo Lagrange, Minister of the Office of Sport and Leisure Activities; Léon Jouhaux, the leader of the CGT; Marceau Pivert of the Socialist Party; and Jacques Duclos of the Partí Communiste Français (PCF). Jean Renoir, Henri Jeanson, and Jean-Paul Dreyfus, the assistant director, urged the crowd to subscribe to a film of revolutionary optimism that would respond to fascism by celebrating the democratic values of the Popular Front. *La Marseillaise* was in production for a little over a year, and on February 9, 1938, opened at the Olympia Theater in Paris. It was the preceding year, however, that had made the film possible, for in 1936 a national election brought a Socialist government to France. From the events surrounding this election the film took its shape.

The Birth of the Popular Front

On February 6, 1934, demonstrations against the government erupted into widespread fighting between civilians and the police in the streets of Paris. Answering the call of the right-wing press, veterans' organizations and fascist groups led the protesters in a night of street violence that left fifteen dead and fifteen hundred injured. The next day the Radical–Socialist premier, Édouard Daladier, resigned, stepping aside for a "national union" cabinet, which tried to restore confidence in the Republic. The parties of the left believed the clash to be a nearly successful attempt by fascist elements, already in command in Germany and Italy, to seize power. The "insurrection" prompted a move toward unified action that resulted in the Popular Front coalition.

In the coming months the PCF took the initiative. Reversing its longstanding enmity toward the Socialist Party, it proposed cooperation, and in July 1934 a "Unity of Action Pact" was signed. The Communists followed with a surprising invitation to the Radical-Socialist Party, the center–left representative of the French petit bourgeoisie, to join the coalition. In a massive demonstration on Bastille Day, July 14, 1935, leaders of the three parties, Édouard Daladier of the Radicals, Léon Blum of the Socialists, and the Communist Maurice Thorez, announced the formation of the Popular Front. A common plan for the election of 1936 resulted in a decisive victory, with the Socialist Party holding 146 Assembly seats, and the Communists registering a remarkable gain, from 10 to 72 seats.

The Popular Front owed its strength to broad support; six days after the violence of February 6, 1934, one hundred and fifty thousand people, with a variety of party affiliations, had rallied in opposition to the fascist leagues at the Place de la Nation. Throughout the period the political leaders, jockeying for position and divided over policy, exhibited less enthusiasm than the masses.[5] Eleven days after the electoral victory of May 3, 1936, workers launched a spontaneous wave of sit-down strikes. Blum, Thorez, and Jouhaux were unprepared for, and indeed alarmed by, the factory occupations, but the workers' initiative prodded the leaders and brought immediate gains for the movement. When Blum presented his cabinet to the Assembly on

June 6, more than half a million workers were on strike. The new Socialist government immediately brought workers and management into negotiations, and the Matignon agreements were soon signed, providing wage increases averaging 12 percent, legal recognition for collective bargaining and other union prerogatives, a forty-hour work week, and paid vacations. In the following weeks the Blum cabinet brought the Bank of France under state control, nationalized defense industries, and outlawed the fascist leagues, such as the Croix de Feu.

Tensions among the coalition leaders soon surfaced, however. While agreeing to support the government in the Assembly, the PCF refused to accept a portfolio in the Blum cabinet. This position allowed the PCF to offer general support for the Popular Front and, at the same time, criticize any particular decision of the government. The opportunity to use its strategic distance appeared with the outbreak of the Spanish Civil War in July 1936.

As the Blum ministry moved to institute reforms, the Spanish Civil War divided the government and the nation. Simultaneous with the 1936 election in France, another Popular Front coalition gained a legislative majority in Spain. On July 17 the forces of General Francisco Franco launched an open rebellion against the government in Madrid. Though initially eager to send military assistance to the Spanish government, Blum hesitated, then backed off. Cries against Spanish intervention came, as expected, from the French right, and they were joined by the British and Blum's coalition partners, the Radicals. A fear that military action might spark a general European conflict, or even civil war in France, increased Blum's caution. Rather than join the conflict, the premier promoted a nonintervention pact among the European powers, which the Germans and Italians signed and then openly violated. The Communists called for armed support of Spanish democracy and attacked the Blum policy. The Spanish crisis exposed a political division within the Popular Front between pacifism and rearmament.

Many in the Popular Front were torn between their abhorrence of war and fear of the military threat posed by fascism. In the years since World War I, the French left, particularly the Socialists, had consistently opposed arms spending and an aggressive military posture. In 1935 the Italians invaded Ethiopia;

in 1936 the Germans militarized the Rhineland in violation of the Versailles Treaty, and Franco's army rebelled against the elected Spanish government. In this climate of danger, the Soviet Union sought a broad antifascist alliance. After years of voting against military spending, French leftists now read that Stalin "fully approves the policy of national defense followed by France."[6] Political anthems were indicative of the shift. The nationalistic "Marseillaise" had once been countered with the "Internationale" of the workers' movement. Now Thorez could proclaim that "by singing the 'Internationale' we have taken up the strains of the 'Marseillaise.' By hoisting the Red Flag we have raised again the Tricolor of our ancestors."[7]

The Popular Front was divided. The Blum government voted for an arms buildup, yet refused support to its allies in Spain. The Radicals fervently pushed militarization, but objected to Spanish intervention. The Communists demanded action against Franco, yet would not join the cabinet. In trying to maintain the political union, Blum became a negotiator among factions rather than a forceful national leader.

Division also stalled Popular Front economic policy. The most significant achievements resulted from the strikes of May and June—from massive popular action rather than a legislative program guided by the politicians. In the cabinet the Radicals supported spending restraint, whereas the Socialists called for a Keynesian program on the model of the American New Deal. Though the Matignon settlement offered a sharp impetus for the Socialist plan, the business community responded by exporting capital, and the economic situation actually worsened. Soon labor's wage gains were wiped out by inflation; unemployment persisted, and Blum, after insisting that he would not, succumbed to economic pressure and devalued the franc late in 1936. In February 1937, the premier announced a pause in the reform program. In June, with the economy still in decline, the government faced a crisis.

Meeting on June 15, the Blum cabinet decided to request extraordinary powers from Parliament to meet the emergency. After a heated debate in the Assembly, Blum overcame objections and was supported by a vote of 346 to 247. When he turned to the Senate, however, his plan was rejected. Many of his Socialist colleagues urged Blum to pressure the Senate by calling for public demonstrations; others pushed for new elections. The Radicals, however, would not endorse such measures. Without their support Blum decided not to press the fight, and he resigned on June 21. Socialists were angry that Blum withdrew without a stronger fight, without an appeal to the public. Joel Colton, in his biography of Blum, writes of the decision:

> There is no doubt that Blum alone was responsible for the decision to capitulate to the Senate without a fight. . . .
> He was convinced that a fight against the Senate could not have remained within political and constitutional bounds. It would have to be a "revolutionary struggle." . . . Once he had convinced himself that it would have been impossible to resist the Senate in a legal and constitutional way and make use of moderate mass pressure, once he saw the break-up of the Popular Front coalition which he believed essential for the defense of republican institutions, once he saw resistance turning into internal conflict and even civil war at a time of grave foreign danger, his capitulation inevitably followed.[8]

The Popular Front was an exuberant two-year campaign followed by thirteen months of ambivalent leadership, internal division, and growing crisis. The popular consensus and political determination of the movement was spent months before the Blum resignation. Viewed in this context, *La Marseillaise* expresses the euphoria of the campaign, the tensions within the coalition, and the disillusionment with leadership.

Cultural Politics and Ciné-Liberté

The Popular Front was engaged in cultural politics, and the government's support was enlisted in the production of *La Marseillaise*. Offers from the national ministries included a reimbursable advance of 50,000 francs, access to national monuments and archives, the cooperation of the army, air time on state radio, and an official showcase as the French entry at the International Paris Exhibition of 1937.[9] Since the Blum government fell before these commitments could be fulfilled, however, the production turned for support to the CGT and independent cultural groups associated with the left. The most important organization behind *La Marseillaise* was Ciné-Liberté.

Ciné-Liberté was formed in the spring of 1936 to combat censorship, screen progressive films, and form a base for production free from the restrictions of the commercial industry. From its genesis it was closely tied to the PCF, which had long been active in the politics of culture. In March 1932 the Party was instrumental in forming the Association of Revolutionary Writers and Artists (AEAR), which established a league of antifascist artists and intellectuals, including André Gide and André Malraux. The AEAR established affiliated groups in various media, and workers in the film industry formed the Alliance for Independent Cinema (ACI) in 1934. In March 1935 the AEAR was transformed into the Maison de la Culture, with PCF member Louis Aragon as its secretary-general. Preparing for the campaign of 1936, the Communists turned to the ACI for an election film. Jean Renoir joined a distinguished crew of filmmakers (including Henri Cartier-Bresson, Jacques Becker, André Zwoboda, and Jean-Paul Dreyfus) to produce *La Vie est à nous*, a sixty-six-minute film that mixes documentary and fictional material to present the politics of the PCF in an unprecedented manner. Because the government censor denied the film a license, screenings had to be restricted to Party meetings. The public never saw it.

The ban had ample precedent in prewar film censorship and in 1928 legislation that established the regulations in force during the 1930s. Broadly authorized to "[consider] the whole of national interests, and especially the interests in the preservation of national customs and traditions,"[10] the censorship commission in practice protected the public from communism and attacks on the judiciary, the military, and other venerable institutions, as well as episodes likely to provoke foreign powers and films deemed "anti-French." It had banned Soviet classics such as *Battleship Potemkin*, celebrated works by Jean Vigo and Luis Buñuel, Nazi films such as *S.A.—Mann Brand* (1933), and Hollywood pictures like *The Mask of Fu Manchu* (1932). For years the commission had fended off attacks, but Radio-Liberté, an organization campaigning for fairness in broadcasting, had demanded equal treatment of political parties, and in a matter of months had gained increased access for the Socialist Party and the PCF. That success and mounting enthusiasm for the Popular Front made the left confident that they too could strike at the film censor. The ban on *La Vie est à nous* became the catalyst for Ciné-Liberté, which sought to drive the censor from the screen.

The first mention of Ciné-Liberté appeared in the Communist newspaper, *L'Humanité*, in January 1936.[11] On April 20, 1936, the Socialist *Le Populaire* reported on the "Programme de Ciné-Liberté," which read in part:

> The ACI will make newsreels and documentaries meant to give an objective image of our time and will organize the screenings of unreleased films and classic films. . . . The ACI leads the campaign against the censor, against the stupidity, against the judge of the film markets, . . . It proposes editing a periodical, a free tribune for all members and a rallying point for the renovation of the seventh art.[12]

On May 20, 1936, an editorial committee including Henri Jeanson and Jean Renoir launched the first number of the journal *Ciné-Liberté*. A vigilant campaign against the censor was the central theme. In the first issue, P. J. Laspeyres stated the objective clearly: "After the magnificent victory the Popular Front has just returned in the elections, to crush the censor should be written on the first line of the list of administrative tasks."[13]

The campaign continued, but the new government would not abolish the censor. Enraged over the Minister of Education's refusal to issue a permit for *La Vie est à nous*, Jeanson published "An Open and Uncensored Letter to Jean Zay" in the July–August *Ciné-Liberté*: "Voilà, some serious words which prove that liberalism is only a form of condescension, only a means of controlling, administering, making compromises with liberty. In one word as in ten, *La Vie est à nous* remains banned. The third of May has meant nothing."[14] Parallel to the government's failure in foreign policy and economic reform was a failure in cultural policy. The mass support that had brought the Popular Front to power could not end screen censorship. Divisions within the government prevented any far-reaching reform.

With the campaign against censorship blocked, Ciné-Liberté's energy shifted to filmmaking. A number of short films were made in conjunction with member unions of the CGT, but most resources were directed toward the feature film *La Marseillaise*. In March 1937 a special issue of *Ciné-Liberté* devoted to *La Marseillaise* urged members to support the subscription drive to finance the project. By August, 350,000 advance tickets had been sold at two francs each, but the sum still fell short of the three-million-franc budget.[15] The production had to look to friendly organizations and investors. A regular joint stock company was formed, with limited title and controlled by the CGT under the name "Societé de production et d'exploitation du film *La Marseillaise* (CGT)." Louis Joly, a trusted member of the PCF and an experienced administrator, became the executive producer. Jean Renoir, leader of Ciné-Liberté, central collaborator on *La Vie est à nous*, and an internationally acclaimed filmmaker, was the obvious choice for director. Shooting commenced on August 23, 1937, and was completed before Christmas.

La Marseillaise sought shelter from the contending factions within the Popular Front in historical fiction. On the one hand, Renoir explained, "It would be impossible for us to make a film on the present political situation; this would risk provoking polemics and being disagreeable to a public which goes to the cinema simply for distraction."[16] With millions of francs invested, it would also have been foolish to provoke the censor to deny a government license to a feature aimed at a mass audience. The polemics of *La Vie est à nous* had to be checked in *La Marseillaise*, but a historical setting could give the film's political message authority and needed distance. At the release of *La Marseillaise*, Renoir could affirm that it was "a film of contemporary ideals. It does not stop with being a fictional or historical film, if you insist on these terms. It is not concerned either with fiction or history—it is concerned only with problems of the present day."[17] The politics of the PCF shaped the film, but their tone had to be muted if the filmmakers were to pacify the censor, balance the views of a fragmented coalition, and revive the enthusiasm that had brought the Popular Front to power. *La Marseillaise* may have failed to realize its grand ambitions, but it bears the marks of its critical moment.

| Allusions to Popular Front Politics

"A chronicle of some facts which contributed to the fall of the monarchy," *La Marseillaise* follows a battalion of Provençal volunteers through the political crisis of 1792. The struggle between the Jacobin and Royalist factions reached a climax on August 10, when members of the popular militia, federal troops, and the National Guard stormed the king's residence, the Tuileries palace. The fall of the monarchy, more than three years after the taking of the Bastille, stands as a central, and controversial, event in the history of the French Revolution. In dramatizing this episode, *La Marseillaise* expresses the political goals and internal tensions of the Popular Front.

The film can be conveniently divided into three sections: the progress of the Revolution from the fall of the Bastille in July 1789 to the crisis in the spring of 1792; the formation of the Marseilles contingent and their march to Paris; and the tense days in Paris from July 29, when the troops arrived from Marseilles, to the attack on the palace on August 10. A brief coda ends the film on September 20, 1792, at the Battle of Valmy, where the revolutionary army defeated the forces of Prussia and Austria to save France for the Republic.

The opening six episodes, nearly one-third of the film, condense three years of revolutionary activity and explain the need for the expedition from Marseilles. Beginning with the attack on the Bastille, the film moves from Versailles to Provence, from Germany to northern France, as the scenes race over the events of many months; characters from each class are drawn with economy and purpose. The exposition combines history with contemporary allusions to present the motifs from which the film's thesis will grow.

The film begins at Versailles on July 14, 1789. The summer routine continues undisturbed as the king's guard precisely executes a change of duty. The camera moves in a long take approaching the royal chamber as a visitor petitions for an audience with Louis XVI. Word passes from servant to secretary to valet, traversing hallways, antechambers, and waiting rooms. Finally the Marquis de la Rochefoucauld appears before His Majesty with news of the attack on the Bastille. Louis XVI has spent the day hunting and napping, and the message interrupts his hearty supper, leaving him startled and confused. Louis XVI is portrayed as isolated, unaware of the grievances of his subjects and baffled by the current carrying the nation to revolution. The failure of leadership is expressed, not in tyranny, but in helplessness and uncertainty. The state apparatus encloses the king. The protocol that shields the throne undermines government by distancing the people from their leader. A similar absence of strong leadership weakened the Third Republic, which was marked by shifting cabinets during the 1930s. The gradually emerging parallel between Louis XVI and Léon Blum begins here.

The clash at the Bastille occurs off-screen, saving the depiction of revolutionary violence for the concluding assault on the royal palace. Several noncinematic strategies seem to account for this decision. First, the Popular Front intended to bring socialism to France in a peaceful and orderly manner. Dwelling on the revolutionary violence of the Jacobins might exacerbate fears already excited by the Bolshevik Revolution and the May sit-down strikes. Second, the filmmakers believed that the Marseillais regiment's reputation as brutal fighters was a slander and wanted to lay this historical misrepresentation to rest. Third, keeping violence in check would calm potential objections from the sizable pacifist element within the Popular Front.

The next scene, set in June 1790 in Provence, contrasts the royal hunt with a commoner's desperation. A peasant who kills a pigeon feeding on his crop is arrested for violating the game laws and condemned to the galleys. The mayor of the town, a convivial bourgeois, intervenes on the man's behalf: While the marquis and the mayor argue, the peasant eludes the guards and escapes through a window. The mayor laughs sympathetically, while the nobleman growls.

The episode portrays the politics of class and the shifting alliances of the bourgeoisie. The contrast between the shabby peasant and the arrogant nobleman conjures up the division between the hardships of unemployed and the wealth and power of the "200 families."[18] The mayor, however, as representative of the bourgeoisie, signifies not simply the middle class, but also the Radical–Socialist Party, the right flank of the Popular Front coalition, whose support came from small tradesmen and craftsmen, and particularly from the rural population. The Radicals regularly led center–left cabinets during the interwar period, and the mayor, governing at the side of the marquis, evokes this role. His quarrel with the nobleman indicates the division within that union and the left shift of the bourgeoisie, and anticipates the alliance of the Radicals with the Socialists and the Communists. As a result of the rift between the mayor and the marquis, the peasant finds an opportunity to regain his freedom.

The law itself is presented as a tool of the aristocracy, alluding to a controversy within the Popular Front and Socialist politics. Over the years Blum had developed a distinction between the "exercise of power" within a parliamentary government and the "conquest of power" by the working class. According to the Blum policy, the Socialists should respect the constitutional system and the legal order while exercising cabinet leadership. Though the time might come for the "conquest of power" and the transformation of the capitalist order, that moment was not at hand. As a result Premier Blum was scrupulously attentive to the constitutional system and refused to employ extralegal action as head of state. Others on the left wing of the coalition, both Socialists and Communists, were not reluctant to challenge the order of the Republic. The film embraces the pact with the bourgeoisie, but tends toward a left perspective in presenting the law as a weapon of the ruling class.

Seeking shelter in the mountains, the fugitive meets Bomier and Arnaud, two middle-class artisans fleeing from oppression in Marseilles. The three make camp, aided by a local priest, and live off the land. The group represents the Popular Front alliance between peasants and bourgeoisie, city and country, clergy and laity. They realize their common interest in a return to nature. The unity of the characters and the locale is emphasized by the framing and depth of the image in a location setting. Nature and liberty are associated with the rising classes, as opposed to the constricting rituals of the courtroom and palace. Smoke from a burning chateau and news of an uprising in the town alert the exiles. The Revolution is active but, like the attack on the Bastille, the violence remains off-screen. The group, united and determined, leave the wilderness to join their comrades.

It is October 1790, and the Revolution has reached Marseilles. With little resistance patriots occupy the royal fortress overlooking the harbor, and a key scene occurs in the aftermath. The commander, the Marquis de St. Laurent, discusses politics with Arnaud, the leader of the rebel band. Concepts like "the nation" baffle St. Laurent; he cannot understand the principles upon which the revolutionaries base their action. Arnaud explains that the nation is a fraternal union of all Frenchmen, to which the marquis replies that he has no bond with these common people: "I serve the king." At that Arnaud politely invites the commander into exile. These Jacobins are reasonable, courteous, and clever. The world is turned upsidedown in polite conversation; a fortress is taken, not with arms, but with rhetoric.

La Marseillaise carries out the Popular Front objective of claiming the nation as the birthright of the left and blesses the popular union with the hand of nature. The conversation between St. Laurent and Arnaud opposes the feudal hierarchy based upon fealty to the king with the nation of citizens united by the mutual consent of the governed. Renoir shoots the dialogue on the ramparts overlooking the bay, so that Arnaud's doctrines are linked with the open sea and nature. In contrast to the prison fortress of the old regime, the seascape glimmers in a spacious depth of field that promises freedom. The film implicates an aristocracy that serves the monarchy but does not understand the concept of the nation. The following episode also alludes to those who looked abroad for economic advantage and political allies, placing personal interest before the good of the country.

The film moves to the Hotel Stadt in Coblentz, April 1792, to observe the émigré aristocrats. Dependent upon German support, the exiles anticipate the conquest of France by the armies of Prussia and Austria under the Duke of Brunswick. The nobles plan to follow in the invaders' wake, avenge themselves upon the revolutionaries, and regain their wealth and privilege. The camera moves among them as they play cards, listen to music, and chat. M. de Fougerolles lauds the German army, proclaiming that the revolutionaries will flee at the approach of a disciplined corps. St. Laurent recalls his encounter with Arnaud and questions his companion's belief that these Jacobins are a cowardly rabble. More significantly, he regrets the émigrés' dependence on foreign armies. The Germans, he fears, will exploit the divisions within France to dominate his country. The scene ends with the nostalgic aristocrats puzzling over the steps of a court dance.

The episode underlines the conflict of class versus national loyalties. St. Laurent is sympathetically treated because of his suspicion of German motives and his concern for the integrity of France. His fellows, however, are fixed on regaining their property at the expense of the nation. Their flight from France finds its contemporary parallel in the flight of capital in response to the Blum program. The film implies that contemporary aristocrats, "the 200 families," will look abroad for investments and support before surrendering their power to a native socialism.

The prologue ends at Valenciennes in April 1792 as the war begins between revolutionary France and the invading German army. The government orders the French forces to take the offensive, but dissension between the aristocratic officers and the common soldiers paralyzes the advance. Throughout the spring action against the enemy is stalled as mistrust grows between the government and the high command. Rumors of a coup are rife. *La Marseillaise* illustrates the crisis in a scene between two soldiers as they huddle by a campfire. A peasant woman off-screen cries that the Austrians have plundered her village without the French army's firing a shot. The soldiers return to their fire, where they roast a crow, complain of a lack of supplies, and speak bitterly of treason. Surrounded by darkness, they curse their commander Lafayette and the officer corps. The scene summarizes the crisis that results in the formation of the Marseillais regiment, a crisis caused by a failure of leadership and the betrayal of the nation by the aristocracy.

The scene at Valenciennes alludes to the division in the Popular Front over the Spanish Civil War. Franco led his army against the elected government of Spain, much as the émigrés and the officer corps maneuver to restore the monarchy. The peasant woman's appeal to the French soldiers evokes the Spanish government's call for help from Paris. Blum's ineffectual non-intervention policy demoralized the common people and sapped the strength of the Popular Front. Like the soldiers in *La Marseillaise*, the masses were prepared to fight for Spain, but were disarmed by a failure of leadership.

The opening section of *La Marseillaise* draws its themes into a series of significant oppositions:

La Marseillaise	versus	The King
Revolution		Old Regime
Nation		Monarchy
Popular unity		Class division
The people		The aristocracy
Power of the masses		Ineffectual leadership
Armed struggle		Legal order
Loyalty		Betrayal
France		Foreign
Liberty		Restraint
Nature		Artifice
Outdoors		Interiors
Landscape		Buildings

The film portrays a series of episodes that link characters with settings and concepts to establish a network of associations. The king and the aristocracy, presented exclusively in imposing buildings—palace, fortress, courtroom—inhabit an interior world dominated by such artifice and restraint that the proper steps in a court dance can become a serious concern. The king and the aristocracy have no concept of the nation as a community of citizens. They inflame class divisions in their ignorance of popular grievances, their strict administration of oppressive laws, and their disregard for the interests of France. The commoners are photographed out of doors, living off the land and in harmony with nature. Their free manner easily breaks down social barriers between peasants, townsfolk, and clergy. The revolutionary order signifies the unity of all people in common loyalty to the nation. The initial scenes establish a network of correlatives that develop the central themes of the film and suggest the need for more militant action, both from the Jacobins of 1792 and the left in 1937.

The Fall of the Monarchy: A Field of Historical Interpretation

"No period of history has so frequently been rewritten in the light of current preoccupations or has been such a repeated battleground of conflicting ideologies as the French Revolution," wrote the historian Georges Rudé.[19] The assault on the Tuileries on August 10, 1792, is a controversial episode in a historical epoch brimming with rival interpretations. The representation of the event asks to be positioned within the field of historical scholarship and investigated for its bearing upon French politics in 1937. In the rhetoric of authenticity that typically surrounds the historical film, Renoir wrote of the project, "Let us combine the two categories of films into one single class and declare that films are neither 'historical' or 'modern' but, quite simply, 'realistic.' I have tried to make out of *La Marseillaise* a film worthy of admission to this honorable class."[20] In its subtitle the film sets a tone of casual impartiality, "a chronicle of some facts which contributed to the fall of the monarchy." However, neither impartiality nor realism faces up to the nature of history as a construction based upon evidence, value, and argument. Let us consider the film's historical sources and investigate their implications for its politics. But before analyzing points of controversy, a review of the commonly agreed-upon events portrayed in *La Marseillaise* is in order.

By the summer of 1792, the Revolution in France had been in progress for three years, and the authority of the monarchy was in crisis. Louis XVI still maintained executive powers, supervised a cabinet of ministers, and held title as commander-in-chief of the army. Outraged by the Revolution, European royalty in league with émigré aristocrats were about to attack France with the declared intention of restoring absolute power to the king. Since Louis had already attempted to flee the country months before, his devotion to the nation was in doubt. On July 30, 1792, a contingent of Jacobin volunteer soldiers arrived in Paris from Marseilles. These troops were leading participants in the August 10 assault on the royal palace. On September 20, the invading army of Prussians and Austrians was repulsed by French troops at the Battle of Valmy. After the engagement the German forces retreated from France, ending the threat to the regime and breaking the power of the monarchy. Subsequently France entered a period of radical government known as the "Reign of Terror." Danton, Marat, and Robespierre, already prominent figures, moved to the center of power, from which they too eventually fell.

The poles of interpretation can be marked by two nineteenth-century histories of the French Revolution written by Jules Michelet and Hippolyte Taine. These multivolume narratives combine dramatic incident, personal testimony, and florid prose with a pronounced political point of view. Documentary evidence, emotional engagement, and historical analysis become inseparable in these enormous works, which rival the most ambitious social novel in scope and impact and provide a wealth of material as well as a narrative model for historical fiction.

The political sentiments of Michelet and Taine, if not absolutely contrary, were quite distinct. Georges Rudé, a modern historian, notes that Michelet's work is "impregnated with the spirit of the Republican democrats of 1848," whereas Taine, publishing his history five years after the Commune of 1871, is disillusioned with popular government.[21] Their contrasting views are apparent in their treatment of the storming of the palace on August 10.

Michelet finds that the attack was imperative and fulfilled not merely the demands of a particular faction, but the interests of the whole French people: "August 10th was a great deed that France did. Had France not taken the Tuileries, it perished."[22] Moreover, "the victors of that 10th of August were not, as has often been said, a band of brigands and barbarians, but the whole people. Every kind and condition and character of man was to be found among them. The most violent passions were present; but the base, the ignoble passions were, in this moment of heroic exaltation, completely absent."[23] As is typical in Michelet's history, France assumes a personal identity. The nation is not merely a collection of people or a geographic region, but an almost mystical union, a manifest spirit striving to realize its destiny. This view of revolutionary politics complemented the ethos of the Popular Front and was comfortably adapted by *La Marseillaise*.

For Taine, the Marseillais regiment were the shock troops of the Jacobin radicals, militants who led the mob in political intimidation and violent action. Chosen with "great care" for a bloody and vicious deed, the troop

> comprises 516 men, intrepid, ferocious, adventurers, from every quarter, either Marseilles or abroad, Savoyards, Ital-

ians, Spaniards, driven out of their country, almost all of the
vilest class, or gaining a livelihood by infamous pursuits,
"the bravos and demons of evil haunts," picked men out of
the bands that had marched on Aix, Arles, and Avignon.[24]

Having retreated from the Tuileries before the outbreak of fighting, Louis XVI ended the battle by ordering his Swiss troops to
surrender. Taine describes the response of Michelet's heroes:

No quarter is given. The warfare is that of a mob, not civi-
lized war, but primitive war, that of barbarians. In the abandoned palace into which the insurgents entered after the
departure of the garrison, they kill the wounded, the two
Swiss surgeons attending to them, the Swiss who had not
fired a gun and who, in the balcony on the side of the garden, "cast off their cartridge-boxes, sabres, coats, and hats
and shout: 'Friends, we are with you, we are Frenchmen,
we belong to the nation!'" They kill the Swiss, armed or un-
armed, who remain at their posts in the apartments. They
kill the Swiss gate-keepers in their boxes. They kill everybody in the kitchens, from the head cook down to the pot
boys. The women barely escape.[25]

Jean Renoir wished to counter this harsh view in *La Marseillaise*. In researching the scenario, the production team went
through the Marseilles Archives for records of the battalion of
1792, checking the Journal of Grievances from the Estates-
General, delving into reports from political clubs, newspapers,
and court logs. The researchers verified that in order to join the
march one had to be innocent of criminal convictions and free
of debt, command sufficient resources to support one's family
while on the expedition, and produce evidence of previous military training. Aiming to redeem the Jacobins, the film builds a
key episode around Bomier's effort to meet the demanding cri-
teria. *La Marseillaise* characterizes the volunteers as upstanding
working folk, who were, in Renoir's words, "quite far from the
troop of bandits so magnificently described by anti-revolutionary
writers. . . . Let us hope that by frequenting this friendly troop
our revolutionary comrades of today will be consoled in the
face of calumnies in which a certain press contrives to impli-
cate them."[26]

Though *La Marseillaise* subscribes to Michelet's description of the recruits, the film comes closer to Taine in treating Louis XVI. For Michelet, the king is a villain, a traitor to France. At the storming of the Tuileries, he remarks, "At that moment the picture was absolutely distinct: on one side, the Assembly and the people; on the other, the King. . . . Face to Face, France and the enemy."[27] Taine views Louis XVI with sympathy, regretting that he lacked strength and political determination:

> If the King had been willing to fight, he might still have defended himself, saved himself, and even been victorious. . . . His good sense, probably, enabled him to see that a retreat was abdication; but his phlegmatic understanding is at first unable to clearly define its consequences; moreover, his optimism had never compassed the vastness of popular imbecility, nor sounded the depths of human wickedness; he cannot imagine calumny transforming his dislike of shedding blood into a disposition to shed blood. Besides, he is bound by his past, by his habit of always yielding; by his determination, declared and maintained for the past three years, never to cause Civil War; by his obstinate humanitarianism, and especially by his religious equanimity.[28]

A hesitant and good-natured king, finally unable to cope with the political storm, finds his way into *La Marseillaise* (illustration 5). As one reads of the monarch's "humanitarianism," "optimism," "equanimity," and fear of civil war, Louis XVI evokes Léon Blum. The film finds an underlying similarity between the head of the old regime and the fallen-Socialist premier.

La Marseillaise also draws on early twentieth-century historiography of the French Revolution, which was dominated by scholars associated with the left. They emphasized economic and social questions, highlighting class struggle rather than heroic personalities, quantitative evidence rather than dramatic incident. Detached political analysis replaced the rhetorical flourish. Between 1901 and 1904, Jean Jaurès, the founder of the French Socialist Party, published a four-volume *Socialist History of the French Revolution* that was praised as a landmark work. In 1903 Jaurès established the Commission for Research and Publication of Documents on the Economic Life of the Revolution, devoted to the collection and dissemination of primary histori-

5 | *La Marseillaise* (1938), production still. Pierre Renoir's hesitant and good-natured Louis XVI cultivates parallels with Léon Blum, leader of the Popular Front coalition. Courtesy Museum of Modern Art/Film Stills Archive

cal materials. Fifty-seven volumes had been published at the time of Jaurès's assassination in 1914, and thirty-six volumes followed. Georges Lefebvre acknowledged Jaurès's achievement: "If anyone cares to assign to me a *maître*, I recognize only him." [29]

Albert Mathiez, the most influential historian of the Revolution between the world wars, argued in favor of the radical phases of the Revolution. Finding in class struggle the engine of revolutionary progress, Mathiez divided the period into four parts: "the revolt of the nobility, 1787–88, the bourgeois revolution, 1789–91, the democratic and Republican revolution, 1792–93, and the social revolution, June 1793–July 1794." [30] His interpretation marked August 10, 1792, as the decisive victory for the democratic revolution. Mathiez also championed the radical Robespierre. Contrary to the longstanding view of the Jacobin leader as a monster of the Terror, Mathiez made a case for him as "a man of incorruptible virtue and unwavering principle . . . a great statesman of the Revolution."[31] With the fall of Robespierre, Mathiez sees the Revolution coming to an end, progress halted.

On Mathiez's death in 1932, Lefebvre succeeded him as president of the Société des Études robespierreistes; after 1937 Lefebvre occupied the Chair of the History of the French Revolution at the Sorbonne, once held by Mathiez. At the time *La Marseillaise* went into production, Lefebvre was recognized as the leading authority on the period, having published detailed studies as well as collaborating on a general history of the Revolution. Lefebvre shifted scholarly attention away from Paris to the provinces, away from political leadership to the lower social orders. He investigated peasant politics and the composition and motives of the revolutionary crowd, frequently finding in them the spearhead of social transformation. Lefebvre's scholarly interests complement both the subject of *La Marseillaise* and the grass-roots initiatives so important for the Popular Front.

These twentieth-century historians, rather than finding in 1792 a contest between the French people and the monarchy, describe a struggle between various factions for command of the state. In this respect *La Marseillaise* takes its interpretation from Michelet, and Popular Front politics are again the key. The film, rather than emphasizing class struggle, sought to portray the Jacobin crusade as a democratic expression of national unity. Mathiez and Lefebvre do, however, share with the movie a belief in the importance of August 10; the fall of the monarchy marks a significant change in the Revolution and the ascendancy of progressive, republican forces. Mathiez writes:

> The fall of the throne amounted to a new revolution. The dawn of democracy was visible on the horizon. . . . The insurrection of August 10 was quite unlike those which had preceded it; it was not directed merely against the throne. It was an act of defiance and a threat to the very Assembly itself. . . . A new situation had been created: legal power was face to face with revolutionary power.[32]

This passage illuminates the historical position of the film and its political meaning in the context of the Popular Front. Celebrating an armed uprising against state authority implicitly criticizes the prudent legalism motivating Blum's resignation. The animating historical episode of *La Marseillaise* favors an aggressive revolutionary stance. The film presents extralegal force as a viable, even necessary, political alternative—a stance that excited fears in the more cautious members of the Front, not to mention those outside the coalition. The film's darker undertone is suggested in Lefebvre's words on the consequences of August 10:

> A second revolution had, indeed, occurred, ushering in universal suffrage, and, in effect, a republic. But it did not have the warm and virtually unanimous support that the nation had offered the first. Events since 1789 had brought difference and divisions: . . . Those who had actually participated in the insurrection or who unhesitatingly approved it were few in number, a minority resolved to crush counter-revolution by any means. The Terror began.[33]

| The Leader and the Romantic Couple: Archetypes in *La Marseillaise*

Just before the battle at Valmy, Arnaud assures his Jacobin comrades that

> before we arrived people just stared at liberty like the lover forbidden to approach his beloved. Now thanks to us the lover embraces his beloved. Of course, she's not yet his mistress and he will have a hard time winning her over. But even if they are parted, they know each other now and one day or another they will be reunited.

The romance and its archetypes, the leader and the couple, have grown as a vehicle of expression throughout the film. *La Marseillaise* portrays the shifting relationship between the individual and the community as a romantic rivalry between Louis XVI and Bomier, between the monarchy and the Jacobins, for the heart of France. The king acts as the ineffectual leader and weak husband, divided between his position as head of state and his class loyalties, between the nation and the queen. Bomier, on the other hand, represents the new unity animating France. He leaves his town in the south to join in a campaign to save the nation and falls in love with a Parisian, Louison. *La Marseillaise* sees the Revolution overcoming the class divisions of the old regime and joining citizens in a new civic bond. Romance, as we have seen, plays an established role in the historical fiction film, and a comparison with other films of the French Revolution will illuminate these archetypes in *La Marseillaise.*

The French Revolution spanned a ten-year period from the fall of the Bastille in 1789 to the coming to power of Napoleon in 1799. On the screen the French Revolution became synonymous with the "Reign of Terror" of 1793–94. The guillotine held the attention of the camera, surrounded by the intrigues of the famous Jacobins—Marat, Danton, and Robespierre. The cinema owed its history more to Charles Dickens than to all the scholars of the nineteenth century. *The Scarlet Pimpernel* (1934), *A Tale of Two Cities* (1935), and *Marie Antoinette* (1937) turned the revolutionary government into a heartless oppressor constantly threatening the romantic couple. The private life of the lovers was perpetually under attack by the public sphere represented by the state; the individual was permanently at odds with society.

La Marseillaise set out to counter a screen tradition that equated revolution with mob violence, political anarchy, and mass murder. To this end the filmmakers moved much of the drama from Paris to southern France, personalized members of the revolutionary crowd, and shifted attention to 1792 to celebrate the triumph of democracy over monarchy. In *La Marseillaise* political action—the transformation of the state and the defense of the Republic—joined men and women. The individual was integrated into society, and the division between the private and public spheres was overcome. The crusade of the Jacobins fostered romance, and the union of Provence with Paris was reflected in the love of Bomier and Louison.

The dominant romantic archetypes marking films of the French Revolution were well established in the decade before 1930. *Madame Dubarry* (1919), Ernst Lubitsch's first international success, portrays the French Revolution in the closing episodes and presents the model for the tragic couple. The heroine, Jeanette, is a clever, good-natured bourgeoise separated from her true love by circumstance, her tempting beauty, and the depravity of the aristocracy. Making the best of her position, she finds her way to Louis XVI's bed and becomes the royal mistress, Madame Du Barry. Throughout the film, injustice, popular unrest, and the decadence of the old regime herald the Revolution. When the uprising breaks out, Jeanette seeks to be reunited with her loyal sweetheart, but it is too late. She is implicated in the crimes of the court, and sent, along with her innocent lover, to the guillotine.

This romantic couple is at odds with society in general and the state in particular. Although the power of the aristocracy divides Jeanette from her lover, the romance sustains itself through years of imposed separation and political obstacles. She is victimized by both the old and the new regime, neither of which respects the needs of the individual or the passion of lovers. *Madame Dubarry* poses a tragic division between the intimacies of private life and the injustice of public institutions.

Similarly, *Orphans of the Storm* (1921) finds in history a conflict between personal happiness and political institutions, a clash between romantic aspirations and community authority. Again people seek redress from a corrupt aristocracy, only to fall under the knife of a bloodthirsty mob. While Lubitsch focuses on passion, Griffith binds the romance to nature, class, and family. *Orphans of the Storm* divides society into three representative families: the heroines are abandoned bourgeoises, and they are flanked by the Vaudrys, aristocrats of the old regime, and the Frochards, a family of city beggars. Thrown into Paris during the Terror, the bourgeois orphans gravitate to the aristocrats, while the urban poor, embittered and vengeful, collect into a vicious mob. Though good and bad exist in each class, the poor have an uncommon propensity for evil, just as the rich are favored by more than their share of grace. Class distinctions are not, however, determined simply by property; ultimately, it is blood that matters. As a result, one of the heroines—unknowingly separated in infancy from a noble mother—gravitates back to her "natural" station and marries a count. In *Orphans of the Storm*, the family serves as the only haven for lovers in a predatory society. As in Lubitsch, the state, whether aristocratic or popular, divides the romantic couple. The individual, rather than being integrated into society, is isolated and finds in the community an oppressor.

Napoleon (1927) valorizes the leader as a godlike genius who stands far above the people he commands. Eschewing romance for a childlike notion of paternal domination, the Abel Gance film portrays Napoleon as driven by a mystical destiny that allies him to nature rather than to the community. An enormous eagle parallels the Corsican's progress from his school days through the march into Italy. Mediterranean winds drive the young soldier back to France; a rainstorm ensures his victory at Toulon. Napoleon literally speaks to the ocean but can create no bond with his fellow men and women. The "child of destiny" is at odds with his classmates; he is driven from Corsica by his enemies. Napoleon is misunderstood, another isolated individual, but in this case absolutely superior to the mass of French men and women.

For Gance's hero, romance and the common people merely obstruct the progress of genius. Bonaparte encounters Josephine at a decadent ball, and the courtship elicits the film's single clumsy note from the general. Immediately after the marriage, Napoleon rushes to the front to take command of the army of Italy, as if fleeing marriage itself. Gance's revolutionary crowd is an illiterate, crazed rabble bent on anarchy and vengeance. Only under the disciplined command of General Bonaparte do the French prove worthy of the ideals of the Revolution. Equality and fraternity do not influence *Napoleon*. The heroic leader, self-sustaining, independent, authoritarian, completely dominates the community.

The three films present different but familiar roles for the leader and the romantic couple. In each film revolutionary politics and the romance are at odds. In conscious response, *La Marseillaise* presents the romance of liberty and the people as a harmonious combination of political ideals and personal aspirations. At the Jacobin meeting in Marseilles, a romantic tragedy does not separate but brings together the volunteers. Louis Vauclair comes from Paris to tell the assembly of her lover, killed at the front because of treason. Her plea stirs the patriots to enlist, march to Paris, and save the nation from sabotage and invasion. Romantic feeling expands to embrace the nation and join the citizens in common cause.

In contrast, Louis XVI's character as a leader and a lover is emblematic of the failures of the old regime. In the king's second scene, he and his cabinet are considering the Brunswick Manifesto, a document, issued by the commander of the invading German army, that threatened Parisians with pillage and executions if the royal family was harmed. Louis is revealed as a weak leader unable to mediate between his class loyalties and his responsibilities as head of state. The throne wavers. Should the document be made public? Will it strengthen the royal position or inflame the populace? After a sober airing of positions, the queen, fearing that she has failed to persuade His Majesty, resorts to a homespun domestic maneuver. She pouts and feigns tears at Louis's inadvertent insult to her relatives, the Austrian royal family. Disarmed, the king retreats from his better instincts and yields to his wife's feelings; giving national policy no more weight than a household quarrel, Louis permits his leadership of the nation to be undermined by his romance with the queen.

La Marseillaise portrays the old regime not as a tragic couple, but as a bad marriage. The queen, identified as a subversive foreigner whose power over her husband threatens national unity, is the chief enemy of the Revolution. That she competes with the nation for the king's affection, wooing Louis away from France, owes much to the coalition politics of the Popular Front. To promote national unity the film embraces figures associated with France and makes the villains exiles and foreigners. Oppression—by implication, fascism—was presented as an imported ideology.

The king's wavering between patriotism and class loyalty is expressed in casting and performance style. The actors from the legitimate stage, where training emphasizes precise elocution and a theatrical manner, play the nobles with the control and restraint typical of their milieu. An easy comic style with boisterous speech, broad gestures, and spontaneous expression animates the Marseillais. These contrasts (which have a precedent in Renoir's *La Grande Illusion* of 1937) do more than bear out class division; they also signify a thematic opposition between the liberty of the revolutionaries and the restraint of the old regime.

Pierre Renoir's performance as Louis XVI brings to life the division between the nation and the aristocracy in a misplaced performance style. The king brings the clumsy manner of a commoner to the constricting milieu of the court. This interpretation of Louis XVI expresses his political ambivalence. The monarch's pedestrian manner and frank opinions seem alien to the deliberate and calculating court. Louis is introduced in a nightshirt. His feasting on a joint of meat links him with the people, for Renoir's commoners enjoy meals, but the king is the only aristocrat who eats. He even recommends that the queen try tomatoes, the new dish that the Marseillais have brought from the south. Louis's discomfort with the style of the nobility and the exercise of power is evident in his ill-fitting hairpiece, which, like his crown, sits uneasily on his head.

Congenial, sympathetic, but overwhelmed by circumstances, Renoir's Louis XVI becomes a misplaced leader in a chronicle about an oppressive monarchy. The characterization departs from the historical interpretation (that of Michelet and the left) that guides the other aspects of the film; the political events of 1936–37 suggest a reason for this departure.

Although *La Marseillaise* was committed to the Popular Front, many of those in the production were affiliated with the PCF and critical of Léon Blum. As noted above, numerous qualities link the two leaders. Both were well-intentioned but failures at exercising and maintaining power. Faced with a divided cabinet, Blum wished to aid Spain but yielded, like Louis, to pressure from the right. Just as the king was trapped between Brunswick's invading army, the Assembly's demand for national defense, and a wife in league with the invaders, so Blum, faced by fascist aggression in Spain, was plagued by division among his political bedfellows and endured fierce attacks from his acknowledged enemies.[34]

In the closing scenes at the Tuileries, the royal guards, largely Swiss mercenaries, fire on the Marseillais troops, bringing to mind the Clichy episode from March 16, 1937. In a Paris suburb members of the fascist Partí Social Français clashed with followers of the Popular Front. The police arrived, along with André Blumel, Blum's *chef de cabinet*. In the commotion that followed, the police fired upon the leftists and, in the process, wounded Blumel. The next day Blum, who had rushed from the opera to the scene in top hat and tails, was criticized by the left for the attack on the demonstrators and mocked for his formal attire. In both instances, the leaders of the state opened fire on French patriots, and their headgear became a sign of their political inadequacy.[35]

Finally Louis yields to the pleas of the Assembly's emissary, Pierre Louis Roederer, and his retreat from the palace echoes Blum's retreat before the Senate's opposition. The king's surrender to the Assembly and his desire to avoid civil conflict strongly suggest Blum's decision not to contest the Senate's no-confidence vote and give substantive meaning to the film's portrayal of Louis XVI.

Louis's romantic rival for the heart of the nation is the Jacobin mason, Bomier. Bomier's romance indicates the love of the people for liberty and the new union between the individual and the state promised by the Republic. *La Marseillaise* finds in romance the basis of Bomier's predicament and the source of his salvation. He acts as Everyman, angered by oppression and full of patriotic emotion. He shouts enthusiastically for the Jacobins to rise to the defense of the nation and assist their compatriots in Paris and at the front. When the men rush to answer the call for volunteers, however, Bomier departs without enlisting. The property qualification (volunteers must be free of debt) prevents him from marching along with his friends. A conversation with his mother reveals that Bomier had financed a shop for a woman named Marie, but both the shop and the romance failed. Marie is linked by name to the queen, and the shop to private aspirations no longer viable during revolutionary upheaval. At first relieved that her son will not go to war, the mother recognizes his disappointment and resolves to help him pay his debt. The crisis overcome, the patriot dances off to enlist with his comrades. The scene presents the constrictions of the past in Bomier's failed courtship of Marie, balanced by the positive tradition embodied by his mother. By volunteering for national service, Bomier strikes a new bond with his fellow citizens, which results in another romance.

Arriving in Paris, Bomier immediately falls in love with Louison. Her name links her with Louis XVI, and she replaces the king in the affections of the common man. The rivalry between the monarchy and the Jacobins for the allegiance of the nation is presented at the shadow play Bomier and Louison attend. On the stage the king unsuccessfully courts "la belle France," who rebukes him for flirting with the invader, Brunswick. While the puppets play out the snubbing of the king, the Marseillais commoner and the Parisian republican link arms in the revolutionary coalition between the provinces and the capital.

Bomier's love is never consummated, for he falls in the attack on the Tuileries, just as the Popular Front cabinet expired after less than thirteen months in office. Though death interrupts the romance between Bomier and Louison, Arnaud reminds his comrades that once liberty has been introduced to the people, their desire is destined to be fulfilled. The Jacobin couple symbolizes the political ideals yet to be realized and points to the Popular Front as the heir to the tradition embodied by the romance.

In the resolution, the Marseillais regiment as the collective hero represents the strength and continuity of the French people. *La Marseillaise* does not valorize the great leader or the isolated couple, but the union and equality of the nation's citizens. So the death of Bomier does not hinder the romantic–political quest, and the regiment marches on to Valmy. The closing victory is a signal for Popular Front revival and the future triumph of democratic ideals. *La Marseillaise* overcomes the division between personal passion and community action prevalent in the historical fiction film. The integration of the individual and the community is realized not in marriage, but in the union and victory of the Jacobin regiment.

| Spectacle and Meaning in *La Marseillaise*

Jean Renoir's direction brought to *La Marseillaise* a rich and meaningful historical spectacle. While most of the historical films of the 1930s (for example, the biographies) depended heavily on characterization, the Popular Front production developed its most significant themes in its spectacle. Here the extrapersonal forces shaping historical change were integrated with the personal experience of community life. As a result, the French Revolution becomes a movement in which social change responds to personal needs. *La Marseillaise* attempted to overcome the divisions between private and public in representing political action as a satisfying endeavor and a vital part of human life. The motion picture organizes its spectacle around three major elements: the volunteers as a collective hero, the food motif as a political and economic commentary, and an opposition between nature and artifice in the composition and setting.

The Collective Hero

The second part of *La Marseillaise* encompasses eight scenes that draw together and heroize the Jacobin recruits. The section concentrates on the Marseillais, following them continuously from their enlistment until their arrival in Paris on July 29, 1792. The shooting style, characterized by the long moving-camera panoramas of massed patriots, expands its frame, indicating the fellowship of the regiment in the collective compositions.

The section opens at a meeting of the Jacobin Club of Marseilles. A working woman from the north of France urges her southern brethren to aid Paris in fighting the royalist traitors who are sabotaging the national defense. The group responds by calling for a volunteer unit to march to the capital. The alliance cements the bond between the provinces and Paris and symbolizes the birth of a commonwealth independent of feudal loyalties and a sovereign monarch. The assembly recalls the Popular Front rallies of February 13, 1934, and July 14, 1935, and the meeting to initiate *La Marseillaise* itself in March 1937.

The remaining episodes of the middle part present the troops being recruited, marching the length of the country, and triumphantly parading into Paris. Composition and casting, music and dialogue combine to shape the collective character of the men. The composition in five of the eight scenes presents huge crowds in extended takes. Panoramic crane shots float down from a high perspective to frame determined groups. To underline the unity of the volunteers, Renoir, following his casting practice for *Toni* (1934), gave the parts to actors from Provence. Their regional mannerisms and patterns of speech emphasize their common bond. "I sought out my characters for *La Marseillaise* from the real world," Renoir wrote, "and I can say truthfully that I've met these men of Marseilles! For the people in the film really are from that city and speak with a local accent which for once in a while justifies the film's title." [36] The attention to regional casting complements the class distinction articulated in the contrasting performance styles discussed above. In this way the composition and casting reinforce the unity of the collective hero.

The anthem "La Marseillaise" unifies the collective hero by gradually gathering the many voices of the volunteers into a single chorus. The song first rises inconspicuously from off-screen as the men register. The volume then grows from scene to scene as more and more people take up the song until all the patriots join in an enormous chorus, a spectacle of sound, as the men depart from Provence.

The exchanges between Bomier and Arnaud portray a political dialogue between the common people and the leadership. Bomier is the voice of popular feeling, while Arnaud acts as the leader, a spokesman for reasoned policy and coordinated action. Bomier allows his feelings to shape his beliefs, and when the mechanics of government become divorced from the experience of daily life, impatience blocks his understanding. He forgets the Jacobin passwords, complains of the strict standard for volunteers, and objects to the new "Song of the Rhine Army." Arnaud functions as his respondent—he is the organizer, teacher, and ideological leader. Always prepared to tame Bomier's disaffection, he explains that "you cannot create order from disorder." Between the lines one senses Maurice Thorez advising the workers occupying the factories that "one must know how to end a strike." [37] Arnaud maintains close ties between principles and action, expressing the sense of history that eludes Bomier's impetuous temper. When Bomier complains of the property qualification for joining the troop, his friend reassures him that "the rich started it [the Revolution], but the poor will finish it." The Jacobin of 1792 speaks to the Popular Front supporters of 1937, asking them to continue their common struggle and bring it to its conclusion. The dialogue between Bomier and Arnaud shapes the collective character of the Marseillais without investing either of them with a distinct personality. In the closing scenes their characters yield to a symbolic function: Bomier's death marks the frustrated aspirations of 1937, while Arnaud marches on to Valmy, declaring to his comrades that obstacles cannot prevent their eventual victory.

The collective hero has roots in Michelet. The nineteenth-century historian expresses a mystical belief in the nation, not as a mere compact among men and women, but as one body ordained by destiny. Of 1792 he writes:

> In those days the sacrifice was truly limitless, vast and universal. Several hundred thousand offered up soul and sinew, others their fortunes, their hearts, all with one same spirit. . . . It must be said there was no party unworthy of France in this holy time.[38]

During the engagement at Valmy:

> A kind of invisible assurance held sway in their lines. Something, something like an heroic glow, hovered over the whole of that young army: something about which the King understood nothing (save that it meant he had to return to Prussia).
> That something was faith.[39]

In the spiritual union drawn from Michelet, the acts of the Marseillais come to represent the will of the French people as a whole. In trying to reunite the left coalition in 1938, the film appeals to the memory of 1792, to patriotic unity in the face of foreign invasion, drawing the tradition of the nation from the history of the revolutionary Republic.

The collective hero had an immediate precedent in the scholarship of Georges Lefebvre. Early press releases about the production mention Brissot, Robespierre, and other famous revolutionary leaders. The impulse toward a heroic figure was typical of the biography films of the 1930s and complemented left historiography: as we have seen, Mathiez devoted much of his writing to rehabilitating Robespierre as an exemplary leader. The film's turn from a central figure to a collective hero can be traced to Lefebvre's regional studies of peasant action and the composition of the revolutionary crowd. Rudé summarizes Lefebvre's approach:

> Previous historians, whether sympathetically portraying participants in revolutionary popular movements as "the people" (like Michelet) or unflatteringly labelling them as

"rabble" or *canaille* (like Taine), had tended to treat them as disembodied abstractions and had failed to probe deeply into the motives that impelled them. Lefebvre insisted on the need to study these particular motives, which, he maintained, were quite distinct from, and often at variance with, those of the revolutionary leaders. But he went on to argue that, in order to understand the causes and nature of these repeated popular explosions, it was not enough to determine the more or less rational impulses prompting individuals: account must be taken also of the "collective mentality" of the crowd.[40]

La Marseillaise did not aspire to scholarly precision, but the impulse behind the collective hero suggests Lefebvre's influence (illustration 6). The focus on mass action rather than individuals mirrors the strength of the Popular Front itself, so enthusiastic as a body, so disappointing in leadership. As an emblem of the left, the common man as collective hero stands as an appropriate centerpiece in the Popular Front film of the Revolution.

The middle section of *La Marseillaise* ends with the arrival of the troop in the capital. Their first encounter with Parisian Royalists serves as a condensation of spectacle elements and a reminder of the film's partisan politics. Michelet, Mathiez, and Lefebvre do not report the episode; Taine's description contradicts the film's:

> Welcomed with great pomp by the Jacobins and by Santerre, they [the Marseillais] are conducted, for a purpose, to the Champs Elysées, into a drinking place, near the restaurant in which the grenadiers of Filles St. Thomas, bankers, brokers, leading men well-known for their attachment to a monarchical constitution, were dining in a body, as announced several days in advance. The populace, which had formed a convoy for the Marseilles battalion, gathers before the restaurant, shouts, throws mud, and then lets fly a volley of stones; the grenadiers draw their sabres. Forthwith a shout is heard just in front of them, *à nous les Marseillaise!* upon which the gang jump out of the windows with true southern agility, clamber across the ditches, fall upon the grenadiers with their swords, kill one and wound fifteen—No debut could be

6 | *La Marseillaise* (1938), production still. The collective hero had a
precedent in Georges Lefebvre's investigations of peasant politics and
the revolutionary crowd. Courtesy Museum of Modern Art/Film Stills
Archive

> more brilliant. The party at last possesses men of action;
> and they must be kept within reach![41]

In the film the provocation comes from the aristocrats, and the
Marseillais rush from the banquet table to the defense of their
friends. The camera expands in a long take over a wooded setting as the rival groups duel across the Champs Élysées until
the grenadiers, drenched by the summer storm and routed by
the Jacobins, retreat into a walled court. Amid the commotion,
Bomier meets Louison and runs off with her to find shelter. The
bucolic, rain-drenched landscape soothingly embraces the fight,
and, rather than focusing on the bloodshed, the film ends the

incident with a blossoming romance. The scene includes all the major spectacle elements—the collective hero in the Marseillais, the food motif in the banquet, and the meaningful opposition between nature and architecture in the setting, with the wood dominated by the republicans versus the enclosed court into which the monarchists retreat.

The Food Motif

In *La Marseillaise*, hunting, cooking, and meals establish a recurrent setting for the drama and allude to the extrapersonal forces shaping history. By the close, the food motif has illustrated how political relations shape the economy of daily life. In the opening scene the king rests from the hunt, the sport of the aristocracy now divorced from any productive function. Louis, of course, never lacks food, and as he hears of the incident at the Bastille, wine and meat are brought to his bedside. The next scene moves to Provence, where a peasant is arrested for killing the pigeon that raided his crop. The old regime has reversed the natural order; while the starving peasants are barred from the bounty of the land, the sated aristocrats turn hunting into sport.

Food continually illustrates how power relations shape common experience. Meals, for example, may express unity or division. When the fugitive peasant finds Bomier and Arnaud in the mountains, their bond is sealed as he teaches them to hunt. Later they exchange the fine points of roasting a hare over an open fire. Divisions between the old and the new, men and women, parent and child, are illustrated when, in spite of Bomier's insistence, his mother stands serving the man of the house while he eats. Food also serves as a visual metaphor. Outside Valenciennes, two soldiers literally eat crow as they grumble over the betrayal of the officer corps. Arnaud and Bomier discuss recruitment policy and the new song, "La Marseillaise," as they fish in the harbor. The casting for food and the open space of the sea are analogous to their quest for answers and their free exchange. The Revolution itself comes disguised as a gift of food. The Jacobins take the fortress at Marseilles by offering the royal troops a barrel of wine, which bursts open to reveal an armed man. New foods herald new ideas. A meal of potatoes, just introduced from America, is seasoned by volunteers with taxfree salt as they express their outrage over the Brunswick Manifesto. Food infuses the film with the politics of daily life and shows how social relations artificially control the fruits of nature. The food motif reminds the audience that the Revolution of 1792 was not based simply on political principles but, like the struggles of the modern era, arose from common hardship, economic exploitation, and political injustice.

Landscape and Interiors

The composition of space and the representation of landscape add a further dimension to *La Marseillaise*. These elements of the spectacle elaborate an opposition between nature and artifice, freedom and constraint, the Revolution and the old regime. The democrats command the expansive exteriors. They are comfortable in nature, and their homes are flooded with sunlight. The aristocrats inhabit opulent salons and chateaus. They are masters of interiors, artifically constructed, rigidly defined, and thoroughly enclosed. The contending classes are characterized by the spaces they inhabit.

The opening scenes introduce the theme by juxtaposing the palace's numerous passageways and guarded rooms to the open farmlands where the Revolution is taking shape. The peasant cornered in the courtroom escapes to the mountains through an open window. In the nurturing hills the exiles join together, their union blessed by nature. At Coblenz the aristocrats' salon is windowless, impervious to sunshine or storm. Bomier's sitting room, on the contrary, looks down into the streets of the town and up at the Mediterranean sky. The long-take panoramas celebrate the fraternity of the volunteers and the unity of the nation. They are exclusive to the commoners, and are concentrated in the middle section of the film. As the Marseillais marches north, the battalion is photographed in medium-long shots parading by streams, fields, and shaded woods. A benign nature is associated with the Jacobins and speeds them to Paris.

The spacious *mise-en-scène* is immediately constricted upon the return to the court. The Tuileries is introduced with a closeup of the king's hand on the proposed manifesto. The scene continues with tight medium-close shots of Louis XVI and his ministers. Only midway through the scene is an establishing view offered, and the entire episode never leaves the interior of the room. When the king finally moves outdoors to review the troops, he seems to cross into foreign terrain, the natural world that is allied to the Jacobins. Even in the courtyard of the palace, the monarch is challenged with cries of "Vive la Nation" and forced to retreat. Leaving the palace, the king's entourage retains a dignified pose as they stroll past the formal gardens until the young prince playfully throws himself upon a pile of fallen leaves. The child's spontaneous gesture, embracing nature's violation of the order of the garden, speaks the language of the Revolution. The king moves to his son and guides him forward, explaining, in an uncertain, faltering tone, "So many leaves. . . . They are falling early this year." The movement into the open marks the defeat of the monarchy. The melancholy mood and premature autumn foretell the king's death. The attack on the Tuileries follows, with the revolutionaries charging from the sunlit streets into the monumental edifice. With the fall of the palace, the collective hero brings down the artificial structure, the labyrinthine interior, that lay at the foundation of the old regime.

| The Reception of *La Marseillaise*

The public exchange that greeted *La Marseillaise* has been largely forgotten, but it offers a valuable perspective. On February 9, 1938, *La Marseillaise* premiered at the Olympia Theater in Paris, attended by an array of Popular Front dignitaries. The success of *La Grande Illusion*, months of press reports, and the unambiguous political aims of the production attracted a critical audience that was primed and alert. Responses immediately divided along partisan lines. The public, however, delivered a serious rebuke of a different kind: They failed to come. In an interview in 1967, Renoir could attribute the lack of interest only to an undefinable mood and his own inability to anticipate the public temper.[42] *La Marseillaise* appeared on the screen during a conspicuous decline in the fortunes of the French left and a mounting international crisis. The Popular Front was in disarray, and the film's call for renewed commitment fell upon a dispirited and downcast population.

Conspicuous omissions from *La Marseillaise* drew heated reactions from those who saw the film. The revolutionary crowd of 1792 derived its power from actions both admirable and infamous. Conservative accounts had distorted the crowd into a grotesque monster, but the Ciné-Liberté production presented the Jacobins as untainted heroes, ignoring the September massacres, in which the Marseillais unit in fact took a leading part. These mass killings were bracketed by the fall of the Tuileries on August 10 and the Battle of Valmy on September 20, the point at which the film concludes. There is no question that the massacres fell within the film's scope.

In 1792, the fears of the approaching German army were augmented by rumors that imprisoned subversives were planning a massive escape now that most of the able-bodied men had gone to the front and left the population unprotected. There was also fear that émigrés and their allies might take Paris, freeing the prisoners to strike back. Many argued for eliminating the Revolution's enemies before facing the invaders. Moreover, revolutionaries, particularly the Marseillais, were eager to avenge comrades who had fallen on August 10.

Historians report the outcome in grisly terms. Taine has no hesitation in assigning blame to "the Federates of the South, lusty fellows, former soldiers or old bandits, deserters, bohemians, and bullies of all lands and from every source. . . . It is their band which, first of all, takes the twenty-four priests from the mayoralty, and on the way, begins the massacre with their own hands."[43] Masses of citizens marched into nine Paris prisons and over the course of five days summarily executed between eleven and fourteen hundred inmates. Though the exact demographic profile of the mob is uncertain, it is acknowledged, even by historians sympathetic to the Jacobins, that Marseillais recruits participated in the slaughter. The vast majority of those killed were thieves, prostitutes, petty criminals, and even juvenile delinquents of no political persuasion. Michelet does not flinch from describing the brutality:

Some two or three hundred in all—went, drunker and drunker, from prison to prison, sinking ever deeper into blood and filth and packing a lifetime of debauchery into three days. On the second, many still found the massacre an effort, but by the third it had become a joy. Bit by bit the thieving began; and then killing of women. By the fourth, there was rape, and children joined the list of victims.[44]

Lefebvre concludes that "the Terror accentuated the political, religious, and social consequences of August 10. No longer were there any who dared defend the monarchy."[45]

The September massacres and the attack on the Tuileries are responsible for the reputation of the Marseillais as a brutal and determined revolutionary corps. The film skips over their role in the massacres but portrays their honorable service on the field at Valmy. As a consequence, even the members of the conservative and moderate press who had praised *La Grande Illusion* and recognized Jean Renoir's talent were quick to attack *La Marseillaise* as a travesty of history and a vehicle for Communist propaganda. In *Esprit* Roger Leenhardt described the film as mediocre and criticized its politics: "It has faithfully followed not history, but legend. Its vision of the Revolution is a children's tale of Jacobin sentiment and idealism."[46] In *L'Action Française* François Vinneuil conceded that Renoir was an eloquent artist, but regarded him as a dangerous partisan. "The communist Jean Renoir has composed a Marseillaise according to instructions from Dimitroff. . . . For the greater glory of the Soviet Union."[47] Pierre Brisson of *Le Figaro* strongly objected to the portrayal of the revolutionaries as so charitable and humane that one could hardly imagine them engaging in the unpleasantries of civil war. He reminded his readers of the massacre of the Swiss Guards and the pillaging of the palace that followed the surrender on August 10.[48] In the left press Louis Aragon was beside himself with praise in *Ce Soir,* comparing Renoir to Charles Chaplin, Gustave Courbet, and even Michelangelo.[49] Georges Sadoul echoed Aragon in *Regards,* finding that Renoir "has achieved the most authentic epic ever produced by the cinema."[50] The reviews remind us how deeply divided France was on the eve of World War II.

Early in 1937, Marcel Achard and Henri Jeanson, both distinguished writers, had been mentioned as collaborators on the screenplay of *La Marseillaise.* As a leader of Ciné-Liberté and a member of the editorial board, Jeanson was in a position to shape the project. By the summer of 1937, both men had dropped out of the production. Their response to the picture suggests the conflicts within the Popular Front.[51]

Achard's review expressed regret that partisan feeling had prevented a fair evaluation of *La Marseillaise*. He praised Renoir's visual craft, but on balance found the film tedious in its weak dialogue and superficial characterization and dangerous in its glorification of civil strife. Indignant at the positive portrayal of bloodshed between political factions, Achard accused Renoir of being an "apostle of civil war" and the film of encouraging political hostilities. One senses the moderate Socialist position of Léon Blum in these words. Achard seems to have objected to the implications of the historical episode itself. The critic's reaction seems to have been sparked by the dominant Communist influence on the production and by the sensitivity of the French audience to the contemporary political allusions.

Jeanson's article, *"La Marseillaise* or Stalinist Deceit," gleefully recounted the tempestuous public meetings in which suggestions from all sides overwhelmed the filmmakers. He described the result as a complete concession to Communist propaganda. For his former colleague Renoir, he contended, the Revolution was "charming, gracious, and refined. . . . His historical film is a film without history." Like Achard he conceded the visual quality of the work and pinpointed the scenario as the source of its failure. Jeanson ended by dismissing Achard's fear that the film would divide France: He was confident that everyone, reactionary and radical alike, would agree that *La Marseillaise* is "beautiful but boring."

The response to *La Marseillaise* confirms that the film's audience understood the work as a partisan address to contemporary issues. Enmeshed in the politics of 1937—the disappointment of the Blum government as well as the divisions in the Popular Front—*La Marseillaise* hardly appears to be the objective document described by Truffaut. As a political artifact, the film continued to spark strong reactions. Five years after the initial release, with France divided and at war, came reports of yet another spirited response.

Harold Salemson, an American officer who did propaganda work for the Psychological Warfare Branch under the Allied Command, was stationed in Tunisia in the summer of 1943, a few months after the Allied Liberation. He observed the enthusiastic reception of *La Marseillaise* by an audience composed largely of French citizens in exile:

> Revived in 1943, it took on a new light. The film had not changed in the five years that had elapsed, but the temperature of the public, its mental processes, and the air it breathed, had been through Munich, war, defeat, occupation and liberation. The spoken lines and physical situations of *La Marseillaise*, only plain statements of truth in 1938, became in 1943 incendiary political material. Before the film had been running three days, it had become a focal point for political thought in the French protectorate. . . . I found that, in the five years that had elapsed, objective events had made of *La Marseillaise* the weapon it had somehow failed to be when first released.[52]

Salemson described standing-room-only crowds and shouts from the audience:

> Innumerable individual incidents and lines of dialogue kept the stream of political comment from the audience alive, and the over-all effect of the film was no less a call to action on the part of the audience. In a quarter century of film-going I have never seen any film, even one turned out for a specific agitational or propaganda purpose in a specific circumstance, elicit the unanimous type of response from its audience which *La Marseillaise* evoked in Tunis in the latter half of 1943.[53]

In North Africa, the Gaullist authorities, unsympathetic to the left politics of the film, had the film withdrawn despite its "more than sold out box office success."[54]

La Marseillaise was the same film in 1938 and 1943, but now combative nationalism was widely shared and sparked a fervent response. The French in North Africa now saw the betrayal of Vichy in the émigrés of Coblentz, and they were ready to take up the Jacobin battlecry for a new nation.

Chapter 3

Hollywood History and the French Revolution: From *The Bastille* to *The Black Book*

> *For through this blessed July night, there is clangour, confusion very great.*
> —THOMAS CARLYLE, 1837

Few Hollywood films progress from the initial concept to premiere screening without change; financial pressures, social forces, and contending personnel all influence a film's development. Sometimes the off-screen drama proves more meaningful than the film itself. In the absence of a commanding figure like Charles Chaplin, David O. Selznick, or John Ford, many films fail to express a unified and coherent view; these are best understood by examining the tensions that arose during production. The making of *Reign of Terror* (1949) is a case in point; Hollywood's meditation upon Robespierre reveals more about its own time than it does about the course of the French Revolution.

On February 11, 1948, *Variety* announced the Walter Wanger production of *The Bastille* at the Eagle–Lion studio.[1] By June the completed screenplay was called *Reign of Terror*, and before the end of the exhibition run the title was *The Black Book*. The title shifts hint at the evolution of this eccentric hybrid of historical fiction and film noir that portrays the crisis of 9 Thermidor 1794.

The tradition of the historical film is one of pomp and solemnity—the lavish sets, thoughtful research, and high aspirations of *Intolerance, Gone With the Wind*, and *Ivan the Terrible* come to mind. Earlier films of the French Revolution, such as *Orphans of the Storm, Marie Antoinette*, and *La Marseillaise*, challenged the resources of the various film industries that produced them; they were beyond the reach of Eagle–Lion, the tawdry factory of crime melodramas. *Reign of Terror* marks the studio's one attempt at a historical film. Georges Sadoul dismissed it as "the worst kind of pseudo-historical melodrama,"[2] but Robert E. Smith expressed a growing fascination with "the most bizarre and baroquely shot of French Revolutions."[3] The film reflects key elements in the relationship between the cinema and historical representation, offering a useful counterpoint to *La Marseillaise*.

| Aspirations and Execution in a Divided Production

In the eighteen months between the announcement of the production in February 1948 and the premiere of *Reign of Terror* in July 1949, the film underwent major shifts in its goals, resources, and personnel. The resulting conflicts and compromises threatened the film's coherence and fostered the contradictory elements that give the work its special quality.

The Eagle–Lion studio operated only from 1946 to 1951. The railroad magnate Robert Young began the operation by purchasing the Producers Releasing Corporation, a low-budget Hollywood studio that had churned out genre pictures since 1940. He then struck a deal to distribute the British productions of the J. Arthur Rank studio in the United States.

The ambition of Young and President of Operations Arthur Krim was to establish a competitive studio on the order of Columbia or United Artists with a mixed program of quality and "B" films. The first Eagle–Lion releases hit the screen in 1947 with limited success, but the seminal picture from the studio, *T-Men*, appeared in January 1948. An urban crime film featuring police procedure and location shooting in the noir manner, *T-Men* garnered favorable reviews and earned a handsome $1.6 million on an investment of $424,000.[4] The success provided welcome income for the struggling enterprise, which faced losses of $2.2 million in 1947. Eagle–Lion tried to duplicate its hit by producing similar crime films such as *Raw Deal, Canon City*, and *He Walked by Night* while pursuing the prospect of quality pictures through a 1947 agreement under which Walter Wanger would make two to four films for the studio. As former president of the Academy of Motion Pictures and one of the leading independent producers in Hollywood—his credits included *Stagecoach* (1939), *Foreign Correspondent* (1940), and *Scarlet Street* (1945)—Wanger brought prestige to a firm largely known for low-budget features. During the spring of 1948, he was developing his initial Eagle– Lion projects: *Tulsa*, and a film about the French Revolution, *The Bastille*.

Wanger was a producer who brought his cosmopolitan sensibility and political convictions to the screen. He had contested prewar isolationism and dramatized his support for American intervention in European affairs in *Blockade* (1938) and *Foreign Correspondent*. Wanger worked regularly with émigré European directors, counting Fritz Lang and Max Ophuls as well as Alfred Hitchcock among his professional associates. Furthermore, he sought to increase Hollywood access to foreign markets and was generally interested in cooperative foreign ventures. The association between J. Arthur Rank and Eagle–Lion encouraged Wanger to strike an alliance with the fledgling studio. Subjects with a European setting expressing transatlantic concerns were attractive to Wanger. In 1947 he was already making a lavish historical spectacle, *Joan of Arc*, which he believed would strengthen Franco-American relations and attract European audiences. The subject of the French Revolution had the additional advantage of representing a popular struggle against an authoritarian regime. Both before and after World War II, Wanger did not hesitate to trumpet antitotalitarian themes in his films.[5]

A disparity between the studio's resources and the producer's aspirations soon became apparent. In Hollywood, historical films were an expensive prospect and their costs carried commensurate prestige. Eagle–Lion, eager to gain recognition for "A" product, found in the historical film a genre that said "quality." The problem was raising the money. In the early months of 1948, the project was developed as an "A" film, with Wanger considering Joan Crawford, Alida Valli, and Victor Mature for leading roles. In May, Wanger and Eagle–Lion negotiated $1 million-plus budgets for *Tulsa* and *Reign of Terror*. One month later, however, continuing losses forced the studio to cut back funding for the high-quality productions Wanger planned. In order to protect funding levels for *Tulsa,* the producer had to accept restrictions on *Reign of Terror.* The big-budget spectacular originally conceived was soon restricted to the resources of a "programmer." (A "programmer" was a feature film budgeted midway between an "A" and a "B" production.) With a budget of $750,000, Wanger, disillusioned and pressed for cash, had to settle for Robert Cummings and Arlene Dahl as the headliners. Yet the key personnel assembled for the project were impressive: screenwriters Aeneas MacKenzie and Philip Yordan, producer William Cameron Menzies, cinematographer John Alton, and director Anthony Mann. Three of these five men would receive the industry's highest honor, an Academy Award, during their careers. Shooting on the film began on August 9, 1948, and was completed in early October.

The screenplay for *Reign of Terror* was composed in two distinct stages. First, the script was developed over a period of months by MacKenzie, a writer specializing in period and historical films. His first screen credits were for Warner Brothers' lavish productions of 1939: *Juarez* and *The Private Lives of Elizabeth and Essex.* His last credit came in 1956 on Cecil B. De Mille's *The Ten Commandments.* The screenwriter was a veteran at integrating historical fact, popular legend, and dramatic action. In the early months of 1948, MacKenzie proceeded with research and writing. After the budget cut, however, MacKenzie was out. Anthony Mann called in his friend Philip Yordan to transform the MacKenzie material from a historical spectacle to a more economical action picture. Yordan had a string of credits for low-budget action fare, most notably *Dillinger* (1945), for which he received an Academy Award nomination. In the 1950s and 1960s he would write distinguished Westerns and historical films for both Mann and Nicholas Ray (*Johnny Guitar, The Man from Laramie, El Cid, 55 Days at Peking, The Fall of the Roman Empire*), as well as the Oscar-winning *Broken Lance* (1954). Yordan claims to have made substantial revisions in the screenplay, but he completed his work quickly, possibly in the six days from June 12, when an Eagle–Lion memorandum reduced financing, to June 17, when he submitted the manuscript to Wanger. Yordan worked without conducting any historical research or consulting MacKenzie. In an interview, Yordan confirmed that Wanger had little interest in the revised screenplay or the picture itself at this point.[6] MacKenzie's and Yordan's shifting agendas begin to explain the unusual hybrid of historical spectacle and film noir and the jocular dialogue that often punctures the solemnity characteristic of historical fiction.

Disillusioned and caught up with the shooting and release of his "A" pictures, *Joan of Arc* and *Tulsa*, Wanger delegated authority as the producer of *Reign of Terror* to William Cameron Menzies. In more than twenty-five years of work, Menzies had gained a reputation as one of the outstanding art directors in the industry and in 1928 won the first Academy Award given in this category. *Gone With the Wind* was among his credits. When Menzies, the art director, assumed the duties of producer on *Reign of Terror*, he proceeded to shape the visual design of the film. In an interview shortly before his death, Mann called Menzies "the most creative art director I ever worked with. . . . it was only through his ability that we were able to achieve any style, feeling, or period."[7] The windmill locale early in *Reign of Terror* seems to be lifted from a famous Menzies set for Hitchcock's *Foreign Correspondent;* the carriage attack and the portrayal of the revolutionary Convention have also been attributed to Menzies. The budget reductions might have provoked carelessness or resignation; instead, Menzies prompted the crew on *Reign of Terror* to tackle the historical setting with imagination and bravado. The result was what Robert Ottoson has dubbed "as bizarre a period piece as one could find."[8]

John Alton and Anthony Mann, the creative bedrock of Eagle–Lion, also made central contributions to *Reign of Terror*. They had already worked on three urban crime films at the studio, *T-Men*, *Raw Deal*, and *He Walked by Night*. On these pictures Alton and Mann developed a visual style that enriched the vocabulary of what later became known as film noir.

Alton had earned a reputation for lighting from the floor and using fast camera setups to hold down expenses. Though he later moved to MGM, where he won an Academy Award for cinematography on *An American in Paris* in 1951, his signature style is wedded to film noir. His oblique camera angles, extreme close-ups, and extensive shadows established a visual texture foreign to the historical spectacle. Alton's foreboding images express the fear of the Terror and camouflage the rudimentary sets by dressing revolutionary Paris in the shade of a midnight alley. His technique is strikingly illustrated by the first meeting of the protagonists, Charles and Madelon. Madelon enters a darkened room to deliver a secret message to an unidentified agent. Through half the scene Alton keeps the two foreground figures in dark silhouette, employing a single light filtered through the wooden blinds of a window in the rear of the set. Finally a candle reflecting off a mirror becomes the diegetic light source for Alton's softly lit closeups of Charles and Madelon. The dim lighting increases the tension of the encounter while eliminating any need to dress the set. Alain Silver and Elizabeth Ward have noted that "Alton created a portrait of eighteenth century France from shadows and silhouettes . . . that, in the noir manner, gives *The Black Book* the dark quality of a milieu mired in despair and turbulent with chaotic activity."[9] By employing the claustrophobic style of film noir, Alton worked against the convention of the historical picture that emphasized the spectacular through panoramic vistas and elaborate sets.

For Mann, the director, *Reign of Terror* came at a career crossroads between his crime films and a celebrated series of Westerns starring James Stewart, which were initiated in 1950 with *Winchester '73*. Mann's crime films and his Westerns are noted for his expressive but contrasting treatments of setting. The crime films confine the action and enclose the characters, whereas the Westerns establish an expansive landscape. His historical films from the 1960s, *El Cid* and *The Fall of the Roman Empire*, testify to an interest in panoramic spectacle closer in style to the fifties Westerns than the crime films from the forties. At Eagle–Lion, however, economy called for a film noir vocabulary for the Paris of Thermidor. If surging crowds and imposing sets had been visualized when the production of *The Bastille* was announced in February, they were no longer possible in August.

Auteurists might look to Mann as the guiding force on *Reign of Terror*, citing his contribution to the production and the noir vocabulary, but even Mann's chief advocates pass over *Reign of Terror*.[10] The film's most striking qualities surely have multiple, even contending sources.

What does the change in subject from *The Bastille* to *Reign of Terror* imply? Both titles allude to important events in the French Revolution, but events of a distinct character. Significantly, the fall of the Bastille resulted from a popular mass uprising against established authority, politically moving France to the left. *Reign of Terror* takes place five years later, in 1794, after the radical party of the Revolution, the Jacobins, have seized power. In this case an oppressive government of the left falls to a political conspiracy organized from the right. The execution of Robespierre ushers in a period of reaction, Thermidor. Wanger could play out antiauthoritarian themes in the context of both historical episodes, but the choice of events suggests a political turnaround. The change displays a different attitude toward the French Revolution and toward parallels in contemporary affairs. *The Bastille*, named after a symbol of oppression overcome by a popular uprising, would probably have celebrated the success of the Revolution of 1789. A feeling of optimism, democratic power, and political progress coalesces around the title. How different is *Reign of Terror*, where the Revolution is discredited, the common people become a bloodthirsty mob, and the historical attitude turns fearful and bitter.

What motivated the change of setting from 1789 to 1794? The evolution of the production suggests a discomfort about the subject. The treatment of popular insurgency was a volatile issue in Cold War Hollywood. In a letter to Mann on October 1, 1948, after the principal shooting was completed, Wanger sensed lingering difficulties. The producer congratulated his director on a "fine job" and left the picture in Mann's hands for editing, but expressed apprehension as well as satisfaction. "I am terribly concerned about the opening [moments of the film]," the producer wrote. "I feel that a great deal of the success of the picture will depend on the audience understanding the spirit of the Revolution—where everything gets out of control and where opportunism reigns supreme." Wanger describes this "spirit" as marked by "distrust, chaos and a carnival of lust." [11]

In promoting *Reign of Terror* to exhibitors and the press, further discomfort with the subject of the French Revolution emerged. Eagle–Lion initially marketed the film as a historical spectacle that portrayed "the spirit of the French Revolution" (illustration 7). The studio press book synopsis began: "France

7 | This advertisement from the *Los Angeles Times* for *Reign of Terror* stresses the historical spectacle but seems less certain about the French Revolution's political implications.

in 1794. The blood-drenched Reign of Terror is at its height. Maximilien Robespierre, evil genius of the terror, has demanded absolute dictatorial powers."[12] Publicity described *Reign of Terror* as "a spectacular epic of the French Revolution in the great tradition of 'Marie Antoinette,' 'A Tale of Two Cities' and 'The Scarlet Pimpernel.'" In addition Eagle–Lion urged exhibitors to link the movie to books set during the period and critical of the Revolution's excesses, particularly *A Tale of Two Cities* and Thomas Carlyle's *History of the French Revolution*. The studio touted "the exceptional authenticity of the French Revolutionary background" and suggested that exhibitors promote the picture with local schoolteachers.

Eagle–Lion's newspaper advertisements, on the other hand, were generalized and even ambiguous in evoking the historical setting of the film. Some ad designs used the guillotine as a central icon, but the copy displayed on opening day in the *Los Angeles Times* eliminated the guillotine altogether. The *Times* ad highlights the heroine under torture, half-undressed and hanging by her wrists. The image evokes the historical spectacle with a collage of figures in period dress spread around her in frenetic activity. The promotional copy allies the production to the tradition of the epic by touting a sweeping panorama of revolution and the battle for empire. A note of hesitation is apparent, however. Instead of luring customers with specific information about the crisis of Thermidor, Eagle–Lion couches its ad copy in historical generalities. The publicity seems uncertain about the implications of the French Revolution.

Reign of Terror opened during the week of Bastille Day, July 1949, at the Orpheum Theater and four other sites in Los Angeles. The first week's take of $29,700 was described by *Variety* as "okay"; in the second week, however, the film's return dropped to a "thin" $11,900.[13] *Reign of Terror* closed after eleven days. Subsequently, Eagle–Lion revised its promotion for the autumn release in New York City and changed the title to *The Black Book* (illustration 8). Central to the shift was a remarkable retreat from its historical subject.

The campaign for *The Black Book* eliminates all the references to history and the French Revolution that had appeared in the *Reign of Terror* publicity. The revised synopsis speaks of the struggle against tyranny and despotism without acknowledging the historical setting of the film or providing many details about the plot. The new title and advertising iconography emphasize anxiety and suspense, linking the movie to the Eagle–Lion crime dramas of 1948. Distressed female figures dwarf the surrounding males in the copy for *The Black Book*. The magnified closeups of shadowed faces emphasize the psychological motifs typical of film noir rather than the expansive mass of tiny figures indicative of the historical spectacle. *The Black Book*'s ad features bold and simple words, whereas the one for *Reign of Terror* gives greater emphasis to ornate language, as if the historical subject required exposition.

Despite such revisions, *The Black Book* proved even less successful in New York than *Reign of Terror* had been in Los Angeles. In a week and four days at the Globe, the Wanger production brought in only $16,500.[14] But the distributor did not give up. Two years after its release, the film had returned its production and distribution costs and shown a small profit of $20,000.[15]

8 | The publicity campaign for *The Black Book* abandoned the historical subject and emphasized mystery and suspense, trying to link the film to Eagle–Lion's crime dramas. Courtesy Wisconsin Center for Film and Theater Research

Given the declining fortunes of Eagle–Lion, its performance, if not outstanding, was still commendable.

| "Don't Call Me Max"

Reign of Terror displays an unusual tension between a detailed incorporation of the historical record and a playful tone that undermines the solemn claims to authenticity typical of the genre. Although reviewers dismissed the film's historical representation, examination reveals a greater attention to historical evidence than one finds in many major productions, such as *Orphans of the Storm* or *A Tale of Two Cities*. What one also finds is a split between a knowing incorporation of historical data and a jocular rendering of the period drama—a split that reflects the film's peculiar attitude toward history in general and the French Revolution in particular.

Reign of Terror follows Charles D'Aubigny, who is dispatched by Lafayette to join the plot to overthrow the Jacobin government in July 1794. Disguised as the infamous executioner of Strasbourg, Charles gains access to Robespierre while making contact with the opposition leaders Tallien, Barras, and Fouché. To his surprise Charles also meets Madelon, his duplicitous ex-lover who is at the center of political intrigue. The plot against Robespierre hinges on fear of the Terror, as the conspirators strive to build a coalition by uncovering the "Black Book," Robespierre's secret list of those to be executed after he gains dictatorial power. Though Charles captures the book and wins Madelon, he must finally surrender the secret list to the unscrupulous Fouché in order to save her. Though Robespierre falls, Charles and Madelon must flee Paris.

Press response to *Reign of Terror* was favorable, if condescending. The critics generally agreed that the film matched technical achievement with a ridiculous history in order to produce commendable entertainment. The visual design made an impact. The trade press in particular praised the sets, photography, editing, and performances—Menzies, Alton, and Mann were regularly singled out. But the press criticized the screenplay and dismissed the historical representation as "façade."[16] One is distracted from appraising the film's treatment of the French Revolution by lines like Robespierre's droll "Don't call me Max."

One is surprised, then, to discover that the plot and the central dramatic conceit are historically informed. Though the film reaches back to the spring of 1794 to include the condemnation of Danton, the narrative focuses squarely on the forty-eight hours leading to the execution of Robespierre, from July 26 to July 28, 1794 (7 to 9 Thermidor, according to the revolutionary calendar). The Jacobin leader's speech to the Convention on 8 Thermidor ignited the fears among the representatives that brought Robespierre down. The idea that the leader of the Committee of Public Safety maintained a ledger, the notorious Black Book, inscribed with the names of those to be executed has the appearance of a preposterous Hollywood contrivance, but just such a fear is widely reported by historians. In discussing Robespierre's speech, the American scholar R. R. Palmer writes that the Jacobin leader "threatened right and left, as in the past; but when asked point blank to name the men he accused he evaded the question. The insinuation of Fouché and others thus seemed to be borne out; any man, for all he knew, might be on Robespierre's list." [17] Lefebvre notes that Robespierre's failure to disclose the names of those he accused "destroyed him, for it was assumed that he was demanding a blank cheque." [18]

The historical literature also informs most of the characterizations. The familiar protagonists of the "Reign of Terror"— Robespierre, Saint-Just, Danton—are presented from a conservative point of view, which juxtaposes Robespierre's and Saint-Just's fanaticism with Danton's humanity. More provocative because they are generally foreign to popular dramas are the men who lead the conspiracy of 9 Thermidor—Fouché, Barras, and Tallien. Joseph Fouché, the terrorist, was a coalition-builder, drawing together adherents of various political persuasions against Robespierre. Jean Lambert Tallien is acknowledged as the first to speak out against Robespierre on 9 Thermidor. Paul François Barras, an officer in the National Guard, led the military contingent that guaranteed the ascendancy of his allies. All three became prominent members of the Directory in the period that followed. Barras was probably the leading member of the French government from 1794 to 1799.

The production's ambivalence surfaces in the troubled portrayal of leadership in the film's opening moments, a scene added after the body of the picture had been shot and in response to Wanger's concern about conveying the "spirit" of the Revolution. A newsreel-like voice announces the date, July 26, 1794, and describes Paris as in the grip of anarchy and fear. Then six characters are introduced in closeup head shots, harshly underlit over a background of flames. The first three are terrorists and villains:

> "Robespierre: a fanatic with powdered wig and twisted mind
> Saint-Just: a connoisseur of roses and blood
> Fouché: the politician, always on both sides, never in the middle"

The last three are honorable men:

> "Danton: soldier, savior of France
> Barras: citizen of France, an honest man fighting for the life of his country
> Tallien: another honest man"

One can dismiss this expressive treatment as growing from the caricatures that routinely transform historical complexity into popular legend. No doubt this rhetoric belongs to that genre, but it is meaningful in a curious way because it splits the historical film's figure of the great leader into two camps of multiple figures, all of whom are historical personalities. In the case of Tallien and Barras, the film's description is drastically inconsistent with either their historical character or their legendary status.

Hardly "an honest man," Tallien was tainted with political corruption and decadent habits, alluded to in the film's tavern and boudoir settings. Robespierre had denounced him at the Jacobin Club as early as May 1794 for conspiring with foreign courts and international bankers. During the Thermidorian reaction, his lavish life excited criticism, and his politics discredited him with both the right and the left. His allegiances were as mercurial as Fouché's but not as gracefully orchestrated.

Barras was no more upstanding. *The Historical Dictionary of the French Revolution* describes the leader of the Directory as "an extreme example of the ruthlessness, corruption and venality that emerged during the Revolutionary period." [19] His willingness to bribe seemed to be exceeded only by his eagerness to accept bribes; his "devotion" to political principle prompted him to serve in turn the Revolution, the empire, and the throne.

In constructing a screenplay around the fall of Robespierre, MacKenzie established a cast of characters drawn from the historical episode. Yordan treated them with a freewheeling disregard for historical evidence and a sense of gallows humor in order to shape the material into a self-deprecating action film. *Reign of Terror*'s cynicism toward the conspirators, the French Revolution, and political activity in general strives to integrate the writers' contending perspectives. The film's opening and closing episodes portray a cycle of political change with no indication of social benefit. The movie begins with Charles being commissioned by the exiled Lafayette, a leader during the early years of the Revolution. After Robespierre's execution Fouché stumbles upon the unknown officer, Bonaparte, foreshadowing the fall of those who have just assumed power. Although the historical reputations of Tallien and Barras are whitewashed, Fouché is presented as a witty but unscrupulous rascal whose cooperation is needed in order to undermine the Terror. As a result the film cynically alludes to the limitations, if not the corruption, of its political leadership.

The romantic couple too presents a curious mixture of historical tradition and Hollywood convention. The heroine, Madelon, is a provocative figure because she appears to be based on the historical Thérésa Cabarrus, daughter of a Spanish court banker. In the months before Thermidor she and Tallien became lovers. Then, in the summer of 1794, she was arrested. Carlyle writes, "And now his fair Cabarus [*sic*], hit by denunciation, lies Arrested, Suspect, in spite of all he could do!—Shut in horrid pinfold of death, the Senhora smuggles out to her red-gloomy Tallien, the most pressing entreaties and conjurings: Save me; save thyself. Seest thou not that thy own head is doomed." [20] With the fall of Robespierre, Cabarrus was freed, and in December 1794 she married Tallien. In the coming years, Cabarrus played hostess to a notorious salon that became a center for Thermidorian decadence and the political right. Lefebvre dubbed her "Our Lady of Thermidor," "a woman of easy virtue" who "set the tone for Parisian society." [21] Eventually Cabarrus deserted Tallien for Barras and became an obstacle to the political cooperation of the two men.

Reign of Terror alludes to these biographical facts in a clever and knowing way. Madelon enjoys a lavish life while embroiled in political conspiracy against the Jacobin government. She is a fickle lover who has betrayed Charles in the past. During Charles's clandestine meeting with her, arranged through Tallien, Barras appears from behind her boudoir curtains. As the plot unfolds, Madelon is jailed by Robespierre's henchmen, and her release is secured as a result of his fall. Thus the filmmakers used some historical knowledge in shaping their material. Why did the studio press book fail to make journalists aware of the movie's historical reliability? Most historical films exaggerate their claims to authenticity; *Reign of Terror*'s ambivalence toward historical representation reflects its discomfort with the Revolution itself.

| Conventions in Contest: The Historical Spectacle in Film Noir Style

Robert Ottoson, Alain Silver, and Elizabeth Ward include *Reign of Terror* in their guides to film noir, even though a contemporary setting is standard for these films. The connections between this historical fiction and film noir are found in central elements of characterization and plot as well as visual style. Madelon is the duplicitous *femme fatale*, Raymond Durgnant's "Black Widow." Richard Basehardt's Robespierre is the villain described in Paul Schrader's "Notes on Film Noir"—"the small time gangster [who] has now made it big and sits in the mayor's chair." *Reign of Terror* also takes its historical attitude from what Schrader cites as "the overwhelming noir theme: a passion for the past and present, but also a fear of the future. Noir heroes dread to look ahead, but instead try to survive by the day, and if unsuccessful at that, they retreat to the past. Thus film noir's techniques emphasize loss, nostalgia, lack of clear priorities, and insecurity, then it submerges these self-doubts in mannerism and style." [22] The filmmakers' lack of clear priorities, and the conflict between the generic demands of the historical subject and their limited resources, are all submerged in the stylish constructs of Alton, Menzies, and Mann.

Charles D'Aubigny, the film's protagonist, is a familiar noir hero. Charles looks to the past, to the long-spent glory of Lafayette and the revolutionary years of 1789 to 1791, and he looks to a future with Fouché as Minister of Police and Bonaparte as emperor. Nostalgia, loss, and uncertainty characterize his romance with Madelon. They are lovers with a bitter past, and move toward each other again through stages of disguise and recognition. Charles and Madelon deceive each other and then their mutual enemies in their progress toward union. Madelon must penetrate Charles's disguise as Duval; later, at the tavern, Charles must see through the mask of a false Madelon. At the prison Madelon appears as Madame Duval in order to confirm Charles's false identity as the executioner of Strasbourg. In the ensuing chase they cooperate in their masquerade as a husband and wife returning to their farm. Finally, Charles must search for and find Madelon imprisoned behind a wall of black books. Near the climax Fouché poses an emblematic choice for Charles: he must decide between the Black Book, which represents knowledge, power, and political commitment, and Madelon, who represents personal feeling and private life. He turns from the original object of his quest, the political goal of the film, in order to renew his romance apart from the entanglements of government. His choice is undermined by the allusion to the real Thérésa Cabarrus, which implies that the lovers' union, like the coalition of Thermidor, has no future.

The spectacle in *Reign of Terror* embodies an equally bleak historical attitude. Historical films generally present panoramic landscapes, exotic locales, surging crowds—spectacles that express forces working in history. Hence the tendency is toward long shots and epic scope. *Reign of Terror* prefers narrow, dim studio streets, constricting enclosures such as the prison cell, the night carriage, or Robespierre's chamber beneath the bakery (illustration 9). *Reign of Terror* presents the antithesis of the historical spectacle, and in that respect it is revealing. For though film noir looks to the past, it fails to find in the past the explanation, the causal relations, that are the object of history. *Reign of Terror* skeptically suggests that the essential political struggles take place underground, among conspirators, in back rooms. Popular forces, political principles, and economic relations exert little influence. The underlying causes of history are submerged and largely inaccessible.

Two memorable spectacles in *Reign of Terror* express this attitude—the meetings of the Convention and Robespierre's inner

9 | *Reign of Terror* (1949), production still. Robespierre's chamber beneath the bakery: Although most of the stills prepared by Eagle–Lion to promote *Reign of Terror* pointedly fail to display the film's distinctive visual style, there were some exceptions. Courtesy Wisconsin Center for Film and Theater Research

office. Mann explained how Menzies developed the image of the crowd at the Convention. The designer squeezed a hundred extras onto a small rising gallery of benches, flooded the set with irregular shafts of light, and then photographed and enlarged the scale of the image. These shots were integrated through rear projection with the foreground of the Convention. The crowd fills the flat space of the background and spills, limitless, over the edges of the image. As a result, the members of a national legislature appear to be an expansive mass closer to a stadium crowd than a deliberative body. Unstable, temperamental, and cruel, the delegates embody an immediate but strangely distant public whose collective brutality swallows any individual sentiment.

The full shots of the Convention emphasize two, at times three, distinct visual planes. The rear projection and harsh underlighting distort the features of the image and undermine the continuity of perspective, as if a canyon separated the space between the visual zones. Clear and stable spatial relations are never established. In the background is the gallery of representatives. Before the crowd on the central podium stands Robespierre, who controls the plastic mass. An additional foreground space is occasionally established by sentries framing an entrance way or the dock initially occupied by Danton and later by Barras. The effect underlines the space between the people and their leader and further accents the spectator's distorted and uncertain perspective as if we were glimpsing a disorienting vision through the frame of history.

The second emblematic spectacle is Robespierre's inner office. Midway through the picture Charles realizes that Robespierre keeps his infamous death list in his private chamber. Joined by Fouché, Charles breaks into the room, rifles the desk, and then illuminates the office. All four walls are covered from floor to ceiling with bookcases holding identical black books. "It will take forever to go through all of this," Charles cries. The promise of knowledge is thwarted by excess, multiplicity, the opaque. The spectacle of the room suggests that there is too much information, but also that the past is impenetrable, and understanding is beyond reach. Humor diverts the audience, but an underlying skepticism emerges. A large hound appears and inadvertently leads the men to the treasured document. Finding the list, Fouché and Charles immediately attack each other. The spectacle of Robespierre's library haunts the film. The rows of books contain the secrets for which men fight and die, but knowledge is hidden, not by scarcity, but in its very abundance.

Underscoring the importance of the library and the Convention, the film concludes by crosscutting between the two sites. In the public arena at the Convention, Robespierre's accusation of Barras backfires as delegates, now presented in a montage of lurching head shots, demand their leader's death after glimpsing the Black Book. Simultaneously, Charles again breaks into Robespierre's office, seeking the imprisoned Madelon in a secret chamber behind the wall of books. Armed with a torch, the sign of his passion, Charles frees his beloved. The crosscutting between the public and the private spheres shows the one to be corrupted by the struggle for power, the other purified by passion. Only politics can thwart the romance, and the lovers must flee to preserve their union.

| Political Ambivalence and the Trail of Allusions

Between the announcement of *The Bastille* in February 1948 and the release of *The Black Book* in the fall of 1949, significant political changes occurred. The shift in the treatment of the Revolution reflects the political mood in 1948, when fear, suspicion, and instability set the tone for public affairs.

Reign of Terror takes France for its subject and suggests parallels with contemporary events in Europe. The film's insertion of three military leaders calls attention to another conspicuous French soldier, Charles de Gaulle. On three occasions the film refers to a military man whose integrity rises above the turmoil of politics and who is sympathetic to the right. Charles D'Aubigny is delegated by Lafayette, a figure invested with American sympathies and identified as a general in exile without an army. More surprisingly, Danton is called "soldier and savior of France." Though Danton's political leadership may have engineered French military victories, he was trained as a lawyer, not a soldier. Finally, at the film's conclusion, Bonaparte appears as a foreboding figure threatening the ascendancy of Fouché. Each of these figures echoes de Gaulle's posture in contemporary France.

In the years following World War II, the Fourth Republic was dominated by a center–left coalition attacked on the one hand by the Communists and on the other by the Gaullists. In *Reign of Terror* the attack on Robespierre is marshaled by figures from the left, the terrorist Fouché, and the right, the party of Barras. In 1947, the Communists were ejected from the governing coalition. Many saw in the strikes that followed in 1947–48 an attempt by the PCF to undermine the Fourth Republic. In 1947 General de Gaulle also reentered politics with his new organization, Rassemblement du Peuple Français. The political group attracted a mass following and was under instructions from the general not to cooperate with the governing regime. During 1947–48, France presented a picture of instability, with strong opposition to the constituted Republic from the right and the left.[23] *Reign of Terror*, with its triple allusions to a sympathetic general standing above the turmoil of partisan politics, points to de Gaulle's stance in 1948.

In the United States the Cold War intensified and politics moved dramatically to the right. The National Security Act of 1947 reorganized the military establishment and institutionalized covert military operations in peacetime with the creation of the Defense Department, the Central Intelligence Agency, and the National Security Council. Frank Freidel and Alan Brinkley note that these acts "transferred to the President expanded powers over all defense activities, centralizing in the White House control that had once been widely dispersed. It enabled the administration to take warlike actions without an open declaration of war; and it created vehicles by which the government could act politically and militarily behind a veil of secrecy."[24] These conditions seem analogous to the consolidation of power attempted by Robespierre in *Reign of Terror*. When the leader of the Committee of Public Safety hands Barras legislation to propose at the Convention, Barras cries, "Why, this would make you dictator of France! We didn't storm the Bastille to make any man dictator." One might object, persuasively, that drawing such a parallel violates the portrait of the Jacobin as a mad tyrant hardly comparable with President Harry Truman. No doubt the film is rife with contradictory impulses; nevertheless, I contend that the production expresses anxiety over the growing concentration of authoritarian power.

Cold War fears escalated in 1947 when Truman signed the Federal Employee Loyalty Program, which reviewed all federal workers for subversive tendencies. The sensational news coverage of the Alger Hiss case kept international subversion and undercover espionage firmly in the public mind. In the months immediately preceding the shooting of *Reign of Terror*, July and August 1948, Whitaker Chambers testified before the House Un-American Activities Committee that Hiss, a distinguished State Department officer, had passed secret information to Communist operatives in 1938. Tales of secret meetings, hidden documents, and international sabotage filled the newspaper headlines. The mood of conspiracy and betrayal set the tone for Eagle–Lion's treatment of the French Revolution.

In these years the politics of the Cold War engulfed Hollywood, where the Motion Picture Producers Association began to take on extraordinary powers. In October and November 1947, HUAC conducted public hearings on Communists in the motion picture industry. Ten prominent Hollywood professionals suspected of Communist sympathies were cited for contempt of Congress after invoking their constitutional right to remain silent. Industry leaders issued on November 26 their famous Waldorf Statement, which established the practice of "blacklisting" motion picture workers tainted with a history of left-wing activity who were unwilling to cooperate in the crusade against subversives.

Walter Wanger at first attacked the anti-Communist extremists within the film industry. In September 1945 he charged the Motion Picture Alliance for the Preservation of American Ideals with making "unsupported charges of Communism in the motion picture industry." [25] Soon, however, he yielded to pressure. In the fall of 1947, he participated in the meeting of industry power-brokers that drafted the Waldorf Statement; in 1950, he became head of the Los Angeles chapter of Crusade for Freedom, a group dedicated to exposing suspected Communist sympathizers. Most likely the longstanding liberal surrendered grudgingly to the political tide washing over the film industry, but he was now eager to demonstrate his loyalty to the Hollywood establishment.

Wanger was clearly aware of the political connotations of *Reign of Terror*. Early in 1948, the scriptwriter John Balderston read McKenzie's screenplay and advised Wanger against integrating the political analogy of the Revolution with contemporary events and the lowbrow appeal of a "rough-house sex-chase." [26] After the film was completed in April 1949, Wanger suggested that studio advertising give a political slant to promotion:

> I think the best way to make a lot of dough with this—I don't know whether you agree with me or not—would be to go all out and maybe have some of the ads warn the public

that we will be going through a REIGN OF TERROR in this country if we don't watch out and that there is a REIGN OF TERROR all over the world. Let this be hailed as the Motion Picture Industry's effort to stop all kinds of totalitarianism.[27]

By this time, Wanger had publicly aligned himself with Hollywood's anti-Communist crusade and tried to overcome suspicions growing from his former associations. One could surmise that divided political sympathies simmered within him, but the crew as a unit seems divorced from any political intent, directing their skills instead toward concocting a profitable entertainment with limited resources.

Some commentators find resistance to the Cold War ethos in the work. Richard Maltby argues that an unconventional foregrounding of hyperbolic noir stylistics invests *Reign of Terror* with a subversive edge.[28] More straightforward evidence also exists. In the opening minutes of the film, for example, Danton responds to Robespierre's accusations, crying to the Convention, "Open your eyes. Tomorrow it may be you standing here accused, condemned, unheard." One might easily speculate that those in Hollywood would associate the Black Book with the blacklist. Matthew Bernstein's assessment that ambivalence finally diffuses any serious political address seems more persuasive than Maltby's claims, however.

The Cold War reaction, economic pressures, and fear of political enemies influenced Walter Wanger and his crew on *Reign of Terror*. Could the struggling Eagle–Lion studio risk a film celebrating the fall of the Bastille in such an atmosphere? Better to turn revolutionaries into villains and venal conspirators into "honest citizens," and wash the project in ironic humor and the despair of film noir. Given the circumstances, one can understand why this peculiar production moved from the optimism of 1789 to the terror of 1794 and then denied its historical lineage to the popular audience.

Chapter 4

Risorgimento History and Screen Spectacle: Visconti's *Senso*

The old is dying and the new cannot be born; in this interregnum there arises a great diversity of morbid symptoms.
—ANTONIO GRAMSCI (1891–1937)

The key to understanding of the spiritual and psychological conflicts is always social, even if the conclusions I reach are always those which concern individuals whose cases I am describing. The yeast, the blood in the veins of history, is always thick with civic passion and social reasoning.
—LUCHINO VISCONTI, 1961

Marlon Brando was the big news of the 1954 Venice Film Festival. Although *On the Waterfront* took second prize while Renato Castellani's *Romeo and Juliet* took first, it was by all accounts the popular favorite. When Jean Gabin was named the festival's best actor, the fans let their preference be known with shouts of "Brando! Brando!" Other films honored included *The Seven Samurai, Sansho the Bailiff*, and *La Strada*, but one noteworthy entry stirred controversy when it was ignored by the jury. Foreign reporters commented on the slighting of the Italian production *Senso*. In *Variety* Robert Hawkins described the film as a "stylist's delight and one of the most beautiful pictures made," and remarked that it went "strangely unrewarded by the judges."[1] John Francis Lane, reporting for *Films and Filming*, claimed that *Senso* "caused considerable embarrassment to the powers-that-be," and noted that the jury's decision to ignore the picture was a "pertinent reflection indicative of the taste and judgment of officialdom in Italy today."[2] Italian response was less reserved. Piero Regnoli, film critic of *Osservatore Romano*, reported a bribe offered by the Christian Democratic Minister for the Arts with instructions that on "no account was a prize to be given to *Senso* because both the film and director were Communist."[3] Tempers eventually erupted in a fist fight between two assistant directors—Franco Zeffirelli (*Senso*) and Moraldo Rossi (*La Strada*).[4] The Italians recognized that this film of the Risorgimento used the representation of the past to speak to the politics of the present.

The film's political meaning is expressed in several ways. Censorship pressures generated the turn to history; historical scholarship then shaped *Senso*'s cinematic spectacle and invested the picture's interpretation with a political meaning. In addition, the historical context of the production and release reveals that *Senso* should not be mistaken for a simple romance. An exploration of that context opens up the political implications of the film, implications demonstrably felt in Italy in 1954. *Senso* succeeds in combining romantic melodrama and screen spectacle in a radical commentary on Italian politics and Risorgimento history.

Senso begins in Venice in 1866, six years after the march of Garibaldi's Red Shirts. Cavour is dead; the most glorious episodes of the Risorgimento are in the past. The "Third War of National Liberation" sets the context, and the film opens in Venice as hostilities between Austria and the new state grow imminent.

This war was a painful experience for Italy. In 1866 Rome and the kingdom of Venetia remained in the hands of foreigners, and Italy had entered into an alliance with Prussia against the Austrians in the hope of gaining Venetia through a military victory. Flanked by hostile armies, Austria divided its troops between two fronts, and the Italian forces, superior in numbers and weaponry, loomed over their enemy. Yet the Italians suffered defeats at Custoza and Lissa as the disorganization, vanity, and incompetence of the high command squandered the military advantage. To the north Prussia smashed the Austrians at Sadowa and negotiated a peace without consulting its allies. Although Austria ceded Venice, the Italians acquired less territory than they had been offered in prewar diplomacy. The year closed in Italy with the civilian government and the military command exchanging accusations and dodging responsibility. Writing in 1925, Arrigo Solmi explained, "The defeats at Custoza and at Lissa had regrettable consequences that pierced the hearts of men of the time, and weighed for two generations on the political life of Italy."[5] Edgar Holt, in a more recent account of the Risorgimento, agreed that "defeat in the field gave the Italians a military inferiority complex which was to last for many years."[6] The historical setting colored *Senso*'s romance in the dark shades of national catastrophe.

The fiction develops around three Venetian aristocrats—the Countess Livia Serpieri, her cousin, the Marquis Roberto Ussoni, and her husband, the count. An Austrian officer, Lieutenant Franz Mahler, animates the melodrama. An illicit affair between Livia, an Italian patriot, and Franz, an enemy soldier, portrays the political divisions plaguing the Italian consciousness at the formation of their new state. The conflicts between romantic passion and civic duty engage the characters as they are caught up in the events leading to the clash of armies at Custoza.

Some have claimed that the historical perspective was obscured by the romantic melodrama. Gianfranco Poggi, for example, complained that "Visconti's attention is mainly on . . . Livia's affair with Franz; the 'public' line of events appears and disappears in the background, but is not integrated with the 'private' line."[7] Although the love affair is central to the plot, politics has a formative influence upon the meaning of *Senso*.

| Censorship and the Turn to Historical Fiction

The genesis of *Senso* reveals the fundamental influence of conditions in the Italian film industry. In 1953 the industry was hostile toward the neo-realist movement. As leading figures in the movement, Luchino Visconti and Suso Cecchi d'Amico had reason to be apprehensive. Visconti's *Ossessione* (1942) was a precursor of neo-realism, and his *La Terra Trema* (1947), a prizewinner at the Venice Film Festival, was a landmark achievement of the movement. D'Amico had already collaborated on screenplays for *Ladri di biciclette* (*Bicycle Thieves*, 1948) and *Miracolo a Milano* (*Miracle in Milan*, 1951) before initiating her partnership with Visconti on *Bellissima* (1951), in which the two filmmakers worked with Cesare Zavattini, the leading theorist of neo-realism. An examination of the developments leading to the demise of neo-realism sets the context for *Senso*'s production.

On February 20, 1949, film workers had demonstrated in the

streets of Rome demanding protection against foreign competition. Italian motion pictures, accounting for barely 10 percent of domestic releases, were losing the home market to Hollywood. The Christian Democratic Party, firmly entrenched after its victory in the elections of 1948, responded with the passage of the Andreotti Law on December 29, 1949. The new legislation influenced production in three ways: The discretionary power of the censorship office was increased, especially in supervising the choice of subjects and scenario planning; encouragement was offered through grants to films of social merit; and the state could ban from export any picture that "might give an erroneous view of the true nature of the country." [8]

The legislation had a serious impact on the Italian cinema. Already hampered by commercial limitations, the neo-realist movement now had to face the state censor and export restrictions. The government, antagonized by the social criticism characteristic of the movement, could now intervene at the scenario stage. Just as intimidating was the threat to foreign distribution. Neo-realist classics, such as *Roma Citta Aperta* (*Rome, Open City*, 1945), *Paisan* (1946), and *Bicycle Thieves*, had garnered a large share of their income from the international audience in cities such as Paris and New York. Cut off from this market, producers could never hope to profit from their investment. As a result, neo-realist projects became increasingly difficult to finance.

Restrictions continued to grow. In 1951 the Venice Film Festival adopted a regulation "prohibiting the showing of films which are 'in any way offensive to the national feelings of any of the participating countries.'" [9] In April 1954 the *Motion Picture Herald* announced that Italian film producers had established a committee to review scripts in order to combat "Communist infiltration." [10] In addition, the Roman Catholic hierarchy exerted a powerful, and increasingly severe, influence upon culture and the arts. As the health of Pope Pius XII declined, a group of more conservative cardinals came to exercise authority at the Vatican and demanded sterner restrictions on the media. Norman Kogan in *A Political History of Postwar Italy* notes:

Under church pressure, censorship became more vexatious. Article 21 of the Constitution prohibits publications and

entertainment "contrary to good morals." While some con-
stitutionalists insisted that only post-censorship was per-
missible under this article, in fact pre-censorship of moving picture scenarios, stage plays, and radio and television
scripts was exercised by a bureau in the executive office of
the Prime Minister. The censorship was exercised so arbitrarily that while many salacious films got through, scripts of
social and political criticism were blocked.[11]

In the 1953–54 *Motion Picture and Television Almanac*,
Dr. Argeo Santucci could write of Italy, "All native and foreign
production is subjected to government censorship on moral and
political standards. . . . Though no law has been issued, the
observance of the current regulations was made stricter during
1953."[12] Carlo Ponti, the producer, asserted before the Association of Cultural Freedom, "Today, anyone intending to produce
a film has to cross a minefield of compromise, intimidation and
all kinds of pressure."[13]

As a filmmaker identified with neo-realism and a public
supporter of the Communist Party, Visconti had reason to be
troubled.[14] Nevertheless, in 1953 he and d'Amico began work on
a scenario entitled "Marcia Nuziale" ("The Wedding March"),
a critical portrait of class and marriage in contemporary Italy.[15]
Exhibiting the markings of neo-realism, the treatment investigates the suicide of a wealthy young mother who killed her two
children before taking her own life. The tale probes the psychological turmoil and social conflicts in a group of characters ranging
from upper class to low. In spite of Visconti's international reputation as a stage and screen director, he was unable to interest
any producer in a project that courted commercial failure and
government censorship.

Putting aside "Marcia Nuziale," Visconti and d'Amico decided to test the authorities to see if the impossibility of finding
a backer was due to the script or to their own involvement with
the project.[16] When Lux Films suggested a film based on Camillo
Boito's nineteenth-century novella *Senso*, Visconti and d'Amico
set to work. Their scenario enriched the story with historical
content and political meaning completely absent from Boito.

Three changes are particularly noteworthy—the characterization of Livia, the addition of Roberto Ussoni, and the explicit historical setting. The novella presents a cynical affair between a married Venetian aristocrat, Livia, and an Austrian officer, Lieutenant Remigio Ruz. In Boito's story, the two are kindred spirits, unscrupulous, vain, and selfish. The film transforms her into a virtuous woman working for the unification of Italy. The scenario introduces Roberto, the political activist, and changes Remigio into Franz Mahler, Roberto's polar opposite. The contrast between the Italian patriot and the Austrian lieutenant underlines the divided consciousness of the heroine and the political contradictions faced by her class (illustration 10). The film also develops the historical spectacle, adding the opening at the Venice opera, the move to the Serpieri country villa, and the battle at Custoza. As a result, the romance is firmly linked to the events of the Risorgimento. Custoza took on a special significance in the production. D'Amico writes of extensive research, including mapping the army maneuvers during the battle.[17] Visconti claims that he wanted to call the film *Custoza*, but "that caused an outcry: from Lux, from the ministry, and from the censor."[18]

The climate of the industry and the reputation of the director kept Lux worried over the production. During the shooting the firm adopted the working title *Summer Storm*, afraid that *Senso*, not to mention *Custoza*, might excite suspicion.[19] In an interview Visconti speaks of his producer's anxiety and the changes required even before the film's release:

> The first final version was quite different from the one seen today. It didn't end, for instance, with the death of Franz: we saw Livia pass through groups of drunken soldiers, and the very end showed a little drunken Austrian soldier— very young, sixteen or thereabouts, blind drunk, propped up against a wall, singing a song of victory. . . . Then he shouted: "Long live Austria!"
>
> Guallino, my producer and a very sympathetic man, came to watch the shooting. He muttered behind my back: "Dangerous, dangerous." Perhaps. But for me this was the perfect finish! We left Franz to his own affairs, we didn't give a damn for Franz! It didn't matter in the least whether he was killed or not. We left him after the scene in the room

10 | *Senso* (1954), production still. Countess Livia Serpieri (Alida Valli) and Lieutenant Franz Mahler (Farley Granger): Their relationship illustrates the divided consciousness of her class. Courtesy Museum of Modern Art/Film Stills Archive

where he shows himself in his true colors. Pointless that he should be shot. We watched her instead, running to denounce him and then escaping into the streets. She passed among whores, becoming a sort of whore herself, going from one soldier to another. Then she fled, shouting, "Franz, Franz!" And we moved on to the little soldier who stood for all those who paid the price of victory and who was really crying, weeping and shouting "Long live Austria!"

But I had to cut it. The negative was burnt. Thousands were spent filming Franz's death but for me this isn't the end of *Senso*.[20]

When the film premiered on September 3, 1954, the producer's anxiety proved justified. After the uproar at the Venice Festival, the Ministry of Defense objected to the portrayal of Custoza as offensive to the soldiers of Italy. A cut was ordered.[21]

The censored scene takes place at the headquarters of the Fifth Division Command as the Battle of Custoza begins.[22] Captain Meucci, a staff officer in the Italian army, is confronted by Roberto. Roberto has led a company of Italian volunteers to fight alongside the regular army, but Meucci dismisses him, claiming, "Experience has always demonstrated that volunteers enrolled in the regular army are meager assistance." In frustration Roberto cries, "The call has gone out everywhere that all Italians should join forces and take part in the war. We have responded to the call. . . . The order that you have given me manifests the repugnance of the whole army, from General La Marmora on down, with regard to the revolutionary forces. It is clear that they wish to exclude those forces from the war."[23] The officer gives Roberto a pass, leaving him to his own devices, and turns to salute the arrival of a general. Roberto, consumed with anger, strides off.

The irregular volunteers and the established Italian army represented opposing factions during the Risorgimento, but Roberto's encounter with Meucci further suggests tensions during and after World War II between the anti-Fascist resistance organizations and the government in Rome. When the Defense Ministry singled out this episode to be cut, it underlined *Senso*'s relevance to Italy in 1954. But to understand the implications of the film, one must look to the competing histories of the Risorgimento and their significance in postwar Italy.

| Risorgimento Histories and Postwar Italian Politics

The return to democracy after twenty years of Fascism led Italians to reflect upon the history of their nation, particularly the Risorgimento. In a debate with serious political implications, intellectuals, artists, and politicians alike asked whether the origins of Fascism were embedded in the foundations of the Italian state. One camp held that the institutions established after the Risorgimento were a sound basis for government; the other argued that their weakness had led to a Fascist takeover.

Dominating the debate were Benedetto Croce (1866–1952), "the greatest and most influential Italian philosopher of the twentieth century,"[24] and Antonio Gramsci (1891–1937), a founder of the Italian Communist Party. Each combined historical scholarship and political philosophy with participation in national affairs. Croce served as a legislator, minister, and central figure in the Liberal Party. He participated in the national government before the ascendancy of Benito Mussolini, and in September 1945, from his seat in the National Assembly, Croce contested the significance of Italian history with Premier Ferruccio Parri. Gramsci, a student of Croce's, turned from his teacher to Marxism and died in a Fascist prison, but not before writing extensively upon Italian history and politics. Both men wrote at length on the Risorgimento.

The Risorgimento ("resurgence") movement was dominated by two factions, the Moderates and the Action Party. Piedmont, a northwestern Italian state, assumed the leadership of the Moderates. Their king, Victor Emmanuel, and his prime minister, Conte Camillo di Cavour, sought to join regional governments into a national federation, and, while maintaining the position of the native propertied classes, drive foreign powers from the peninsula. Piedmont exercised the traditional weapons of European power politics—international diplomacy, military alliances, and its armed forces—in order to achieve these aims.

The Action Party, led by Giuseppe Mazzini and Giuseppe Garibaldi, adopted the radical spirit of the French Revolution, calling for social justice, democratic rights and political freedoms as part of the Italian renewal. These revolutionaries organized underground networks, equipped volunteer units, and plotted for a popular uprising against established authority, foreigners and Italians alike—without, however, developing a unified front or a coherent program for social change.

In 1848 the Moderates and the Action Party failed in a bid for power. Uprisings occurred in Palermo, Venice, and Milan; Piedmont declared war against Austria. But the Piedmontese army was defeated at Custoza and Novara, and the popular revolts were subsequently put down throughout the peninsula. Within the year Austria reasserted control. After this First War of National Liberation, prospects for Italian unification seemed distant, but in 1859 another war erupted. Piedmont, supported by France, waged a successful campaign against Austria and occupied most of northern and central Italy. Then, in the spring of 1860, Garibaldi landed in Sicily with one thousand volunteers, and, to the astonishment of Europe, his "Red Shirts" marched north to Rome, capturing Naples and all of southern Italy. Piedmont consolidated its position, and its army advanced through the Papal States, linking up with the Red Shirts south of Rome. There Garibaldi offered his conquests to Victor Emmanuel, and the Kingdom of Italy was declared in March 1861. Rome and Venice, however, remained apart from the nation.

In *A History of Italy, 1871–1915* (1928) and *A History of Europe in the Nineteenth Century* (1931), Benedetto Croce praises the achievements of the early Italian state and implicitly attacks the Fascist regime. The Risorgimento, in its promotion of liberty and national self-determination, was, for the scholar, a glorious episode in the history of Europe:

> If it were possible in political history to speak of master-
> pieces as we do in dealing with works of art, the process of
> Italy's independence, liberty and unity would deserve to be
> called the masterpiece of the liberal-national movements
> of the nineteenth century: so admirably does it exhibit the

combination of its various elements, respect for what is old and profound innovation, the wise prudence of the statesman and the impetus of the revolutionaries and the volunteers, ardour and moderation; so flexible and coherent is the logical thread by which it developed and reached its goal.[25]

Croce also praises the role of the Piedmont monarchy in the national crusade. Its leadership, especially after the defeats of 1848, is judged crucial: "The path of salvation and honor was one alone, to proceed in close union with Piedmont and her policy. . . . The 'war of the people' now found its true form in a state that represented a nation, in an army that was to grow into the army of this nation."[25]

Cavour, the chief minister of Piedmont and master of continental politics, was blessed with heroic stature: "It is impossible not to admire Cavour when one looks through his life and his letters, and sees what genius, what versatile labor, what discretion and courage, what passion and poetry, what suffering and rage at times . . . this labor cost him to which he had been called by history."[27]

The liberal ideals of the unification movement became the guiding principles of the Italian government. In the first decades of the new state, Croce finds Italy moving steadily toward the goals set during the Risorgimento. The nation instituted parliamentary government, centralized administration, expanded the suffrage, sponsored education, and promoted economic growth. In spite of occasional setbacks, Croce believes that this program brought progress and unity to Italy. Then came the World War, and the consensus holding the nation together collapsed. A costly victory brought personal suffering and economic turmoil; the political order was challenged by parties on the right and left; severe social divisions undermined the constitutional system. Within a decade after the armistice, Mussolini and his Fascists had taken control of the state. For Croce, the fall of Mussolini opened the way for a resumption of progress and a renewal of the liberal values engendered during the national movement of the nineteenth century.

During the 1930s Gramsci, writing in a Fascist prison, responded to Croce, his teacher in notebooks that appeared posthumously after the war had ended. The historian A. William Salomone explains that "from 1947 to 1952—when Antonio Gramsci's *Prison Notebooks* were being published . . . —the 'great debate' on pre-Fascist democracy became obsessively acute."[28] Their differences are marked by contrasting attitudes toward the parties of the Risorgimento. Croce praises the cooperation and balanced program of the Moderates and Action Party leaders. Gramsci emphasizes their division, not only from each other, but from the mass of the population. He finds their distance from the needs of the people indicative of the unstable foundation upon which the state rested.

Gramsci claims that the Risorgimento incorporated the interests of the landed aristocracy with the ascendant power of the bourgeoisie, yet the needs of the masses, especially the peasants, were ignored. Divorced from broad popular support, the state was unable to survive the crisis of World War I, and the government proved vulnerable to a Fascist takeover. The Italian ruling class, Gramsci concludes,

> said that they were aiming at the creation of a modern State
> in Italy, and they in fact produced a bastard. They aimed
> at stimulating the formation of an extensive and energetic
> ruling class, and they did not succeed; at integrating the
> people into the framework of the new State, and they did not
> succeed. The paltry political life from 1870 to 1900, the fundamental and endemic rebelliousness of the Italian popular
> classes, the narrow and stunted existence of a sceptical and
> cowardly ruling stratum, these are all the consequences of
> that failure. A consequence of it too is the international position of the new State, lacking effective autonomy because
> sapped internally by the Papacy and by the sullen passivity
> of the great mass of the people.[29]

Gramsci's analysis of the Risorgimento focuses upon the Action Party's failure to address popular needs and offer an alternative to the Piedmontese monarchy. Lacking a concrete political program, the radicals consistently yielded to the policies engineered by Cavour. Even after the astonishing march of

Garibaldi's Red Shirts, the revolutionary leader bowed to the authority of the king:

> The Moderates represented a relatively homogeneous social group, and hence their leadership underwent relatively limited oscillations . . . ; whereas the so-called Action Party did not base itself specifically on any historical class, and the oscillations which its leading organs underwent were resolved, in the last analysis, according to the interests of the Moderates. In other words, the Action Party was led historically by the Moderates.[30]

The inability of the Action Party to arouse mass enthusiasm with a popular program left the common people indifferent to the new state. For the peasants the Risorgimento was only a change in masters, and their political alienation left the country weak and unstable. Yet Gramsci claims that an alternative existed in what he describes as a "Jacobin" policy, similar to that pursued by the radicals of the French Revolution:

> In order to counterpose itself effectively to the Moderates, the Action Party ought to have allied itself with the rural masses, especially those in the South, and ought to have been "Jacobin" not only in external "form," in temperament, but most particularly in socio-economic content. The binding together of the various rural classes, which was accomplished in a reactionary bloc by means of the various legitimist-clerical intellectual strata, could be dissolved, so as to arrive at a new liberal-national formation, only if support was won from two directions: from the peasant masses . . . and from the intellectuals of the middle and lower strata.[31]

But agrarian reform and an ideological offensive were not put forward by the Action Party. Memories of the French "Terror" of 1793 frightened the bourgeois nationalists, and the suppressed revolts of 1848 sapped conviction in the power of popular uprisings. As a result the Action Party compromised with the ruling strata rather than leading the lower classes in a bid for power. In *Italy: A Modern History,* Denis Mack Smith characterizes the situation:

The Risorgimento was, as one would expect, a movement not of the populace but of an elite. In Garibaldi's Thousand there were not peasants, but rather students, independent craftsmen, and literati. . . . Because the Risorgimento was a civil war between the old and the new ruling classes, the peasants were neutral except in so far as their own perennial social war was accidentally involved. They certainly had no love for United Italy, and probably no idea what the term signified until it came home to them in higher prices, taxes and conscription.[32]

The contending views of the Risorgimento had practical meaning for postwar Italy. Those sharing Croce's liberal perspective believed that the pre-Fascist institutions, with a few revisions, could be reestablished and political progress renewed. For Croce Fascism was an aberration, an unforeseeable consequence of World War I. Gramsci believed Mussolini's rise was the result of class antagonism and a political structure built upon a narrow base of popular support. A simple return to the old institutions would set the stage for the growth of neo-Fascism. The Marxists urged fundamental changes in the social and political structure in order to reconstruct the state on a firm ground. If the new government was to unite the nation and integrate the masses into the political system, a serious challenge to the old propertied class and the former political system was in order.

Gramsci's perspective was a familiar part of Italian popular culture in the decade after the war. Pierre Sorlin points out that while the debate on the Risorgimento was going on (1949–54), twelve Italian films, including *Senso*, were set during that period. During the seven preceding years and the six following years, the industry avoided the subject.[33] Significantly, the twelve films turned from the glories of Garibaldi's march to troubling episodes that portray the weakness of the Risorgimento and testify to Gramsci's revisionist history. *Pattuglia sperduta* (*The Lost Patrol*, 1952) dealt with Piedmont's defeat at Novara; *Camicie rosse* (*The Red Shirts*, 1952) and *Cavalcata d'eroi* (*Cavalcade of Heroes*, 1951) focus on the unsuccessful uprisings of 1848. Circumstances suggest that the revisionist attitude was widely disseminated.

As a scrupulous researcher and an acknowledged Communist

who intentionally incorporated the Risorgimento into the film, Visconti must certainly have consulted Gramsci while preparing *Senso*. The Battle of Custoza sequence, and the censored episode in particular, testify to the historian's influence.

Gramsci's views suggest the motive behind the elimination of the scene between Roberto and Captain Meucci. While Croce emphasized the unity marking the Italian national struggle, Gramsci probed the points of division. The tensions between the regular army of Piedmont and the Action Party volunteers was just such a point. The Piedmont command was envious of Garibaldi's success, and the ruling circles were fearful of armed units independent of their authority. With the outbreak of the Third War of National Liberation, the army was determined to exercise control over radical elements and reap the political rewards of military victory. The General Staff rejected Garibaldi's services and, when forced to accommodate him, assigned the hero to an insignificant backwater. The success of his minor Alpine campaign was not sufficient to offset the defeats inflicted on the regular forces. Gramsci writes of the ambivalence and suspicion of the Italian authorities:

> The volunteers were viewed with disfavor and sabotaged by the Piedmontese authorities. . . . The right wing tendencies in Piedmont either did not want auxiliaries . . . , or else would have liked to have been helped for nothing. . . . In real life, one cannot ask for enthusiasm, spirit of sacrifice, etc. without giving anything in return, even from the subjects of one's own country.[34]

It is the rivalry between the army and the volunteers, the Moderates and the Action Party, that is portrayed in the encounter between Roberto and Meucci. The scene was therefore suppressed by the Christian Democratic government, a government in sympathy with the traditional politics of the Moderates.

The elimination of one scene did not essentially alter the meaning of *Senso*. Gramsci's influence on the production is evident throughout the picture, and a detailed examination of the Custoza spectacle makes the influence clear.

The Battle of Custoza: Historical
Meaning in the Film Spectacle

The Battle of Custoza is a key episode in *Senso*. Although it appears near the conclusion of the film, it was among the first sequences to be shot.[35] Visconti emphasized its importance for the film:

> First and foremost it's slanted toward the historical aspect.
> I even wanted it to be called *Custoza*. . . . My idea was
> to mount a whole tableau of Italian history, against which
> the personal story of Countess Serpieri would stand out,
> though basically she was only the representative of a particu-
> lar class.[36]

The Custoza sequence follows Roberto as he strives to make contact with his unit of volunteers and join the battle. The obstacles he encounters—the maneuvers of the regular army and the passivity of the peasants—present an allegory for Gramsci's analysis of the failure of the radical leadership during the Risorgimento.

Just as the Action Party was controlled and manipulated by the policies of Piedmont, Roberto struggles toward the battlefield against the tide of military traffic. He is told that to join the volunteers he must circle the left wing of the army. Screen direction marks the meaning of Roberto's journey; the movement to the left bears its common political significance. The first shot of the Custoza sequence introduces the movement motif. As the camera swings to follow Roberto, he immediately begins striding to the left, opposing the direction of the general and his escort. Shot two finds Roberto moving against the military traffic on the bridge, where he engages a peasant and his gig.

While the army represents the policy of the Moderates, the peasants signify the political alienation of the common people. In shots three through five, troops, supplies, and artillery are blocked on the country roads by peasants hauling the harvest. Indifferent to the new government, the farmers undermine the effectiveness of the Italian forces, yet the strength of the nation rests upon their labor. The film eloquently visualizes the concept in shot fourteen of the Custoza sequence as a bugler sounds the call to battle before an apparently empty field of wheat shocks, and, in response, an armed infantryman steps from behind each stack of grain to fill the field with troops. Shot six underlines the political indifference of the peasants as the camera finds troops at rest among peasants threshing grain. The farmers appear oblivious to the imminent conflict; the battle is of no concern to them. They continue their traditional task, unaffected by the turmoil of the "Wars of Liberation." Shot three expresses Roberto's helplessness, frustrated by forces he fails to understand. Reversing his screen direction and moving right, his gig crawls along a road overflowing with troops and supply wagons. The foreground of the frame is held by the soldiers, and the view of Roberto is significantly blocked. Eventually his slow movement is halted completely when a peasant haywagon moving in the opposite direction appears from off-screen and obstructs the advance. Obviously Roberto must change his approach in order to make progress.

The two allies Roberto engages in his journey suggest Gramsci's history. The peasant driver of the gig wears a bright red shirt, emphasizing the Marxist overtones of the potential popular alliance with the Action Party. When Roberto stops for fresh directions in shot six, a Neapolitan advises him to turn left. Gramsci's belief that the Action Party should have sought allies among the peasants and especially in the south is reinforced by the *mise-en-scène*.

Senso portrays the failure of the upper classes to provide the moral and intellectual leadership for the Risorgimento. For Gramsci the capacity for leadership is a crucial element:

> The supremacy of a social group manifests itself in two ways, as "domination" and as "intellectual and moral leadership." A social group dominates antagonistic groups which it tends to liquidate, or to subjugate perhaps even by armed force; it leads kindred and allied groups. A social group can, and indeed must, already exercise "leadership" before winning governmental power . . . ; it subsequently becomes dominant when it exercises power, but even if it holds it firmly in its grasp, it must continue to lead as well.[37]

Roberto's confusion at Custoza exemplifies the failure of the Action Party to provide effective leadership, just as Livia's passion undermines the moral hegemony of her class. Roberto rushes desperately to join the volunteers, but fails to find his way through the maze of combat. In the opening encounters he continually seeks directions, and though he is always advised to "go left," he is unable to reach his unit. As the battle disintegrates, he stumbles along baffled and asks passing soldiers, "What's going on?" During the retreat Roberto, significantly abandoned by his peasant driver, exchanges his civilian clothes for a tattered Italian army jacket, suggesting the Action Party's submission to the Piedmontese monarchy. Wounded and disillusioned, he joins the army in its retreat. Lacking the necessary understanding, Roberto never grasps the political situation or recognizes the possibility of alliance with the peasants. He is isolated and ineffectual to the end, and his energy never contributes to the Italian cause.

The cut back to the Serpieri villa before the close of the battle links Livia's moral collapse to Roberto's aborted leadership. Livia has received a letter from Franz in Verona, and all her energy is directed toward rejoining her Austrian lover. When Roberto's comrade, Lucca, arrives with news of Italian victories, the countess is alarmed at the prospect of being cut off from Verona. The peasants crowd around her, beaming with anticipation of victory, but Livia's passion has obliterated concern for the cause. She retreats into the shadow, muttering, "We'll be cut off." In directing the battle spectacle, Visconti portrays his protagonists as thwarted by the forces of history. As representatives "of a particular class," Roberto Ussoni and the Countess Serpieri personify the limitations besetting the progressive leadership during the Risorgimento.

A comparison of *Senso*'s Custoza and the attack on the Tuileries in *La Marseillaise* is instructive. In both the collective, extrapersonal elements command the spectacle, but *La Marseillaise* presents a victory, and *Senso*, a defeat. In the French film the Jacobin republicans, the collective hero, overwhelm the king; whereas at Custoza, the machinations of the army and the passivity of the peasants disarm the isolated Roberto. In Renoir's film the opposition between the revolutionaries and the old regime is simplified into a visual counterpoint—the open streets commanded by the people versus the imposing edifice of the palace. *La Marseillaise* sets the stage for a triumphant climax as the crowd storms into the royal residence. *Senso* employs the natural landscape and a more complicated movement between camera and players. The director succeeds in ordering the perception of the viewer while evoking the confusion and helplessness of the protagonist.

In portraying his Risorgimento battle, Visconti adapts his formal organization to Gramsci's political analysis. The weaknesses that doom the Italians (the Action Party's naive politics, Piedmont's self-serving army, and the alienation of the peasantry) are expressed through the narrative organization and the visual design. The spectacle of combat evokes Roberto's disillusionment and the plight of the individual overwhelmed by the forces of history. The representation of the past seldom strays far from the controversies of the present, as an examination of Italian politics in 1954 demonstrates.

The Postwar Crisis and the Specter of Fascism: Italy 1954

Senso suggests disturbing similarities between Risorgimento politics and conditions in Italy during and after World War II. In both periods movements for social transformation were blocked by entrenched interests determined to protect the status quo.

D'Amico has explained that the scenario for *Senso* "tried to underline a comparison with the last war."[38] Relations between the regular Italian army and the volunteer forces of the Risorgimento correspond to the treatment of the partisan resistance against the Nazis. From 1940 to 1943 the Italian army suffered defeats in Greece and Africa; finally, their homeland was overrun by German and Allied forces. Nevertheless, after Mussolini was deposed in 1943, an army commander, Marshall Pietro Badoglio, and the monarch represented authority in "liberated" southern Italy, while bands of irregular partisans, volunteers from the general population, fought a guerrilla war with the Fascist armies in the north. As Rome and then the rest of Italy were freed from the Nazis, the partisan movement demanded a purge of former Fascists from the government and a share in power. Smith notes the parallel with the Risorgimento:

> Some of the very best elements in the country were prominent in the Resistance, and it provided a fine training in

social consciousness. . . . Never before had so many citizens participated so actively in national life. . . . The impression emerges that the liberating war against Mussolini and Hitler penetrated far more deeply into the people's conscience than the nineteenth-century Risorgimento had ever done. . . . During the five months premiership of Parri, who followed Bonomi in June 1945, Italy came closer to a radical process of social and political change than at any time since 1861. That the country stopped short of drastic social changes was due to the conservative instinct of so many of her people and the entrenched strength of vested interests.[39]

Badoglio was forced out; the king was deposed in a national referendum. After the new constitution was instituted, divisions between the established order and those demanding deep-seated changes reemerged. *Senso* as a whole, and the censored episode in particular, alluded to these conflicts, suggesting a connection between the Piedmontese monarchy in the 1860s and the Italian governments during and after World War II, between the Action Party and the resistance.

Although national unity and prospects for reform peaked in 1945, the social divisions that plagued Italy persisted, laying the ground for political crisis and perpetuating fears of a neo-Fascist resurgence. National unity cabinets joined the Communists, Socialists, and Christian Democrats from 1945 until just before the 1948 elections. In preparation for that campaign, the Christian Democrats forced the left out of the government, and went on to win a parliamentary majority. But despite economic recovery, division continued to threaten the state.

The policies of the Roman Catholic Church, the peninsula's oldest and most pervasive institution, contributed to the instability. The Vatican had refused to recognize the Italian state from its beginnings in 1861 until 1929, when the pope signed the Lateran Treaty with Mussolini. During the Fascist regime the Catholic community showed widespread support for the dictator. Although the disastrous war had prompted the Vatican to renounce Mussolini, Fascist sympathies lingered. Serge Hughes notes that in postwar Italy, "Many Catholics who turned into Christian Democrats did so simply because Fascism had been defeated and because they lived in terror of the Communists.

They were undoubtedly more Fascist than Catholic."[40] Although the Lateran Treaty was renewed by the postwar government, the pope fostered political schism through his fierce opposition to the parties of the left. In July 1949 Pope Pius XII excommunicated all Communists, thereby severing from the Christian community, the second-largest political party in the country and the leader of the opposition.

Tensions between Church and State were matched by divisions between the prosperous industrial north and the backward agrarian south. In the south, per capita income was less than half that of the rest of the country; one in four southerners were illiterate; and unemployment ranged between 33 and 50 percent in the rural areas.[41] Although the economy continued to expand into the 1960s, there was an unsettling contrast between increasing productivity and widespread unemployment, prosperity in the north and poverty in the south. Between 1951 and 1955 Italy's average annual growth rate exceeded 5 percent, while unemployment hovered around 10 percent and reached a peak in 1954, the year of *Senso*'s release, with well over two million people out of work.[42]

Recent history only reinforced the regional division. During the final years of the war, the south was liberated by the Allied forces and governed by the Badoglio regime. The north, in contrast, had erupted into a powerful anti-Fascist resistance that fought the Nazis and served as a wellspring for the parties of the left. As a result the Communists and Socialists had their strongholds in the north, while the Church, the Christian Democrats, and the Mafia were more dominant in the south.

In spite of postwar recovery, the elections of 1953 resulted in a setback for the centrist politics of the Christian Democrats and gains for both the Communists and the extreme parties of the right. The year 1953 and the early months of 1954, the period of *Senso*'s production, were a volatile, troubling time for Italian politics. In the weeks following the voting, the Christian Democrats struggled to form a stable coalition, but fragmentation and uncertainty hung over the state. The divisions between Church and State, north and south, wealth and poverty, infected the country; Gramsci's warnings and the specter of Fascism hovered over national affairs.

In the short history of the Italian state, the national leadership, unable to solve internal problems, had more than once sought to win unity and control by drawing the country into unnecessary wars. In 1866, General Alfonso La Marmora turned down favorable diplomatic offers only to face crushing defeats from the Austrians. Neutral in the initial years of World War I, Italy finally entered the war and suffered severe casualties and economic strain. Although Italy was on the winning side, the resulting social unrest led to Mussolini's takeover. In 1940, believing the Germans already victorious, Mussolini jumped into the war, against the counsel of his military advisors. The conflict ended with the peninsula ravaged by the contending forces of Germany, Britain, and the United States. After the elections of 1953, the national government, faced with crisis, inflamed militaristic fervor over demands for Trieste, animating a fateful tradition. The war of 1866 had been fought to gain northeastern provinces for the new nation, and a similar territorial claim generated an international confrontation during the period of *Senso*'s production.

The most immediate parallel between events in *Senso* and the politics of postwar Italy grew from the Trieste controversy. The peace treaty ratified in 1947 awarded most of Venezia Giulia and the Istrian peninsula to Yugoslavia, but Trieste and some of the neighboring area had been designated a Free Territory under United Nations supervision. The Free Territory's zone A, predominantly Italian, was occupied by Anglo-American troops and included Trieste; zone B, populated by people of Slovenian origin, was occupied by the Yugoslavs. Since the close of the war, the recovery of the entire Free Territory had been a major objective of Italian foreign policy. During the 1948 election campaign, the British and Americans supported Italian claims for the return of the Free Territory, hoping to aid their political allies, the Christian Democrats. However, when President Tito of Yugoslavia broke with Stalin shortly after the elections, the Allies backed off in order to foster dissension in the Soviet bloc. In Italy nationalist elements were bitter about this betrayal. Before the 1953 elections, the Americans pressed Italy to accept a settlement based on the current division of zones A and B, but the Italians refused to give up their claim to the entire territory.

After the 1953 elections the Christian Democrats, no longer a majority in the legislature, failed to form a stable, working cabinet. A "provisional administrative" cabinet was established to conduct ongoing affairs while negotiations between parties proceeded. Giuseppe Pella, a right-wing Christian Democrat with only a modest political following, was leader of the "provisional" government. He seized upon the Trieste issue as a means of converting his temporary political position into one of long-term ascendancy. Pella demanded a plebiscite in the Free Territory and pressured his European allies to support Italian claims. The British and Americans invited the Italians to replace them as administrators of zone A, but Tito announced that an Italian move into Trieste would be viewed as an act of aggression. The confrontation escalated, rioters in Trieste were fired upon by British police, and the Italians and Yugoslavs both ordered divisions to the border. The leadership of the Christian Democratic Party detected personal ambition behind the prime minister's grandstanding. Pella was removed, as both sides backed down from a confrontation.[43] The following year the issue was settled quietly.

The Trieste controversy is indicative of the temper of Italian politics during the period of *Senso*'s production. In Kogan's words:

> It is evident that the Trieste issue, no matter how sincerely felt, had been manipulated to build up domestic political positions and to appeal to nationalistic and right-wing sentiments. These were years of reaction and obscurantism in Italian public life. Anti-Fascists were called saboteurs of Italian national honor. The resistance movement was denigrated; partisans were characterized as bandits, murderers, and even Communists. The Communists had been trying to take all the credit for the resistance, but now the opposite extremists just granted them the credit as a favor. Interest in ideas and in political action had drastically declined. Compared to the heated and tense atmosphere of the immediate postwar years, this decline might be interpreted as a growing acceptance by the general public of the institutions of the new republic, and of the political system. This would be an incorrect inference, however. The decline of commitment was no indication of any such consensus, rather it

marked a privatization of personal and family life, signifying an exclusive concern with immediate, materialistic goals.[44]

Visconti, who had once stood before a Fascist firing squad, must have greeted the drift to the right with the gravest alarm.

| Georg Lukacs and the "Typical" Character in *Senso*

For Visconti the meaning of *Senso* was both historical and immediate. As a thoughtful Marxist, he realized that men and women are shaped by history and, in turn, affect its course. This relationship between history and human agency is basic to Visconti's understanding of politics and society as well as to his conviction that historical melodrama is an appropriate vehicle for exploring contemporary issues. When criticized for turning from a commitment to neo-realism, Visconti declared: "They've tried to make out that neo-realism involves questions of form, but that doesn't mean anything. . . . Neo-realism is first and foremost a question of content, and that's what matters. *Senso* is in every way a realist film."[45] But the relationship of the illicit affair of a nineteenth-century Venetian aristocrat to Italian politics in 1954 is not readily apparent. Georg Lukacs, another Marxist who considered the representation of history and the politics of culture, sheds some light on Visconti's intentions.

In *The Historical Novel* (1937), Lukacs argues that historical fiction is the logical outgrowth of the social novel in the realist tradition:

> One sees that its classical form arises out of the great social novel and then, enriched by a conscious historical attitude, flows back into the latter. On the one hand, the development of the social novel first makes possible the historical novel; on the other, the historical novel transforms the social novel into a genuine history of the present.[46]

To serve as "a genuine history of the present," the work has to develop from the social problems and collective consciousness of an epoch, and characterization must balance a detailed and complex psychology with motives and acts that penetrate to the foundation of social experience. In the realist novel, the "typical" character is drawn with heroic dimensions, whereas the "average" exhibits the limitations of ordinary people. A contrast between Balzac and Flaubert illustrates the difference. Balzac's Rastignac and Vautrin in *Père Goriot,* for example, dominate their stories with superhuman qualities, whereas Flaubert strips Emma in *Madame Bovary* and Fréderic Moreau in *Sentimental Education* of any heroic dimension. Lukacs praises the "typical" character as an extraordinary summation of the essential feelings, thoughts, and issues of the time, acting as a microcosm of social consciousness. The drab limitations of the average or the simplicity of allegory can never balance the psychological complexity and social synthesis that Lukacs demands:

> A work of literature can rest neither on a lifeless average, as the naturalists suppose, nor on an individual principle which dissolves its own self into nothingness. The central category and criterion of realist literature is the type, a peculiar synthesis which organically binds together the general and the particular both in characters and situations. What makes a type a type is not its average quality, not its mere individual being, however profoundly conceived; what makes it a type is that all the humanly and socially essential determinants are present on the highest level of development, in the ultimate unfolding of the possibilities latent in them, in extreme presentation of their extremes, rendering concrete the peaks and limits of men and epochs.[47]

The typical character for Lukacs becomes the nexus of the personal and the social, a vessel of consciousness expressing the ties between the individual and history.

If the historical archetype of the leader is to function as a "typical" character, he or she must manifest the collective social consciousness balanced by distinct human traits. On the one hand the leader must avoid broad allegory, so as not to dissolve into a pale generalization. On the other hand, the figure must guard against a messianic tendency to rise above the affairs of men and women and exalt in spectacular personal achievement or saintly moral superiority.

Consider the shortcomings Lukacs might find in *The Life*

of Émile Zola (1937) and *Spartacus* (1960). Both Zola and Spartacus are outsiders crusading for social justice on the basis of moral principle. They endure oppression but persist. While Zola succeeds in overcoming the philistines, gaining recognition as a writer, and bringing the plight of Dreyfus to public attention, Spartacus, after initial triumphs, is executed. These heroes of conscience pose a conflict between morality and politics, between high-minded personal ethics and corrupt public practice. Rather than presenting great leaders as representative of a broad movement, the films tend to valorize them for their moral courage. An elevated moral status for the leader can reduce his or her significance as a historical phenomenon. A moral emphasis can privatize the hero, implying that significance lies in personal behavior rather than social consequences. The historical attitude, in contradistinction, requires that the impact upon the community, the ability actually to change public practice, holds priority. Politics, not morality, takes precedence in historical representation.

For the romantic couple to function as "typical," their love must signify more than a private passion. Just as the historical film often poses a conflict between morality and politics for the leader, for the couple it pits romantic love against social action. Such a tension implies that private experience and public life are mutually exclusive, even antagonistic, rather than integrated. For example, in *The Scarlet Empress* (1934), Catherine is betrothed for political advantage to the mad Grand Duke; later, her love for Alexei is destroyed by palace intrigue. Only when Catherine forsakes her longing for a genuine love can she gain power and become empress. In *Mary of Scotland* (1936) the outcome is reversed. The Stuart pretender turns from the throne and, remaining loyal to her lover, is overcome by the Virgin Queen, Elizabeth. The division between romantic love and political power poses a split between personal feeling and social action that undermines a comprehensive view of human experience. Lukacs finds it naive to believe that moral courage or a rich emotional life can exist apart from its public context and historical condition. The interaction between the personal and the public, the individual and the collective, constitutes the dual perspective that makes the "typical" character an integrated totality and allows it to speak as a "genuine history of the present."

Films that aspire to a distinctly historical, and even leftist, perspective may also fail to satisfy the Lukacs model. One suspects that *La Marseillaise* does not develop "typical" characters. The Jacobins lack the psychological detail necessary to construct deeply felt and convincing personalities. As the film progresses, the volunteers become little more than allegorical figures, so that the death of Bomier has more symbolic than emotional force. Louis XVI, on the other hand, is a complex and fascinating figure, but fails to embody any social phenomena. While an intriguing construct, the monarch conveys an awkward presence because he cannot be integrated into a coherent historical perspective. His character speaks more of the political contradictions besetting the production than of an understanding of events in either 1792 or 1937.

Visconti has described Livia as a "representative of a particular class," and a case can be made that the relationships among the leading characters of *Senso* portray the divided political consciousness of the Italian ruling class. These characters rise to the status of "typical" in a series of acts and emotional expressions that integrate private passion with the course of history.

Roberto Ussoni, the leader, embodies the progressive ideals of the liberal aristocracy, but his political naivete undermines his cause. From the beginning his leadership is ineffective; the demonstration he organizes at the opera results in his arrest and exile; the funds he entrusts to his cousin are given to an enemy soldier; the volunteers he marches to Custoza are dismissed by the military command. Never reaching his unit, he wanders the battlefield in confusion until he is finally wounded by a stray shell. Roberto exercises no authority because he seeks political reorganization without marshaling the support of the common people. The gap between the ideals of national unity and the social and economic realities prevents his political development and deprives him of the power that can only grow from within the community. Ussoni's limitations embody the misguided and immature politics of the Action Party as analyzed by Gramsci.

Count Serpieri represents the opposite response of his class to the national movement. Hardly naive, the aristocrat understands that his power rests upon his property and position, and he is utterly self-serving in his drive to maintain them regardless of political ideals or national allegiance. In an introductory scene, the count shares a box at the opera with the Austrian general staff. He dismisses the demonstration as "adolescent pranks," and his relative, Roberto, as an idiot. When the ceding of Venice appears inevitable, however, the count asks Roberto to intercede on his behalf with the Italian authorities. The landed nobility—collaborators with the Austrians and, later, the Fascists, and in contemporary Italy comfortable as Christian Democrats—engineer their transition through each crisis with little loss of position or influence. On this point Gramsci contrasts the class politics of the French Jacobins with the accommodation of the Action Party:

> In Italy, although a similar connection, both explicit and implicit, did exist between Austria and at least a segment of the intellectuals, the nobles, and the landowners, it was not denounced by the Action Party [and] . . . it did not become a real political issue. It became transformed "curiously" into a question of greater or lesser patriotic dignity.[48]

The count's unprincipled opportunism illustrates the failure of his class to exercise national leadership. Like many of the large property holders, he is prepared to go along with any regime as long as his interests are served. At his country estate the count is anxious over the harvest and worried that the war may damage the summer crop. In defiance of law, the nobleman is hoarding grain in order to profit from the fighting, but expresses no interest in the outcome of the battle. These episodes at the Serpieri villa, added by Visconti and d'Amico, underline Gramsci's view that "the relation between city and country is the necessary starting-point for the study of the fundamental motor forces of Italian history, and of the programmatic points in the light of which the Action Party's policies during the Risorgimento should be considered and judged."[49] The portrait of the count shows the dependence of the nobility, living largely in the city, upon the productivity of the countryside. Serpieri seizes upon the patriotic war to reap profits in the urban grain markets. He has no interest in a social union with the peasants who work in his fields. The peasants themselves represent the countryside. In their passivity they seem to recognize that the war, a contest between factions of the ruling class, will have no effect upon their lives. The Action

11 | *Senso* (1954), production still. Livia (Alida Valli) with her
husband, Count Serpieri (Heinz Moog): Although tied to his
traditional values, she is repelled by his lack of patriotic idealism.
Courtesy Museum of Modern Art/Film Stills Archive

Party has no program to offer the mass of the people, and the
relationship between city and country will remain unaltered.

The Countess Livia Serpieri is at the center of the melodrama, positioned between the count, her cousin, and her lover
(illustration 11). Her divided allegiances represent the conflicts
plaguing her class during the Risorgimento. Livia is tied to the
traditional values and allegiances of her older husband, though
she is repelled by his lack of patriotic idealism. Livia calls
Roberto, her principled cousin, "the person I admire most in the
world," and she assists his crusade for a united Italy. Lieutenant
Franz Mahler appears to combine the count's traditional loyalties
and cynical egotism with Roberto's youth and military bearing.
Upon their second meeting, Franz describes himself as Livia's

shadow, and he becomes the specter of a perverse synthesis. The film insinuates Franz into a provocative relation with Roberto; a pattern of substitution and opposition emerges in which Livia becomes entangled in her effort to resolve the conflicts between political activism and class interest through her romance.

Senso opens with the confrontation at the opera between Roberto and Franz, which Livia witnesses. The pattern of substitution begins immediately, when Livia sees Roberto after the challenge, and then calls Franz to her box, intending to intervene for her beloved cousin. Franz responds with flirtation veiled by an officer's decorum. Days later, after Livia bids goodbye to Roberto, who has been ordered into exile, Franz appears to offer his escort. He successfully cultivates the persona of the courageous and persecuted Roberto, following Livia through the streets and winning her sympathy by describing himself as a homesick soldier separated from his sweethearts in a foreign land. When they discover the body of an Austrian trooper, Livia is drawn to Franz, her sensibility roused by his danger. Later as they stroll lovingly, Franz dismisses patriotism and declares, to Livia's amazement, "I've never been able to get excited over war, or politics, or borderlines, or occupations of territories." Thus Franz replaces Roberto in Livia's affections while hinting at a cynicism typical of the count.

The pattern of substitution is most dramatically realized when Livia searches for Franz after he fails to keep their rendezvous. She rushes to a strange address, followed by her suspicious husband; desperate and weary, she turns to face him as she reaches her destination, declaring her adulterous passion and expecting Franz to appear as the door opens. Instead, to Livia's disappointment, Roberto, just returned from exile, greets them. He agrees to intercede with the Italians on the count's behalf and gives the countess funds collected by the patriots, which she later passes on to Franz.

Lieutenant Franz Mahler, cynic, cheat, womanizer, punctures the illusions of Roberto, the count, and Livia. He scorns Roberto's opera demonstration, responds to his challenge by having him arrested, and finally steals the money raised by the Action Party to escape from the battle Roberto longs to join. Franz's egotism matches the count's, and he reaches for the pleasures of the aristocracy: He seduces the count's wife, breaks into his villa, and, lounging atop mounds of hidden grain, preys upon the countess for money. Livia's illusions make her his chief victim. Even after her lover ignores their meetings, after she is told of his many flirtations, after she sees the tokens of her love discarded, Livia persists in clinging to the object of her passion. Her delusion speaks of the divided consciousness motivating the Italian aristocracy, which hoped for a national revival without disturbing property distribution or class relations. Both Livia and Roberto are misguided. In the conclusion, Roberto stumbles in confusion on the battlefield, and the countess drives to Verona, where she finds Franz entertaining a prostitute with the money she has provided. Humiliated when forced to confront the truth, she reports him as a deserter to the Austrian authorities. As he is dragged to a summary execution, Livia wanders deliriously through the war-torn city calling out for him.

Senso's characters reflect the limitations of the social formation, and the contradictions in the political community give rise to the pathos of private life. Roberto, the leader who serves the Risorgimento with energy, is overcome, not by the Austrians, but by his Italian compatriots, the self-serving politics of the army, the count's opportunism, and Livia's betrayal. Any moral superiority he might have claimed is denied by his ineffectiveness; rather than rising above the limitations of his class, he embodies them. Livia and her class succumb to the romantic delusion that rendered them incapable of transcending self-interest and constructing a genuine political union. The "typical" characters of *Senso* serve as a synthesis of the historical crisis of the Risorgimento. In their story, politics is bound to romance, and the intensity of inner feeling is projected into the public realm.

Chapter 5

The Politics of the Spectacle:
The Rise to Power of Louis XIV

*All knowledge is rooted in a life, a society, and a language
that have a history; and it is in that very history that
knowledge finds the element enabling it to communicate
with other forms of life, other types of society, other
significations: that is why historicism always implies a
certain philosophy.*
—MICHEL FOUCAULT, 1966

*In the living world there are no individuals entirely sealed
off by themselves; all individual enterprise is rooted in a
more complex reality. . . . The question is not to deny the
individual on the grounds that he is the prey of
contingency, but somehow to transcend him, to distinguish
him from the forces separate from him, to react against a
history arbitrarily reduced to the role of quintessential
heroes.*
—FERNAND BRAUDEL, 1950

The Rise to Power of Louis XIV ends in contemplation. The king,
triumphant at Versailles, retreats from his courtiers to a private
room to meditate upon the maxims of La Rochefoucauld. After
deliberately taking off his gloves, hat, sword, wig, necklace, sash,
and outer jacket, Louis puts on a simple coat and reads aloud:

> There is a loftiness that does not depend on fortune. It is a
> certain air of superiority that seems to destine one for great
> things. It is a prize that we award ourselves imperceptibly.
> This quality enables us to usurp other men's deference and
> places us further above them than birth, rank, and merit
> itself.

After repeating the final phrase, the king continues, "Neither the
sun nor death can be faced steadily." Again he repeats the maxim,

pauses in reflection, looks to the book, and reads quietly. Here the film ends. The pregnant, introspective conclusion reverberates back on all that preceded it. The film offers the maxims almost without inflection, inviting the viewer to join Louis in thought.

The words of La Rochefoucauld address issues central to the film. The first passage asks how the influence of great leaders like Louis XIV can be understood historically; what is this "loftiness that does not depend on fortune"? The second passage obliquely responds to the first, suggesting the practice of the film itself. In approaching the radiance of the sun or the finality of death, the text counsels indirection. Essential forces resist access by straightforward investigation; instead, one must wrestle with these forces through their consequences, study their adjacent manifestations, ponder apparently disconnected phenomena in order to achieve understanding. The two passages suggest the historical method of the film, a method that reveals the power of the state in the routine experience of daily life. The enigmatic conclusion of *The Rise to Power* also invites a critical response informed by its indirect allusions—the constellation of circumstances, intentions, and influences that invest the film with a provocative fertility.

The Rise to Power divides itself almost equally into three sections, progressing through a distinct evolution in style and meaning. The film opens on March 8, 1661, just before the death of Cardinal Mazarin, the chief minister of the crown during Louis XIV's minority. The king is only twenty-two, and the passing of His Eminence brings the struggle for power into the open. The first section portrays the contending parties at the Vincennes palace as they hover around Mazarin's deathbed. The second part covers the months following the cardinal's passing, as the young monarch resists the ambitions of the Queen Mother, Anne of Austria, and overcomes a challenge from the Superintendent of Finance, Nicolas Fouquet. This part concludes in September 1661 with Fouquet's arrest. The concluding section presents Louis' ascendancy at Versailles in the 1680s, his domination of the state absolute.

The Rise to Power appears to address no contemporary social issues. Compared with *La Marseillaise,* so closely associated with the Popular Front, or *Senso*, which strove for political engagement under the cover of history, the story of the Sun King seems detached from current events. Instead, Roberto Rossellini speaks of his "search for objectivity. . . . My purpose is never to convey a message, never to persuade but to offer everybody an observation."[1] The director stresses his accurate depiction of the seventeenth-century court, equivocates upon the film's contemporary meaning, and resists immediate parallels.

> I think it's enough to know what happened, there's no need to think up fables. The world is always the same because it is shaped by men. It's easy to find parallels with things that happen today—it's a matter of chance, and I have no interest in picking them out. *La Prise du pouvoir par Louis XIV* describes the technique of taking power—which is a useful thing to know.[2]

One should hesitate before bowing to Rossellini's stated intentions. "The technique of taking power," Rossellini tells us, is central to the film, and, no doubt, a political act. The theme is inscribed into the title, more accurately translated into English as "The Seizing of Power by Louis XIV." Historical films are historical objects themselves, and as such they testify to the moment of their making. As a complex, collective product, movies often incorporate unintended, even contradictory, meanings that may become increasingly apparent as time passes. The chief tension informing the work arises from an apparent endorsement of de Gaulle's Fifth Republic, which sponsored the project, versus a complex of associations linking the film to left-wing French politics in the mid-1960s. Contending motives and meanings surround this French television production.

History on Television under the Fifth Republic

The Rise to Power of Louis XIV, a film produced by the Office de la Radiodiffusion-Television Française (ORTF), was first aired on French national television on October 8, 1966. There were three major collaborators—ORTF itself, the historian Philippe Erlanger, and the director, Roberto Rossellini.

ORTF as an Agent of the
Gaullist Regime

The rise to power of Charles de Gaulle and his Fifth Republic
sets the political context. Eight years before the film's release,
the Fourth Republic, paralyzed by the colonial crisis in Algeria,
turned to General de Gaulle, who took power through a series of
deft maneuvers. By 1962 the general had consolidated his position and extricated France from its fading empire. A challenge to
the Anglo-American leadership of the Western Alliance followed.
He blocked British entry to the Common Market, threatened
the monetary supremacy of the dollar, and developed an independent nuclear force. At the same time the consumer culture
generated by accelerating postwar prosperity transformed French
life. Among the noteworthy developments was the spread of
television, which in France was under the control of the central government. In December 1965, de Gaulle's ascendancy was
confirmed by his reelection to a presidency shaped to his dic-
tates. Less than a year later, *The Rise to Power* was televised to the
French nation.

The common qualities of de Gaulle and Louis XIV illuminate
the political undercurrents in the film. Modern French politics
can be divided into two traditions. The parliamentary tradition is
represented by the Revolution of 1789 and the First, Third, and
Fourth Republics; the authoritarian tradition is associated with
state centralization under Louis XIV, and with Napoleon Bonaparte, Napoleon III, and de Gaulle's Fifth Republic. This latter
tendency has been defined as one

> where most of the power is in the hands of the executive,
> and where the power of the legislature is weak or merely
> fictional.
> . . . The powers of the executive were strengthened by
> the use of what was then known as a plebiscite (now called
> a referendum)—an appeal to the people on specific issues,
> like the establishment of a new regime. . . . The use of the
> plebiscite conferred on these authoritarian regimes an aura
> of democracy. . . . We may consider the Fifth Republic an
> undoubted descendant of the authoritarian/plebiscitarian
> tradition rather than of parliamentary government.[3]

If analysts placed de Gaulle within the same political tradition as Louis XIV, the general willingly played out the role of national leader as shadow monarch. Echoing the Sun King's legendary "*L'état, c'est moi,*" de Gaulle said, in 1964, that "the indivisible authority of the State is confided in its entirety to the President by the people who have elected him, that no other authority exists, neither ministerial nor civil nor military nor judicial, which is not conferred and maintained by him."[4]

The participation of ORTF links the production directly to the Gaullist establishment. French television was notoriously under the control of the central government. An attempt to reform the system with legislation in June 1964, "changed nothing," one history of modern France notes. "The views of government were still presented to the virtual exclusion of others, journalists continued to lose their jobs because of their political views."[5]

Though *The Rise to Power* stands removed from the daily controversy of political journalism, the representation of French history, particularly the ascendancy of the Sun King and the consolidation of a strong central government, must have been immediately attractive to the officials at ORTF. Draped in the authority of history and the benevolence of public education, the film could implicitly endorse the Fifth Republic and valorize Le Grand Charles.

After preproduction negotiations were successfully concluded, ORTF did not intervene in the project. No problems arose during the filming, and the network officials were confident of the production's political allegiances. The participation of Philippe Erlanger offered immediate assurances. A popular historian of conservative reputation who was already serving as a high official in the Office of Education, he had published in 1965 an award-winning biography of Louis XIV. The filmmaking itself went forward with remarkable efficiency. The shooting took only twenty-three days; the editing took less than a week; and the final cost was a modest $160,000.[6] The relative independence of the film is indicated by the color photography, since ORTF at the time could only transmit in black and white. The network, satisfied, gave the film extensive publicity and showcase treatment, scheduling the premiere for Saturday at 9 P.M.

Philippe Erlanger: Historian as Catalyst

The catalyst for *The Rise to Power* appears to have been the friendship between Erlanger and Rossellini. In 1946, at the first Cannes
Film Festival, Erlanger was instrumental in awarding a prize to
Rossellini's *Rome, Open City,* and the two had been friends ever
since. Rossellini "read and read my biography of Louis XIV,"
Erlanger recalled, "and thought he could find in it what he
needed to make the kind of film he imagined."[7] Rossellini found
ready access to ORTF support through Erlanger.

Who's Who in France describes Erlanger as a "diplomat, historian, art critic, and journalist."[8] Robert Coles, writing in the *New
Yorker,* describes him as "a well-known historian and a cultural
services impresario . . . a sort of model of a modern cultivated
Frenchman."[9] Surveying more than twenty-five works published
by Erlanger between 1935 and 1980, one finds a series of French
political biographies mainly dealing with the sixteenth and seventeenth centuries, including *Louis XIII* (1946), *L'Itrage Mort de
Henri IV* (*The Strange Death of Henry IV*, 1957), *Le Massacre de
la Saint-Barthbelemy* (*The St. Bartholomew's Day Massacre,* 1960),
and a three-volume work on *Richelieu* (1967–70). Erlanger was
also a founding member and continuing president of the Cannes
International Film Festival, Director of Artistic Exchange for the
Foreign Ministry from 1946 to 1968, and the Inspector General of
the National Education Ministry from 1960 to 1968. An energetic
and influential scholar, man of the arts, and government administrator, he could ensure his friend the funding and the freedom to
make the film he wanted.

Erlanger's contribution to *The Rise to Power* extended from the
earliest stages of negotiations through postproduction publicity.
As the basis for the screenplay, Rossellini asked him to sketch a
series of episodes from his biography, "1) To show how a young
boy who seemed very shy and not very intelligent could become
the Sun King; 2) to use as much as possible the words he had
really said (the same for the others); 3) to show in a very realistic
manner his way of life and the etiquette of the court."[10] From
Erlanger's outline and the historical materials he gathered, Jean-
Dominique de La Rochefoucauld and Jean Gruault prepared the

scenario under Rossellini's supervision. Erlanger continued to act as the production's chief historical consultant.

Erlanger appeared at the initial screening at the Venice Film Festival and gave interviews before the television airing. He endorsed the film as "the best introduction to the understanding of the reign of Louis XIV. The only important mistake is the part of the Queen Mother, Anne of Austria, who was very different." [11]

Roberto Rossellini: Professional Renewal and Didactic Mission

After a period of personal malaise and professional uncertainty Rossellini had embraced the historical film with enormous enthusiasm. By 1958, if not earlier, Rossellini's confidence was undermined by critical and commercial failure. His extended collaboration with Ingrid Bergman from 1949 to 1954 was at first attacked, and then generally dismissed. Subsequently he returned to episodes from World War II (*Il Generale della Rovere* [*General della Rovere*, 1959], *Era Notte a Rome* [*It Was a Night in Rome*, 1960]), and historical films on the Risorgimento (*Viva l'Italia*, 1960; *Vanina Vanini*, 1961), but the sense of disillusionment lingered. In a 1958 interview with André Bazin and Jean Renoir, Rossellini spoke of his many failures with the public and the difficulty of finding subjects.[12] David Degener notes that, during this period, "Rossellini seems to have spent a good deal of his time 'giving film up' or at least talking about giving it up." [13]

In 1964 a series of history films for television renewed his enthusiasm. For the initial project, *L'Eta del Ferro* (*The Age of Iron*, 1964), Rossellini acted as producer; his son directed, and the film received little attention beyond its airing on Italian television. *The Rise to Power* appears to be the breakthrough film in the series. "These were the first two," Rossellini remarks, "and they're experiments trying to show what could be done in this field. After that the real educational project began." [14]

In history Rossellini sought authority and purpose as a shield against the criticism and uncertainty that had marked his career. In a manifesto published in October 1965, the filmmaker attacks the relative values of contemporary life and particularly modern art, finding in history a positive alternative:

There is a vague feeling abroad that our civilization is only temporary, and already inwardly eroded. Agitation, violence, indifference, boredom, anguish, spiritual inertia and passive resignation are all expressed at every level, by individuals and socially. . . . And the chief testimony to all these developments is modern art. . . . We wish, again, to present man with the guidelines of his own history. . . . We are convinced that with this kind of work we can help to develop information media which, with education, will be indispensable to the process of enlightenment through which man will be able to win back happiness, by giving him an understanding of his own importance, his own position in the history of the world.[15]

Rossellini himself seemed to "win back happiness" and develop a sense of "his own importance" through a concept of film as an educational information medium.

In later interviews Rossellini speaks of *The Rise to Power* as a "historical essay" based upon objective data and firm evidence:

Yes, it is all in the documents, nothing is invented. Let me think, is there anything invented? No, I don't think so. The dialogue with the tailor is invented in a sense because there was no such dialogue in the records, but the argument that Louis XIV uses in the scene is one he had used a thousand times before in other contexts.[16]

The filmmaker associates his work with a simple notion of facts as truth and of history as a knowledge independent of interpretation:

When I am working, I make a choice of facts. Facts are facts. I collect things. I don't want to give any message. I don't want to have any sort of philosophy. I want to offer observations for those who want to look at those kinds of things, things as they are. So I am not magnifying them, I am not exalting them. I am not doing anything to them.[17]

Rossellini's conviction that history is a stable, epistemologically verifiable field of knowledge led to an uncomfortable ambivalence as to the significance of his historical films. Asked,

"How does this [*Louis XIV*] relate to us today?" Rossellini replies, "I don't know and I don't care. What is relevant is to know the facts of history."[18] On other occasions a contrary emphasis, stated in highly generalized terms, emerges. "All my films are absolutely political,"[19] Rossellini contends, or he points to history's function as "not to celebrate the past but to guide us, and guide us better, toward the future."[20] In speaking to *Cahiers du Cinéma* he notes that "art has always had an important role: to give significance to the historical period in which one lives, a significance which is accessible to everyone."[21]

As a result of his faith in evidence, Rossellini rejects the need for a working hypothesis or a critical methodology as a means of dealing with historical materials. His resistance to a conscious historical method is clearly stated in an interview with *Cahiers du Cinéma:*

> *Cahiers:* Do you believe in ideologies . . . ? For example,
>   Marxism as a method of knowing history?
> Rossellini: No, it is necessary to know things apart from all
>   ideology. All ideology is a prism.
> *Cahiers:* Do you believe that one can see without one of
>   those prisms?
> Rossellini: Me, I believe it. If I did not believe it, it would
>   render my life so difficult. The point of departure is there,
>   one can be right or completely wrong: Either one has faith
>   in man or one does not. If one has faith in man, one can
>   believe him capable of all that is possible. If one doesn't
>   have faith, all discourse is pointless. Me, I believe man
>   capable of everything—if he knows. . . . All ideology
>   has some good and some bad. But it limits you in your
>   freedom. And freedom is the central motivation behind
>   everything.[22]

Unable or unwilling to confront the difficulties of weighing evidence, the significance of historical method, or the political implications immanent in a representation of the past, Rossellini invested his confidence in "facts" and a sense of history as a verifiable field of certain truth. This faith provided him with a mission as an educator and renewed self-confidence as a film-maker. However, as I argue below, Rossellini's distinctive style as a filmmaker led to a mode of presentation that constituted an implicit historical method and resulted in a noteworthy historical interpretation.

The international film community greeted *The Rise to Power* with enthusiasm. The picture was programmed for major festivals in London and New York, and the French press welcomed the television airing with extensive coverage and lavish praise. Feature articles appeared in *Le Monde* and *L'Humanité; Paris Match* and *Le Nouvel Observateur* ran interviews with Rossellini, Erlanger, and other collaborators. *Cahiers du Cinéma* published an extensive interview with Rossellini, followed in a later issue with a critical article. The *New Yorker's* "Letter from Paris" described the television production as the "most talked about entertainment of the week" in the French capital.[23] At the New York Film Festival the following year, Rossellini claimed to have reached sixteen million viewers in France and fourteen million in Italy.[24]

The press reprinted and echoed Rossellini's claims to historical objectivity. Jacques Siclier wrote in *Le Monde* of "that extraordinary climate of a true documentary . . . a history lesson where minute realism is allied to the most precise psychology."[25] In *L'Humanité* comparisons were drawn with Brecht, Watteau, and Fragonard; Jérôme Favard was beside himself, declaring that Rossellini was "reviving cinema by way of television."[26] No one appears to have questioned the film's political allegiances or its scholarly predisposition. Drawing the film into the context of political discourse and cultural debate, however, reveals countervailing influences that help explain the variety of interpretations that began to develop around it.

| The Passing of the Old Regime and the Crisis of Succession

The Rise to Power begins on March 8, 1661, as the court awaits the death of Cardinal Mazarin, the chief minister of the crown and master of the state. Slow in tempo, constricting in space, somber in tone, the opening sequence speaks with foreboding of the crisis of transition, the coming struggle to succeed His Eminence.

The train of visitors to Mazarin's chamber represents the contending parties, ideological and political, in that struggle. The opening scene alludes to the uncertain foundations of the state itself. Commoners eating their midday meal before the Vincennes palace talk of the execution of King Charles in England, suggesting that the authority of the monarchy must be continually reasserted. Then the camera follows the court doctors into the sickroom. But these men of science merely accelerate the prelate's death with their primitive treatment. The confessor, rather than soothing a troubled soul, intimidates the dying man in order to secure property for the state. Mazarin's political secretary follows with reports of intrigue and corruption, but the cardinal only advises reconciliation with the Superintendent of Finance. Finally the king, the living symbol of the state, appears to reclaim his dominion. In a coda, the young monarch visits his mother, Queen Anne, and speaks of the turmoil of his minority in which the crown was threatened by the Fronde rebellion. Louis expresses his gratitude to Mazarin, who, fighting from 1648 to 1652, overcame the rebellious nobility and reestablished royal authority. He states his determination to rule after the cardinal's death, but the Queen Mother asks, "Govern, has any king of France ever governed? . . . His Majesty was not being serious." The sequence, approximately one-third of the picture's running time, ends after the minister's death with the king's announcement of a meeting of his High Council.

Twin issues in this opening sequence—the crisis of succession and the representation of social manners as political discourse—find points of contact with France in 1966. The political transition invites a comparison between the Sun King's early reign and de Gaulle's reelection campaign, while the writings of Michel Foucault suggest a telling parallel on the plane of knowledge, representation, and power.

The Rise to Power of de Gaulle
and the Fifth Republic

> *Press:* What is your response to comparisons drawn between
> Napoleon, Louis XIV, and yourself?
> *President de Gaulle:* Personally I feel more like Joan of Arc.[27]

A central issue in the French election of 1965 was the succession—*l'après-gaullisme*, as it came to be known. De Gaulle's major opponents were Jean Lecanuet, the centrist candidate, and François Mitterrand, a man of the left in his first presidential campaign. Both were untainted by the party intrigues of the Fourth Republic; their youth contrasted boldly to the general's seventy-five years. Nevertheless, no one believed de Gaulle's tenure was threatened, so that attention focused on leadership after de Gaulle's departure.[28] The Rossellini film went into production only months after the election, when the succession issue still occupied the public mind.

The Rise to Power alludes not merely to the succession, but to the events that ushered in the current regime: Rossellini described it as "an essay on the technique of a coup d'état." [29] Of course, Louis XIV did not threaten the state with armies or dismantle traditional political institutions as did his contemporary Oliver Cromwell. Rather, under the guise of continuity, the young king moved from government by a council of ministers to government in which all power emanated directly from the throne. How reminiscent of the last coup d'état in France, when the Fourth Republic, paralyzed over the Algerian crisis, accepted its demise and invited General de Gaulle to assume command. De Gaulle's "coup," embodied in the constitution of the Fifth Republic, replaced parliamentary government with an authoritarian structure centered around a dominant president.

The rise to power of Le Grand Charles, like that of Rossellini's Louis, passed through a period of crisis. During the first years of the Fifth Republic (1958–62), the Algerian troubles persisted and the president faced challenges from the native French living in North Africa, the army, terrorists, and the leftist opposition. In 1962, after the Algerian settlement, de Gaulle initiated, contrary to procedures established by his own constitution, a referendum on the direct election of the president. The measure was opposed by all parties as an illegal and authoritarian attempt to consolidate power in the presidential office. But the public endorsed the move, and the general emerged victorious. These years were a time of consolidation for the regime in which the official powers of the government had to be gradually realized by effective action. De Gaulle's reelection in 1965 confirmed that the Fifth Republic was firmly established. Rossellini's commemoration of an earlier rise to power was a historical homage at the moment when de Gaulle's supremacy was confirmed.

From the perspective of *l'après-gaullisme,* the dying Mazarin may be associated with the aging de Gaulle. Mazarin consolidated the power of the state against the rebellious Frondurs, just as de Gaulle preserved the nation against the civil unrest generated by the Algerian troubles and overcame the partisan divisiveness of the Fourth Republic. Mazarin trained the young Louis to assume power after his passing, just as de Gaulle cultivated the institutions of the Fifth Republic. Queen Anne questions whether Louis will be able to exercise authority, one senses the uncertainty of the French public as to the fate of de Gaulle's republic after the great leader was gone.

Another perspective engenders a different reading, however. One could associate the dying cardinal with the passing parliamentary tradition of the Fourth Republic, noting the similarity of his role as the chief minister in a coalition and representative of the old order to the prime ministers of the Third and Fourth Republics. The team of doctors, in verbose but ineffectual consultation, would then parallel the impotence of the legislative tradition, bloated with rhetoric but unable to take decisive action. The confessor attempts to pass on the legacy of the old order, Mazarin's wealth, to the young king, who instead adopts new methods. Both readings offer rich analogies between the politics of succession in the film and in recent French history. But another major issue of the 1965 presidential campaign deserves attention.

The campaign rhetoric posed a debate between the parliamentary and authoritarian traditions of French politics. Initiated by the Gaullists, the debate coalesced around calls for national unity and tacitly demanded support for the new institutions of the Fifth Republic, particularly a strong president. De Gaulle assumed an Olympian position above the fray, attempting to personify the national interest removed from the parties, factions, and interest groups that weakened, and finally destroyed, the Fourth Republic. The president renounced the two hours of television time to which he was entitled in the first round of the election campaign, making only a brief broadcast:

> In announcing his decision [to run] on November 4th he
> sounded no new note, but repeated the old appeal against
> "the State abandoned to the parties and sinking into chaos
> . . . but this time without hope of redress." Every Gaullist
> spokesman took up the theme, which critics summarized in
> a phrase he never used as *Moi ou le chaos.*" [30]

Though the president defined the election as a choice between national unity and divisive weakness, the real issue lay in the distinction between rule by a strong president, as in the Fifth Republic, or by a cabinet government run by a coalition of parties, as in the Third and Fourth Republics. The Third Republic's ignominious collapse before the Nazi advance and the Fourth Republic's inability to lead the nation out of the colonial quagmire left the opposition with little choice. All the candidates endorsed "national unity," disassociated themselves from the old party organizations of the Fourth Republic, and embraced the presidential system of the Fifth Republic. De Gaulle received 54.5 percent of the vote in a runoff against Mitterrand. To no one's surprise, the general moved with serene self-assurance into his second term.

In this context, the feeble Mazarin, surrounded by doctors and priests and plagued by reports of palace infighting, is a positive figure, a man who preserved the state in the face of civil strife. But his vast wealth, reported in detail from the deathbed, testifies to questionable practices. Although the film establishes close contact with contemporary issues and pays a subtle homage to de Gaulle, the connotations become increasingly ambiguous and complex as the film unfolds.

The Political Succession and the Power of the Episteme

The Rise to Power is a multivalent text that seems to support the Fifth Republic while offering a critique embraced by the opponents of Gaullism. For example, James Roy MacBean proposes a Marxist reading and praises the film's "materialist mise-en-scene"; he points to its "essentially political nature" as an "act of demystifying history." Nevertheless, he is troubled by the sponsorship from ORTF and the film's acceptance by the middle-class audience. In contrast MacBean points to Jean-Luc Godard's *Le Gai Savoir* and Marcel Ophuls' *The Sorrow and the Pity*, also produced by the national network but never aired because of their sharp political content.[31] The subversive thrust of *The Rise to Power* arises from its representation of the daily life of the court, which suggests a complex interpretation of the past and a probing critique of the present.

The interviews at Mazarin's deathbed portray political discourse at a decisive juncture, a critical moment that precedes a fundamental shift in the methods of the modern state. The left's enthusiasm for *The Rise to Power* grows from its interpretation of this political shift especially as it relates to concepts gaining prominence in the French cultural milieu of the mid-1960s. Michel Foucault's *Les Mots et les choses* (*The Order of Things*) illuminates these issues.

The Order of Things was published the year of the film's release. It was remarkable not merely for its conceptual demands, but also for its widespread popularity. Foucault's philosophical–historical tract became a bestseller that went into a third edition in less than eight weeks, turning its author into an unexpected celebrity. Sales of the French edition alone exceeded fifty thousand, and, as a result, the scholar's earlier works, until then largely unnoticed, were reissued.[32] Though there is no evidence that *The Order of Things* had any influence upon the film's production, the book serves as a gauge of the public mind. Moreover, Foucault's ideas find ready associations with the Rossellini history.

Focusing on early modern Europe, the period portrayed in the film, Foucault analyzes how systems of knowledge—the episteme—shape intellectual discourse and social behavior. *The Order of Things* portrays the "epistemological space specific to a particular period" and attempts "to reveal a positive unconscious of knowledge."[33] Historically variable, epistemes function at the base of social relations, influencing not merely scholarly endeavors, but the entire range of human activity. Foucault's argument grows from a conviction that "in any given culture and at any given moment, there is always only one episteme that defines the conditions of possibility of all knowledge, whether expressed in a theory or silently invested in a practice." [34]

Foucault develops a connection between the episteme as a "discursive regime" and political power. The dominant episteme gains authority by shaping routine social practices, incorporating itself into the unconscious behavior of a people. "Discursive practices are not purely and simply ways of producing discourse," Foucault writes. "They are embodied in technical processes, in institutions, in patterns for general behavior, in forms for transmission and diffusion, and in pedagogical forms which, at once, impose and maintain them." [35] Changing the reigning episteme is therefore a crucial means of gaining or maintaining power. [36]

In *The Rise to Power* the succession from the old to the new order is portrayed not through the overt use of force, the clash of heroic personalities, or the outcome of a significant event; rather, the struggle for power takes place in maneuvers around social practices—court etiquette, medical procedures, shifts in fashion—that transform the daily routine into a political discourse. In detailing the peculiar customs of the seventeenth century, the film reveals the mechanics of politics, and this anthropological (Foucault might say "archeological") perspective demonstrates the social force of apparently insignificant, even silly, customs. Here lies the key to the film's political critique.

In locating the basis for power in the discursive regime, Foucault limits the impact of the individual and undercuts the influence of great men and women upon history. If the political apparatus is diffused throughout society in subconscious patterns of thought and behavior, even persons of enormous authority are constituted and confined by the reigning episteme. Foucault writes that "in thinking of the mechanisms of power, I am thinking rather of its capillary form of existence, the point where power reaches into the very grain of individuals, attitudes, their discourses, learning processes and everyday lives." [37] Likewise, *The Rise to Power of Louis XIV* presents its powerful figures—Mazarin at the beginning and the king at the end—as in many ways limited and controlled by the practices central to their regime. The cardinal's illness is only exacerbated by the doctor's "cures," and

Louis is as much restricted by the court fashion as the aristocracy he seeks to dominate.

Foucault's ideas can be applied to the interviews at Mazarin's bedside. The doctors invite an association with Foucault's study of medical practice in *Folie et diraison* (*Madness and Civilization*, 1961) and *Naissance de la clinique* (*The Birth of the Clinic*, 1963). Their solemn tones and deliberate movement, the devotion of the cardinal's retinue, and the slow tempo of the long takes invest the scene with high seriousness. The intention is not to debunk the past as backward and ignorant. The leading physician insists upon empirical details, feeling the minister's brow, smelling his perspiration, and inspecting the chamber pot. Like modern scientists, these screen doctors search for tangible and reliable physical data. After conferring over the evidence, the team recommends bleeding the patient for the fourth time in a single day, explaining, "A man has twenty-four quarts of blood. He can lose twenty without dying. . . . The more one removes foul water the purer the well." In spite of the careful observation and group consultation that characterize science, the viewer witnesses a practice that rushes the sick toward death. The presentation of one of the most notoriously counterproductive methods in the history of medicine alerts the audience to the domination of the reigning episteme: Even the most powerful man of the age, Mazarin, is victimized by the flawed beliefs and practices of the reigning scientific discourse. The emphasis on empirical analysis, widely honored and practiced today, suggests that the contemporary episteme may be flawed as well. The film goes on to demonstrate that, like science, political discourse is historical and malleable, even as it assumes a power beyond any verifiable truth.

After the doctors concede that Mazarin's death is imminent, the men of science yield to the man of God, the cardinal's confessor. The exchange between priest and penitent portrays the fading strength of the religious episteme. The medical examination was handled in an open, public manner, with expansive, smoothly choreographed zoom movements that framed as many as six active figures in the composition. The confessional dialogue, in contrast, is presented in a constricting alternation of stable two shots of cardinal and priest, suggesting a need for secrecy and a fear of doubt that go beyond the privacy demanded by the ritual. Mazarin openly expresses his doubts: "I feel no fear and that is what saddens me. I know I shall die. I should tremble at the prospect of meeting my maker and my judge." Instead he is concerned for the fate of the country. The confessor acts not as a messenger of God, but as an agent of the state. He wants to know "to whom you will leave the gold . . . the money . . . all the treasures you have amassed?" The inquiry reviews the minister's holdings—twenty-eight abbeys, the harbor at Brouage, the North Company, as well as sales of offices, which have made the cardinal one of the wealthiest men in Europe. The confessor gives no comfort to Mazarin's soul, but engineers the transfer of his wealth to the crown. Reluctantly His Eminence concedes to the terms of inheritance pressed upon him by the priest. Almost ironically he asks, "What must I do to be able to face God?" The diminishing authority of the Church is represented in the tension between the prelates' religious vocation and their dominant secular concerns. The last rites become a stage for political struggle in which the mission of the clergy bows before the primacy of the state.

The social manners ordering the daily life of the court will become the king's major political tool in *The Rise to Power*. The elaborate court etiquette is seemingly trivial but forceful in its ability to control men and women. A metaphorical allusion to the rise of the new order is suggested in the transition scene from the death of the cardinal to the introduction of the young king. Louis has just awakened, and the bedside ceremony—the attending courtiers, the call and response at prayer, the morning toilet—is presented in meticulous detail as a means of social control that structures behavior and cultivates, in a latent, even subconscious, manner, a system of values. Religious ritual becomes a political gesture in the morning liturgy. Surrounded by his courtiers, Louis leads them in a prayer that he mumbles with such speed and lack of articulation that the invocation loses all reverence and instead becomes an index of domination. What appears to be an exaggerated but superficial ordering of routine becomes, as the film progresses, a vital engine in the machinery of power.

After Mazarin settles accounts with the Church, he attends

to matters of state, welcoming his personal secretary, Jean Baptiste Colbert. Their conversation reveals that the king's Council, the basis for royal government, is rife with division. Colbert reports on the corruption of Nicolas Fouquet, the Superintendent of Finance, and seeks authority to take action against him. His Eminence, however, remembers that Fouquet has served him well and therefore asks Colbert to mend the breach in the interests of peace. Just as medicine appears at odds with health and the Church distant from God, so too does the corruption of the bureaucracy seem to be undermining the good of the state. The cardinal closes the meeting by requesting an audience with the king.

The rising authority of the bureaucratic regime is central to the meeting. Turning his head from the king, Mazarin reluctantly offers Louis his fortune, but the young man declines the inheritance because the size of the gift exposes the weakness of the throne. Approving Louis's judgment, the cardinal offers a more acceptable means to the same end. He commends his personal secretary to the king's service. Later in the film Colbert manages the transfer of Mazarin's wealth to the crown through more subtle means. Appearances are honored, the king maintains his regal superiority, yet the substance of the succession—the transfer of wealth—is consummated. The agents of the transfer act as crucial indicators of the shifting power of competing parties. The fading hold of the Church and the rising power of the state bureaucracy are expressed, not simply in the cardinal's death and the king's rise, but in the rejection of the confessor's methods and the embrace of Colbert, the state bureaucrat. The scenes at Mazarin's deathbed indicate a shift in the discursive regimes ordering politics. The new order is about to be born.

Though the king assumes authority at the cardinal's death, he must still consolidate his power by constructing a new politics, a discourse to match the shift in regimes. The second section of *The Rise to Power* presents the king's struggle in terms of the historical romance as Louis contests the claims of family and resists Fouquet's challenge.

| The Struggle for Power and the Representation of Romance

The second part of *The Rise to Power* portrays the intrigue at the court from Mazarin's death in March 1661 until Fouquet's arrest in September of the same year. The struggle for power emerges as a personal contest between the young king and two rivals—Queen Anne and the Superintendent of Finance. In the opening section the drama's spatial center was the cardinal's bed. Religious rites and Church officials played a prominent role. In the middle section, ellipses of time and locale condense the six-month period into episodes shaped by the romantic motif so prominent in the historical film. At the meeting of the High Council following Mazarin's death, Louis announces his intention to rule with the famous declaration of March 10, 1661:

> Monsieur, I have called you, together with my secretaries and ministers of state, to tell you that up to this moment I have been pleased to entrust the government of my affairs to the late cardinal. It is now time that I govern them myself. You will assist me with your counsels when I ask for them. Outside the regular business of justice, which I do not intend to change, Monsieur the Chancellor, I request and order you to seal no orders except by my command, or after having discussed them with me, or at least not unless a secretary brings them to you on my part. And you, Messieurs, my secretaries of state, I order you not to sign anything, not even a passport . . . without my command; to render account to me personally each day and to favor no one.

After the council adjourns, the political opposition is introduced. The camera witnesses an exchange between Fouquet and Michel Le Tellier, the War Minister, in which the superintendent alludes to his plan to assume power as Louis's determination wanes. "The king likes his pleasures. He will soon grow weary of the role he wants to play. In a month or two everything will be normal again." In the following scene Colbert approaches the sovereign with a petition from Queen Anne, who wants to resume her position on the High Council. Louis instructs his secretary that neither his mother nor his brother is to join the ruling body.

Fouquet and Queen Anne have close ties at the court. Colbert reports to the king that the superintendent, as a result of favors and gifts, has made Anne his friend. In the gaming room Fouquet stands at her side. Later, she vigorously protests against the plan to arrest him. With Fouquet's departure, she also disappears from the film. They can be seen as a couple representing the established political tradition in rivalry with the new order coalescing around the crown.

In their contest with Louis, Anne and Fouquet represent the diffusion of power. She presses the claims of the royal family for influence; he serves as the voice of the nobility on the High Council. Each assumes that a council under the authority of a chief minister will continue to rule in the monarch's name. One could associate them with the collective leadership and coalition of interest groups typical of the parliamentary tradition in French politics. The influence of Gaullism again becomes apparent, for the film presents the Queen Mother and the superintendent as usurpers motivated by personal pride and selfishness and neglects the traditional nature of their claim to power sharing.

Louis strives to concentrate authority in his own hands and create a new political order based on royal absolutism. He rises above the petty concerns of his rivals to rule in the interests of the state, and fights the corruption of Fouquet's Treasury and the divisive provincialism of the Fronde rebellion. His ascendancy, presented favorably, is informed by its association with the politics of ORTF and de Gaulle.

A key element in the second part of *The Rise to Power* is romance, although close scrutiny is needed to reveal romance as a predominant means for representing the power struggle. In part one religion serves as the passing mode of power. In part two a more secular means emerges, indicating that the new institutions of the state require new signs and ceremonies. The tension between personal emotion and calculated detachment, intimacy and politics, romance and spectacle, develops until politics submerges romance into the spectacle of the new absolutism.

Louis's introduction in the first part presents the ceremonies of romance, religion, and fashion as a basis for royal power. As the dawn breaks, the curtains are pulled back from the royal bed, and the chamber fills with courtiers. Queen Marie Thérésè claps from her pillow, announcing to the gathering that Louis has performed his conjugal duty. The intimacies of romance have become a public spectacle. Then the king leads the group in morning prayer, asserting his authority through the rites of the Church. Finally, his grooming, dressing, and breakfast become a ceremony in which the nobility express their submission and loyalty. The shifting and the development of all these ceremonies are a major current throughout the film.

The contenders for power are linked in a web of understated romantic relations. Louis is married to Queen Marie Thérèse, attends to his mistress, Louise de la Vallière, and wrestles with the primal attraction to his mother. Queen Anne intervenes on behalf of Marie Thérèse and cultivates political ties to Fouquet. Fouquet's character is developed in his conversations with his mistress and confidante, Madame Duplessis. To her he reveals his schemes, and through her he attempts to lure the king's mistress into his cabal. Though declarations of passion are completely absent, these romantic connections serve as a means to portray the political conflict.

The emotional tenor of the queen's political maneuvers underscores the importance of romance in the struggle for power. The duel between mother and son comes to the fore in Anne's attempt to regain her place on the High Council.[38] After Louis tells Colbert that the Queen Mother may not join the Council, the following shot finds Anne facing the camera, flanked in a tight two shot by her son. His head slightly bowed and turned to the left he listens passively (illustration 12). "Your debauchery is unworthy of a Christian king," Anne fumes, ". . . you have gone beyond all limits . . . as if the queen [Marie Thérèse] did not exist." The camera holds the scene in a single take, tightly framing the couple's movements. As her words descend, Anne circles the young man, trying to face him, but Louis turns away, resisting her look. The mother acts like a betrayed wife, scolding the king for his infidelity. But her rage quickly reveals a political motive. Gradually her tone yields to a deeper wound as she confesses, "I do not understand why I am not on your Council. . . . Have you lost all self-respect and affection for your wife and for me? . . . I am now rejected by my own son." Louis says nothing, continuing to evade her as she circles, seeking his eyes, trying

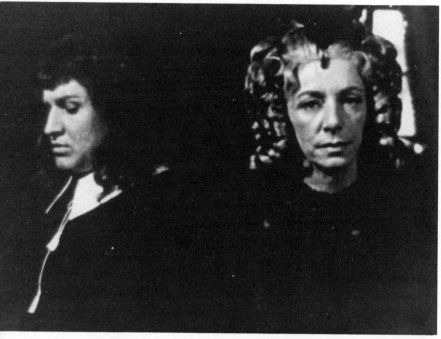

12 | *The Rise to Power of Louis XIV* (1966). Romance as a vehicle in the struggle for power: The duel between Anne, the Queen Mother (Katharina Renn), and her son, Louis XIV (Jean-Marie Patte). Leger Grindon collection

to penetrate his cool exterior. Finally she threatens to retire to a convent, like a discarded lover, and her son, seemingly overcome, covers his eyes with his hands, and then buries his face on her breast, asking for forgiveness. But when Anne extends her arms to embrace him, Louis pulls away, keeping his face hidden. A cut finds the king jauntily descending the stairs and donning a flamboyant hat. He appears self-assured and unmoved by the encounter. Approached by Le Tellier, the queen's confidant, the king firmly replies, "Neither my mother nor my brother shall sit on the Council."

In the encounter Anne takes on various poses with pronounced romantic overtones in order to pierce Louis's political will. First she takes the position of a lover betrayed; then she cultivates the king's feeling for his family; finally she threatens to lock herself away. Reserved and detached, Louis resists her passion just as he avoids her look. The outburst fails to undermine his determination to remain independent of his family in the exercise of royal power.

The scene conveys a conflict between passion and detachment. As if warning the audience, the episode advises caution in the face of emotion, finding calculation and duplicity behind affective display. Rossellini chooses not to resolve the confrontation in the central scene, but rather delays the outcome until the meeting with Le Tellier, when Louis's manner and dress express his resolve and confirm his triumph. The concluding declaration leaves no doubt that "romantic" ties to mother and wife are no obstacle to policy.

In the contest with Fouquet, romance again gives form and meaning to the political struggle. Control over the spectacle of the throne is the lynchpin: Fouquet hopes to seize power by confining the king in elaborate ceremony and distracting him with extravagant pleasures. Louis reverses the gambit and uses the pomp and activity of his daily life to control the court. His life is transformed into a spectacle in which the aristocracy reenacts its submission to the crown. The royal performance becomes a mask through which Louis elevates his person and behind which he dominates others.

In the middle section the king's relations with his wife and mistress appear at the center of the spectacle. In a series of personal exchanges with his own mistress, Fouquet reveals his plans and enlists her in an attempt to undermine the loyalty of the royal mistress. A counterpoint emerges between the spectacle of the king's romance and the more personal contact between the superintendent and Duplessis.

Visual treatment also distinguishes the encounters between Louis and Anne from his skirmish with Fouquet. The king and Queen Mother confront each other directly, and their scenes are generally handled in long, tight shots, often single-take scenes. Though she fails to appeal to his feelings, the encounters are relatively intimate and personal. In the Fouquet affair, distance and indirection are the norm. Louis discusses the superintendent with Colbert or his mother; Fouquet details his schemes with Duplessis; but the rivals never confront each other directly.

Scenes with the minister are more highly edited than those with Anne, and indirect means, such as the metaphor of the hunt and gambling, are employed to portray the contest.

In their confrontation, the king avoided meeting Anne's look. Gradually the visual motif of looking and being seen evolves into a relationship between sovereign and court, of spectacle and viewer. An intensification of this visual motif is central to the contest with Fouquet. As the political contest develops, Fouquet views and comments on the spectacle of the king without participating, whereas Louis's activities are the source of the spectacle itself. Their opposing roles form a significant current in the drama: Fouquet as passive outsider versus the king as active participant; Fouquet as viewer versus the king as vision; Fouquet as the speaker of the word versus the king as the orchestrated spectacle. Their relationship is played out in three scenes—the hunt, the gaming room, and the arrest.

The hunt offers a metaphor for the pursuit of power. A deer running through the forest is the trophy that, like power itself, is being chased by the royal entourage. The chase weaves together four elements, which are intercut in full long shots: a deer in flight, dogs in pursuit, the king and followers on horseback, and finally another group of nobles, including Fouquet and Duplessis, looking on from a distance. The king and his company capture the deer, just as they are destined to seize power, while Fouquet remains a passive observer. After the successful hunt Louis takes his mistress with the same silent determination with which he took the deer. The king rides up to the waiting entourage, abruptly takes the hand of Louise de la Vallière, and strolls with her into the bushes while his attendants ceremoniously bow. The royal lovemaking offers an occasion for the minister and his confidante to discuss their plot. He reassures her that the king "can be ruled if he is kept amused." He is unimpressed by the youth's commitment to state affairs, dismissing his current eagerness and declaring, "Within a month you will see me as Prime Minister."

In contrast to Fouquet, Louis indulges his appetite for game, women, and power. Rather than being confined by his court, the king incorporates the nobles as auxiliaries. The episode closes when Louis and Louise reappear from the shrubs and join the court in a panoramic picnic. Both the hunt and the royal romance are public ceremonies through which the throne asserts its domination.

The gaming room offers a metaphor for Fouquet's play for power, which pivots on the loyalty of the king's mistress. The scene opens with Louis in an awkward position, for he must sit next to his wife, but decorum does not prevent him from openly flirting with Vallière. Fouquet stations himself in a position of strength, standing at the chair of the Queen Mother. Duplessis glides around the room, finally approaching Vallière with a gift from the superintendent—a gift that carries with it an invitation to join their cabal.

Fouquet's attempt to exploit the king's romance fails, however. Even though Louis is vulnerable, with his affections publicly divided between wife and mistress, he seizes control of the situation. When Vallière reports Fouquet's offer, Louis responds with a call for the High Council to meet at the superintendent's provincial stronghold, Nantes. Duplessis is alarmed, but Fouquet dismisses her fears, finding in the announcement an honor for the throne's dutiful servant.

The young monarch confirms his ascendancy with Fouquet's arrest. Here Louis displays his absolute command of the political spectacle. After planning the action with his musketeers and disclosing his intentions to his mother, the king stages a Council meeting for the unsuspecting minister. The episode begins with a full shot of the Council ending its session; as Fouquet prepares to depart, the king beckons him to remain and silently goes over to the window. A distant point-of-view shot reveals a large coach and a troop of horsemen waiting in the square below. Seeing that all is ready, Louis dismisses his minister and returns to the window.

Louis's political domination is incorporated in the film's presentation as the camera watches the spectacle of Fouquet's arrest from the king's towering viewpoint (illustration 13). A high overhead shot frames the seizure, and the distant perspective is complemented by a nearly silent soundtrack. As Fouquet leaves the palace, Duplessis and a troop of five musketeers greet him simultaneously. The romance is over. Helpless and unprepared, the superintendent surrenders his sword and is escorted to the prison wagon. Powerless, Duplessis trails the guards, and is left

13 | *The Rise to Power of Louis XIV* (1966). The camera watches the spectacle of the arrest of Fouquet (Pierre Barrat) from the king's towering viewpoint. Leger Grindon collection

alone in the square as the coach departs. A cut brings the image back to Louis, observing from the window. Without commenting upon the arrest, the king turns to the waiting Colbert.

The minister's plan to confine Louis in his symbolic role has failed. The mute soundtrack smothers the superintendent's vain commentary just as the coach drives him to prison. The king's detachment is matched by the distant perspective, and his lack of response is underlined when he resumes his discussion with Colbert as if nothing had happened. The arrest confirms that reserve has triumphed over feeling, the vision over the viewer, the spectacle over the word.

With the defeat of Anne and Fouquet, romance is subsumed into the political spectacle. Not only is Fouquet separated from Duplessis, but Anne, Marie Thérèse, and Vallière disappear from the film. In his function as the great leader, Louis eclipses intimate emotions, and private experience is transformed into a public spectacle. This transformation indicates the coming order of the secular state. The language of power has changed its discursive basis in its evolution toward state absolutism. The conversion of romance into spectacle indicates the alienation of private life, as its public display makes it another aspect of politics. The ascendant spectacle of the king as embodiment of the state becomes the focus of the conclusion of *The Rise to Power*.

| Film Style and Historical Interpretation

After the film's first public screening at the Venice Film Festival, Erlanger declared to the audience, "Everything that's in the movie is in my book, but I still found it fascinating. Everything was completely correct and yet there wasn't a thing that I recognized. I discovered a whole new world." [39] Comparing Erlanger's biography with Rossellini's film confirms the observation. The two works are remarkably different in spite of their many points of contact because the filmmaker's methods are so distinct from Erlanger's approach. To elucidate the relationship between historical representation and film style, let us examine the methods of various historians, compare the options presented by the cinema, and consider how the selection of episodes and the approach to filming shape an interpretation.

Louis XIV and the Historians

We can begin with the work of the film's credited historical consultant. In reviewing Erlanger's *Louis XIV*, the *Times Literary Supplement* complained that "judging from the references M. Erlanger has not given much attention to recent research on Louis XIV's reign," and pronounced the work "no more than a competent piece of popular historiography." [40] Robert Coles detected a strain of national chauvinism: "Erlanger is less confident about justifying Louis's wars, although he sometimes appears to have difficulty understanding why foreigners were not happy to become French whenever opportunity, in the shape of Louis's invading armies, knocked." [41] These commentators judged Erlanger knowledgeable but not a historian of the first rank.

In dramatizing major events and famous figures from his nation's history, Erlanger employs little quantitative or economic data, and he appears insensitive to the experience of the general population. In response to reports of widespread deprivation during the reign of Louis XIV, he writes:

> The same complaint was repeated hundreds of times. . . . Yet these same Frenchmen, nine-tenths of whom were said to be suffering without respite, were to gain the hegemony of Europe, hold its combined forces at bay, win several wars, annex five provinces, transform the structure of their country, rebuild their towns, construct palaces, fortify frontiers, give birth to countless geniuses and impose their style and culture on the western world. Either the laws of economics are nonsensical, or else this phenomenon never happened. France could not have become predominant in war, culture and splendour while the majority of her sons were foundering in poverty.[42]

This passage appears to dismiss as untenable the coexistence of misery and extravagance, while equating the glory of the state with the prosperity of everyone living in it, no matter how far removed from the benefits of the elite.

There is little doubt that Erlanger's work had a significant influence upon *The Rise to Power*. Its mark can be found in screen episodes such as the confrontation between Louis and the Queen Mother (taken almost directly from the chapter entitled "The Science of Tears"), or in the unequivocal verdict against Fouquet.[43] Even more central to the film is Erlanger's thesis on the revolutionary character of Louis XIV's regime:

> A new and revolutionary phase in the history of France and the world was beginning. Until the early twentieth century, men always thought of revolutions as movements originating among the people and intended, at least in theory, to liberate or serve them. The meaning of the abrupt change that took place in 1661 has thus been distorted. In the eyes of an historian who has observed authoritarian revolutions in

our own times, some of them originating at the summit, it stands out far more clearly. When Louis XIV made up his mind to rule, he was not behaving like the respectable heir of an ancestral monarchical tradition, but as an individual, as a Caesar might have done following a plebiscite, perhaps a coup d'état.[44]

The treatment of the Fouquet affair brings into perspective Erlanger's influence upon and distance from the film. Both biography and film portray Fouquet as a corrupt schemer who poses a threat to royal authority. The king, with the best interests of the state in mind, curbs the minister with a firm and fair hand. In the film, just before Louis walks to the window and witnesses the arrest, he remarks to Colbert, "I do not know M. Fouquet's fate. My justice will decide it." Yet other reports cast doubt upon this impartial characterization of royal justice.

According to John Wolfe, a contemporary American historian, Louis XIV was hardly a disinterested observer—on the contrary, he went to extraordinary lengths to convict his minister. The result was a sensational trial. A royal ploy to remove Fouquet from the established judicial channels preceded the arrest. As a member of Parliament, the superintendent could appeal to that body to conduct his trial. This was politically intolerable for the king, who spent months trying to persuade the nobleman to sell his seat. Once Fouquet succumbed, the arrest followed. The superintendent was charged with treason and tried by a special commission appointed by the king and packed with Colbert's friends and relatives. Fouquet's wit and eloquence in his own defense inspired gossip and admiration. Though the commission revealed his wide-ranging network of influential allies, the serious charges proved flimsy: "One thing came to light: Fouquet may have lived lavishly, but he was not a rich man on the scale of a Mazarin, or a Sully, or even of a Colbert a few years later . . . the evidence did not support the charge of greater dishonesty than was usual in and around the King's treasury."[45] The monarchy failed to get the death sentence, but Louis insisted on permanent imprisonment.

Sympathetic to the regime, Erlanger glosses over the irregular circumstances of Fouquet's conviction with a contemporary comparison. "The Fouquet trial is a prototype of cases that have become common in the twentieth century, in which the passion of those who mete out justice and their contempt for its forms almost constitute extenuating circumstances for the guilty."[46] The editorial "almost" and "guilty" offer an apology for Louis's "passion" and anticipate the film's allusion to royal justice.

Equally revealing is Rossellini's divergence from Erlanger. Erlanger devotes almost a full chapter to the Fouquet trial. Many filmmakers would have relished the confrontation, but Rossellini passes over the episode for more subtle political maneuvers. From the earliest instructions to Erlanger, one learns that Rossellini was not interested in courtroom drama, but "to show in a very realistic manner [Louis's] way of life and the etiquette of the court." Here is an indicator of the film's historical method—one that is at odds with Erlanger's approach. Rossellini turns from the emotionally charged event and the heroic personality. His reserved treatment and subsequent elimination of the romantic elements in the film illustrate his lack of interest in a personalized and dramatic history. After the end of part two, as we have seen, all the characters associated with the romance disappear. Though Rossellini adopts ideas and episodes from Erlanger, his representation of them results in a different interpretation.

Almost simultaneous with the appearance of *The Rise to Power* and a year after Erlanger's biography, Pierre Goubert's *Louis XIV et vingt millions de Français* (*Louis XIV and Twenty Million Frenchmen*) came off the presses. A distinguished professor at the University of Nanterre and president of the Society of Demographic History, Goubert was well known for his scholarly *Beauvais et le Beauvaisis de 1600 a 1730*. His book on the Sun King, however, was addressed to a popular audience.

The contrast in Goubert's and Erlanger's approaches is immediately apparent. One has only to compare the title and chapter headings: Erlanger's read, "The Open Mystery," "The Child of Discord," and "The Queen and Frère Coupechou"; Goubert begins with "Demography," "Economy," and "Society." Erlanger's king is at the center of a story whose tone is close to that of a novel. For Goubert, the twenty million other Frenchmen carry equal if not greater importance. Goubert can conclude, "The major event of this year [1661] was to be not the death of the Italian cardinal [Mazarin], but one of the worst famines of the century." [47] His quantitative rigor and attention to common experience present a distinctly different seventeenth century from the one found in Erlanger.

Goubert worked within the historical school known as *Les Annales*. He describes it in a bibliographical note to *Louis XIV and Twenty Million Frenchmen:*

> Founded in 1929 by two of the best French historians, Marc Bloch and Lucian Febvre, the *Annales d'histoire economique et sociale* have exercised a decisive influence, for better or worse, upon a whole generation of historians, in and out of France. This review has been the determining factor in many historical careers. A kind of "school" has grown up loosely around the *Annales*. The general trend is against pure scholarship, slack chronology, and traditional political and military history, and towards the primacy of the intellectual, social and economic aspects of comparative and interdisciplinary studies, strong reliance on statistics, economic patterns, recent sociological work, ethnology, linguistics, symptomatic studies and so forth. [48]

Fernand Braudel was the leading figure in the group after World War II. Braudel has elaborated on the Annalists's shift from the dramatic event or the heroic personality to a history of routine social experience investigated over an extended period:

> All individual enterprise is rooted in a more complex reality. . . . The question is not to deny the individual on the grounds that he is the prey of contingency, but somehow to transcend him, to distinguish him from the forces separate from him, to react against a history arbitrarily reduced to the role of quintessential heroes. We do not believe in this cult of demigods. . . . Narrative history consists in an interpretation, an authentic philosophy of history. To the narrative historians, the life of men is dominated by dramatic accidents, by the actions of those exceptional beings who occasionally emerge, and who often are the masters of their own fate and even more of ours. . . . It is precisely our task to get beyond this first stage of history. The social realities must be tackled

in themselves and for themselves. By social realities I mean all
the major forms of collective life, economies, institutions,
social structures, in short and above all, civilizations—all
aspects of reality which earlier historians have not exactly
overlooked, but which with a few outstanding exceptions
they have all too often regarded as a backdrop, there only to
explain or as if intended to explain, the behavior of the exceptional individuals on whom the historian so complacently
dwells.[49]

The concern with community life and deeply embedded
social patterns leads the Annalist to distinguish between three
temporal perspectives—the event, the conjuncture, and the long
view. Braudel writes:

On the surface, the history of events works itself out in the
short term: it is a sort of micro-history. Halfway down, a history of conjunctures follows a broad, slower rhythm. So far
that has above all been studied in its developments on the
material plane, in economic cycles and intercycles. . . . And
over and above the "recitatif" of the conjuncture, structural
history, or the history of the *longue durée*, inquires into whole
centuries at a time. It functions along the border between
the moving and the immobile, and because of the longstanding stability of its values, it appears unchanging compared
with all the histories which flow and work themselves out
more swiftly, and which in the final analysis gravitate around
it. . . . The *longue durée* is the endless inexhaustible history
of structures and groups of structures. . . . This great structure travels through vast tracts of time without changing . . .
and in the final analysis its characteristics alter only very
slowly.[50]

Braudel searches for the stable, nearly unrecognized social
patterns in striving to define the historical trajectory of a civilization. In *Civilisation matérielle et capitalism* (*Capitalism and Material
Life, 1400–1800*, 1967), he analyzes a four-hundred-year period
on a world scale, bringing into his investigation the effect of trans-
continental population movements, comparative modes of grain
cultivation, and the influence of housing, clothes, and fashion.

Contrasts between the Annalists and a more traditional approach might be sketched as follows:

Annalists	Traditional Historians
Social and economic history	Political and military history
Stable, routine patterns of daily life of the common people	Significant events or the lives of important figures
Community, civilization, epoch	Individual, nation, event
Preference for quantitative data as evidence	Preference for personal documents (letters, reports, etc.) as evidence
Belief that social patterns shape individuals	Belief that great individuals shape social life
Long term studied as a stable, unified field	Key event or individual life studied chronologically
Impersonal quantitative discourse	Dramatic, personal narrative

Erlanger's *Louis XIV* appears oblivious to the debates on historiography of the preceding generation. His practice represents methods from which the Annalists turned. The Annalists' new perspective on the past grows not simply from new and different evidence, but also from a distinctive treatment of that evidence.

Rossellini's Film Style

The Rise to Power displays an affinity with Annalist methods, not an allegiance; Rossellini shuns association with any historical approach and, in his many interviews, never mentions the Annalists. But the film's treatment suggests a move away from Erlanger's perspective. The change in titles from *Louis XIV* to *The Rise to Power of Louis XIV* signals a shift from a hero to a political process. Rossellini's initial directives to Erlanger assume that the basis of history is to be found not in the willful genius of any individual, but in the patterns of daily life. Though Louis XIV maintains a central presence, it is the details of court life, often trivial ones, that emerge as the lynchpin of Rossellini's interpretation.

The preference becomes increasingly clear when one considers the episodes Rossellini selects or discards from Erlanger's book. Instead of portraying the international rivalry with the Dutch, the Fouquet trial, or the King's amours, the camera follows Louis to the royal tailor. For Rossellini, fashion reveals more about the generation of power than foreign policy, military forces, or dramatic confrontations. The Annalists share this perspective. A Frenchman watching Louis's instructions to the royal tailor on the screen could turn to Braudel and read:

> Costume is a language. It is no more misleading than the graphs drawn by demographers and the price historians. In fact the future belonged to societies which were trifling enough to bother about changing colors, material and style of costume, and also the division of social classes and the map of the world. Everything is connected. . . . Fashion is also a search for a new language to discredit the old, a way in which each generation can repudiate its immediate predecessor and distinguish itself from it. . . . "The tailors," ran a text in 1714, "have more trouble inventing than sewing."[51]

Rossellini, like Braudel, seeks the mechanics of domination in the routine of daily life, though it happens to be the etiquette of the court rather than the habits of a peasant.

Rossellini's film style, carefully examined, reveals how cinematic method shapes historical interpretation. Three aspects of the director's practice invite attention: the planning of the scenario, the handling of performances, and the direction of the *mise-en-scène*. Each reveals a concern for the social over the personal, the public over the private, and the routine over the dramatic.

In planning the scenario, Rossellini shifted the emphasis from the king to the political process. Though Rossellini assured interviewers that the material for his film is "all in the documents" and that "facts are facts," his interpretive edge emerges in his earliest directives, beginning with the three guidelines he gave Erlanger. Though Erlanger's biography follows Louis from birth to death, the film concentrates on the brief period (March–September 1661) in which he takes power. The move away from character is apparent in the attributes the directive ascribes to Louis—"very shy and not very intelligent." In noting the weaknesses of "a young boy," Rossellini is pushing the scenario to seek explanations other than the monarch's personal qualities.

The second point in the guidelines demands a solid foundation in historical evidence, but insisting on "the words he really said" sets the stage for stilted dialogue. Historical documents generally contain what people wrote, rather than what they said. Meticulous fidelity to sources can rob a film of the spontaneous rhythm and psychological inflections associated with normal conversations.

The third point calls for attention to the routine activities of royal life, particularly the etiquette of the court. The desire for a "very realistic" portrayal of daily life weighs the film toward routine habits rather than extraordinary events, toward the quotidian rather than the dramatic. The earliest stages of scenario preparation reveal an interpretive drive consistent with all three points.

Rossellini's handling of performance has been characterized by the film scholar Peter Brunette as "dedramatization."[52] Here the director accents visual and not verbal expression. In casting the film he avoided performers with dramatic training, preferring those who matched his vision of the character:

> I search for people who fit with the characters. I don't care if they are great actors or stars, we don't need them. I manage with little actors, amateur actors and nonactors. Louis XIV was played by Jean-Marie Patte, a friend of mine who at the time was an employee of a ministry. . . . The professional actor is there with his own capacities and he wants to be present. But I don't think that is the way to do the thing. What I want to do is to convey a very precise thing, so there must be a mind. What is important is somebody's expression.[53]

Though the expression is the performer's, the mind appears to be Rossellini's. For in working with the actors he did not invite collaboration in the conception of character or a psychological investment from his players; rather, he offered "just physical, geometrical indications, nothing else. I tell them to go from here to there, to lift their head or bend it down or to do a little move-ment with the hand. All that is purely physical."[54] The visual expression of figure and movement is thereby integrated into the social setting. People and the milieu develop a balanced force in the composition, and a balanced presence in history.

Rossellini's direction of dialogue strips conversation of casual intimacy or interpersonal contact, emphasizing public ceremony rather than psychological insight. Introspection is unusual and when presented tends to be ritualized, as when Mazarin says to his confessor that he does not fear death; displaced, as when Anne, seeking a place on the High Council, attacks Louis for his infidelity; or ambiguous, as in the closing scene of the king in contemplation. Rossellini does little to accommodate the tone of the historical documents to normal speech patterns. The dialogue tends toward long declarations rather than verbal interchange, and as a result lacks the revealing give and take of conversation. The delivery is generally flat and uninflected, and the actors sel-dom look at each other. Fouquet, for example, looks out toward the camera in speaking to Duplessis at the hunt or as the gam-bling scene closes. More explicit is the scolding scene, in which the king avoids Anne's gaze. The direction of dialogue engen-ders a feeling of alienation of one character from another and a complementary sense of personal isolation and political vulnera-bility. The direction of performance highlights physical gestures and the position of the characters within the composition while repressing psychology and the impact of individual acts.

Rossellini's direction of the *mise-en-scène*, a third aspect of his film style, underlines the importance of the image. The film-maker controls the scene through the manipulation of the camera as the performance is in progress:

> I can zoom from an angle of 25 degrees to one of 150 de-grees, and this opens up enormous possibilities. I can oper-ate it myself, it's a very easy thing to use and you can im-provise with it during shooting. If an actor isn't quite in the right spot, for example, you can follow him with the zoom lens. It saves a lot of time and it may improve the actor's performance. . . . The camera works more like an eye, and so you can develop a system of constant direct participa-

tion, because when you have organized the scene and begun shooting, you can see if it's going well, and if not, you can stop. . . . We always shoot in sequences, which reduces montage to a minimum. This optical mobility makes it possible to base it all on organizing the scene, and this means you have to know the set very well. You have to establish it. . . . It's all linked in the context of the scene, which has to follow a certain pattern and bring over a particular meaning. I have to know exactly where the actors are and make the meaning very clear. With this kind of mobility I can do that.[55]

Central to the method is the integration of the players in the composition rather than editing juxtaposition or development through dialogue and dramatic action.

The shooting style undermines a heroic view of personality; consider, for example, the handling of Louis XIV. Closeup re-action shots magnifying personal feelings and enlarging a char-acter's psychological presence are avoided. The film also avoids, until the very last scene, showing the king alone. Louis's relation-ship to others, his position in a well-defined historical landscape, allows one to recognize how the social context comes to influence politics. Furthermore, the camera position accentuates the king's small stature and boyish, almost clumsy, gait by maintaining a medium to distant setup. This perspective places the monarch in relation to those taller and more self-assured than himself, al-lowing his common bearing to puncture, and even contradict, the exalted treatment he receives.

A unified, continuous *mise-en-scène* is fostered by planning the sequence around the long take. At one point in the film, from the meeting of the High Council after Mazarin's death to the king's encounter with Le Tellier at the staircase, four consecu-tive scenes are shot with a single take. "When you conceive that way," Rossellini explains, "you conceive by sequence, by plan, no longer by cut. You have everything tied together, you can have a scene of a thousand feet, or six hundred feet and everything is inside with the movements of the actors and the zooms."[56]

The method presents men and women as shaped by the

historical environment rather than consciously dominating the flow of events. André Bazin noted these qualities years before in Rossellini's neo-realist work. He remarked in "In Defense of Rossellini" that the director's camera

> looks on reality as a whole, not incomprehensible, certainly, but inseparably one. . . . Gesture, change, physical movement constitute for Rossellini the essence of human reality. This means, too, that his characters are more apt to be affected by the setting through which they move than the settings are liable to be affected by their movement.[57]

So Rossellini is not particularly interested in momentous historical acts; rather, he accents the routine, common gestures structured by the mores of the period, searching for the qualities central to the historical epoch. His patient attention to seemingly trivial details finds its methodological basis in his use of rhythm.

As early as 1954 Rossellini told interviewers, "The thing that matters most to me is the rhythm."[58] Cinematic rhythm is a multivalent quality arising from the interaction of many formal devices. Growing from the tempo of the editing, the shifting scale of shots, the blocking of performers, the delivery of dialogue, and the musical score, as well as camera movement, film rhythm is impossible to quantify with precision. But there is little doubt that Rossellini cultivates a slow, contemplative, even solemn rhythm that retards narrative development. "In the film the main thing used to be the tempo, you know, to go fast, fast, fast," Rossellini explains, "but through that you will reduce the architecture of thought. So now I am trying to develop another kind of thing."[59]

In striving to engender "the architecture of thought," the filmmaker shifts attention from the dramatic climax toward the observation of routine action. Rossellini speaks of the importance of "the wait":

> The only thing that matters is the rhythm, and that is something that you just do not learn; you carry it around inside you. I believe that the scene is the important thing; it is always resolved. . . . It always comes to a head at a certain

point. People like to dwell on this *point*. I don't; I think it's a mistake: it detracts from the drama. . . . The thing that matters to me is the wait; that's the part you have to get into.[60]

The direction of *The Rise to Power* is characterized by long takes, a medium to panoramic shot scale, deliberate gestures and blocking, a slow speech tempo, matched by a steady, calm zoom and a panning camera. A viewer anticipating dramatic intrigue will find the pacing ponderous, for the film's style is based on waiting, watching, allowing the seventeenth-century dress and decor, the peculiar habits of Louis's entourage, to absorb one's thought.

The direction cultivates detachment and contemplation in the audience. To promote reflection, Rossellini strips his work of high-pitched emotion. The director is emphatic about the tone of his address: "I don't want to convey my emotions and I don't want to capture through emotions. . . . It would be easy to make people cry. . . . To remain detached is very hard."[61] In another interview Rossellini equates emotion with drama, which he contrasts with his intentions: "I try to be tremendously objective, detached. I don't want to use any sort of seduction. . . . If you build a film with ingredients of drama, you underline, you emphasize things, you guide. I don't want to do that."[62] Rather, his direction aspires to a clarity of concept through the unity of the image:

> When you are inside, when you have an idea, it penetrates everything. So you must select every detail keeping in mind the recreation of the idea. . . . My purpose is to go straight to the truth, and the fact is that the image is very suggestive. . . . I try to interfere the minimum possible with the image, my interference is only to find the point of view and to say what is essential, no more.[63]

Like the Annalist, Rossellini turns away from dynamic pacing, dramatic confrontation, and the heroic personality. The film gives more attention to the doctoring of Mazarin than the intrigue reported by Colbert. The potential excitement of Fouquet's arrest is defused with long-take silence. Though the picture covers a short period, far from Braudel's *longue durée*, the slow tempo complemented by the long-take format invests the film with a rhythm that evokes the slow, almost unchanging, historical continuity that Braudel cultivates. Presenting routine activities in a unified historical landscape, Rossellini, like the Annalist, reveals a political discourse embedded in the structures of everyday life.

A Man for All Seasons

The significance of Rossellini's film style can be better understood through a comparison with another historical film from 1966, *A Man for All Seasons*.

Numerous similarities link *The Rise to Power* with *A Man for All Seasons*. Both films portray political intrigue and state power in early modern Europe; both begin with the death of a cardinal minister and address the issue of succession; furthermore, the rivalry between ministers to the throne—Colbert versus Fouquet, Thomas More versus Thomas Cromwell—is central to both plots.

In other respects the films are utterly different. Formal practices are a key to the contrasting interpretations: A review of scenario, performance, and shooting style will highlight the contrast between a heroic moral drama and a historical vision that finds in the conditions of social life the basis for political ascendancy.

The two scenarios offer contrasting emphases—dialogue versus gesture, word versus image, language versus spectacle. Fred Zinnemann and Robert Bolt, the director and screenwriter for *A Man for All Seasons*, based their film upon Bolt's successful stage play about Thomas More. The conflict between allegiance to the state and the imperatives of conscience focuses upon a careful reading of the law. By dramatizing More's attempt to shield himself from the state by invoking the letter of the law, the film underscores its foundation in the word. The scenario is constructed around verbal duels cultivating psychological nuances or moral distinctions, as in Henry VIII's visit to More's home, and the grand speeches culminating in More's final address to his jury. For Rossellini, dialogue is secondary, and his actors often speak in monotone; he builds his film around rituals, greetings and gestures, or acts completely emptied of speech, such as Fouquet's arrest. In *The Rise to Power*, speech is subservient to spectacle, the personal bows before the social, and morality has no meaning for the political struggle.

The handling of performance illustrates the historical positioning of the individual. While Rossellini submerges the great events of Louis's early reign, *A Man for All Seasons* promotes the heroic character of its protagonist. The grand stature of Bolt's characters is embodied in a cast of stage veterans—Paul Scofield, Wendy Hiller, Robert Shaw. Their vocal delivery infuses the dialogue with powerful inflections, pauses, and nuances that echo years of theatrical experience and position the film primarily in the aural register. Zinnemann's performers, with their eloquent voices, broad gestures, and imposing physical presence, could hardly be more unlike Rossellini's troupe of nonprofessionals. The king's small stature and increasingly absurd costumes, Fouquet's silly, egotistical posing, Colbert's clumsy postures and uninflected monologues, present a circle of power divorced from heroism, if not personality. Draped in artifice and weighed down by decorum, the salons of the court channel the perception of its inhabitants and guide their actions. The personal detachment marking the king's speech becomes an index of control, an emotional vacuum removed from the troubles of conscience and therefore allowing the free exercise of power. *A Man for All Seasons* builds a heroic, moral tale upon the vocal skills of highly trained performers; Rossellini turns from individual expertise and the extraordinary personality to portray a political process that draws its force from emotional reserve and artificial gesture.

The directors' shooting styles complement the scenario and the performances. *A Man for All Seasons* could serve as a casebook for orthodox Hollywood editing and camera placement. The typical pattern sets the scene with a full establishing shot; cuts to middle range, framing characters in waist-level two shots as the dialogue proceeds; moves to closeup for head shots at the dramatic climax; and finally returns to a broad scale for ending the scene. Interaction between characters centers the composition and motivates the editing. The introduction of Thomas More in the second scene is only the first of many examples. Visual metaphors are equally predictable in their traditional "beauty" and conceptual orthodoxy. Stone gargoyles on ecclesiastical buildings introduce the hard, cold statecraft of Cardinal Wolsey.

Nature speaks in knowing, simplistic analogies: Before the cardinal dies abandoned, the camera films a distant long shot of horsemen riding across a barren, snow-covered landscape; More, out of favor and fearful, walks home through a wind-swept forest. Zinnemann employs a lively rhythm that draws its energy from the pacing of the dialogue, continuity editing, and narrative development. The drama sweeps the viewer along, without an opportunity to question a character's motivation or wonder at the historical perspective.

Rossellini, as we have seen, prefers a slow camera movement, full shots, and a lingering pace: He cultivates "the wait." *The Rise to Power* maintains the visual relation of characters with each other and the locale; compositions, rather than dialogue, are the dominant formal device. Zinnemann's direction expresses the conscious force of deliberate language and personal will. Rossellini's long-take shooting embeds his characters firmly in their historical milieu.

A Man for All Seasons follows More's execution with the note that Richard Rich, the Judas of the tale, became Prime Minister and died peacefully in his bed. Nevertheless, the picture applauds the heroic struggle between conscience and a corrupt state. An unbridgeable gap is portrayed between the private conscience and the public life; essential human experience is portrayed as interior and timeless. As the title implies, the film presents a soul standing above changing social conditions. The perspective is ahistorical, heroic, and fundamentally moral, finding no shelter for ideals in the sordid annals of history. *A Man for All Seasons* is not about history or politics; it is a sermon in ethics.

In *The Rise to Power*, the political process is the subject, and the film finds that social conditions, created by men and women, offer the key to historical understanding. "What do exceptional men matter to us?" Rossellini asks. "I'm quite unmoved by the myth of the superman. . . . It is the little things that strike one." [64] In moving away from the imposing personalities of history, the director strives to define the underlying conditions that constitute men and women. In witnessing the practices of the seventeenth-century court, one is prompted to reflect on the power of contemporary manners. Just as people are determined by the conditions of their culture, they determine those conditions and may work to transform them. This view, Rossellini's vision, depicts the process of power and indicates the prospects for change. As such, it is emphatically political and historical.

| The Ascendancy of Spectacle at Versailles

The third and concluding part of *The Rise to Power* portrays the sovereign's program for the new state as Louis embarks on a politics of spectacle. First the king decrees a change in dress and designs a new palace at Versailles. In the closing episodes Louis's ascendancy is presented in the royal meal and a stroll among his subjects in the Versailles gardens. "One rules minds by appearances," Louis confides to Colbert, "not by the true nature of things." After Fouquet's fall, the king consults with his minister on the means of consolidating royal authority. "In the kingdom, each must derive all from a monarch as nature derives all from the sun." The young ruler plans to secure the loyalty of the people by promoting prosperity while simultaneously emasculating the nobility: "They must look to the King for everything . . . privileges, honors, money." As Brunette notes, the "film focuses expressly on Louis' seizure of power, which he accomplished precisely through the mounting of spectacle." [65]

Louis instructs Colbert to call the master tailor for a meeting "of great importance." Ever more ribbons and lace are ordered as the king propels a merry-go-round of fashion, so that the "nobles will be able to think only of their doublets." The regime of appearances becomes increasingly opulent and bizarre as the king buries the political prerogatives of the aristocracy under the weight of luxury. A political hierarchy based upon dress, etiquette, and architecture culminates in the court's move to Versailles in 1680. The modern state raises a subject to do its bidding and creates a new discourse for its politics; the spectacle of the state becomes an elaborate design in which the relations of sight and image, viewer and vision, the subject and representation, act as indicators of power.

The Significance of Formal Development

The politics of *The Rise to Power* are expressed in a formal progression that complements the three-part organization of the narrative. The chief elements are temporal range, the organization of space and movement, and the motifs of vision.

The plot's timeline parallels the growth in the king's authority. Though each of the three parts takes approximately one-third of the film's screen time, the period presented varies enormously. Mazarin's death occupies about two days of diegetic time; the contest with the Queen Mother and Fouquet stretches to six months; the final part, presenting Louis's triumph at Versailles, embraces a twenty-year period. At each stage Louis's power increases along with the span of the episodes.

A distinct organization of space and movement characterizes each of the three parts. Initially the drama is confined to the Vincennes palace, and an uneasy activity grows as the cardinal's death approaches. The second part opens onto a broader field: The choreography is more flexible and wide-ranging, movement more relaxed and playful. In the third part the film returns to a setting marked by regimentation and restraint.

In the opening scenes Mazarin, the source of power, acts as the magnet for the drama. His immobility leads to the constriction of diegetic space as his bed becomes a nucleus drawing all the contending personalities into its orbit. While Mazarin, like a fading star, is confined to his apartment, the king displays the energy of a dawning sun. He is introduced waking in the morning; the curtains are pulled back from his bed, the shades are opened, the light of a new day greets the rising monarch. The king strides through the corridors to visit his minister, moves restlessly at the cardinal's bedside, and proceeds to meet his mother, who paces around her chair in self-absorbed conversation. Then, just as impulsively, he departs. Louis's frenetic activity contrasts with the exhaustion of Mazarin and anticipates the second part.

In part two, vibrant activity in open spaces portrays the contest for power. A key image is the deer running through the wood. Open play and a relative ease of movement mark these episodes: One sees the hunt and the picnic in the forest, cards at the gaming tables, and the musketeers lounging on the lawn.

Even the arrest is presented through broad movements across the expansive plaza. A comparative liberty marks the visual organization during these scenes, in which power is not centralized in any single authority.

Movement becomes deliberate and constrained as royal absolutism takes hold in the concluding part. The key image, a counterpoint to the deer, is the king strolling through the Versailles garden. Louis walks among his courtiers, and the immobilized aristocrats surround the sovereign like well-trimmed shrubs. No longer is power open to contest; the game is fixed, the order firm. Though the radiance at Versailles contrasts with the moribund Vincennes, power is once again established, grounded, centered. All movement is controlled by the king; a suffocating regimentation pervades.

Motifs of vision, the relation between the observer and the observed, complement the other formal elements in the political struggle. In part one Mazarin absorbs the visual attention of everyone. The picture opens with commoners looking toward the palace and speaking of the cardinal's illness. Then the doctors take up a detailed examination of the prelate's body, followed by the confessor, the personal secretary, and the king. Power lies in the object viewed, and it is only the monarch whose vision is guarded against the spectacle. Before Louis's visit to the sickbed, Mazarin has cosmetics applied to his face. After the death the king marches to the cardinal's chamber, but tradition forbids him to look upon the corpse. The sovereign, as the symbolic source of authority, is shielded from the reality of power removed from his person, as if to protect him from the contradiction that power rests with another.

The struggle between the king, Anne, and Fouquet is played out along sightlines. In the scolding scene Anne circles her son, trying to capture his look, as if his eyes were the avenue to power. Louis listens, head bowed, turning away from her eyes, until he finally places his face in his hands. Recognizing the assault, the king protects his vision, eventually shielding his sight with tears. Fouquet's ambition and authority express themselves through his observation and commentary. At the opening of the Council he shares his observations with Le Tellier; later he watches the hunt and the afternoon romance with paternal condescension. In the gaming room he stands by the Queen Mother's chair, observing the court at cards, watching Duplessis, but not participating in the entertainments. At the conclusion of both scenes Fouquet looks outward to the camera, offering his remarks as if his vision granted him control over events. During the arrest his position is undercut. Fouquet no longer looks upon the king, but is observed by him. The camera takes on the sovereign's sightlines as he peers down into the square. Fouquet's look, even his facial reaction, are banished, just as his person is permanently removed. The shot of the arrest, the most explicit point-of-view perspective in the film, markes the firm grasp of power by the king.

In the concluding section the king commands both poles of perception, absorbing the vision of others and dominating them in a reverse field with his elevated gaze. Louis's vision is privileged at the tailor's, observing the construction of Versailles, and in the scene at court in which he rebukes a courtier. Likewise he commands the attention of his entourage as he triumphantly turns his life into a continuous performance.

Every sight is organized to please the king, and his gaze comes to embody his authority, as when, during a meal, he calls forth a courtier, M. Lorraine, or dismisses an elaborate dish. His look also expresses disdain, staring almost blankly over his subjects as if they were unworthy of his sight. The king finds himself elevated and isolated. The only fit subject of his gaze is the spectacle of his own person, the embodiment of the state.

The camera position, however, maintains a cool neutrality. Point-of-view shots are almost absent; even during the arrest, there is no cutting back to the observing king. In alternating two-shot conversations, such as Mazarin's confession or the conferences between Colbert and Louis, the camera does not position itself over the character's shoulder, but occupies a neutral space between the performers. So the power struggle between viewer and vision embodied in the diegesis does not enclose the spectator. The viewer, removed from the sightlines, can maintain perspective and reflect upon the historical vision itself.

The Spectacle of the State and the Constitution of the Subject

The Rise to Power portrays a historical landscape in which the "taking of power" involves a reconstitution of the individual's relationship to the state through a politics of spectacle. When Louis instructs Colbert to call the royal tailor, he intends to lay the foundation of his state by constituting a new subject, particularly a subservient aristocracy—and to do so by shaping the habits of their daily existence. The mode of life functions as a political discourse in which noble prerogatives are to vanish into an obsession with gesture and appearances.

The king's methods were not obscure to his adversaries. An eloquent witness to the politics of Versailles was the Duc de Saint-Simon, whose private journals offer an intimate view of the court during the last twenty years of Louis's reign.[66] Saint-Simon understood well the motives underlying the king's extravagance:

> In everything he loved magnificently lavish abundance. He made it a principle from motives of policy and encouraged the Court to imitate him; indeed, one way to win favor was to spend extravagantly on the table, clothes, carriages, building, and gambling. For magnificence in such things he would speak to people. The truth is that he used this means deliberately and successfully to impoverish everyone, so he made luxury meritorious in all men, and in some a necessity, so that gradually the entire Court became dependent upon his favors for their very subsistence. What is more, he fed his own pride by surrounding himself with an entourage so universally magnificent that confusion reigned and all natural distinctions were obliterated.[67]

Caught up in the sumptuous spectacle at Versaille, the aristocracy allowed the king to encroach upon their authority. The nobles, ever more dependent upon royal favors, lost more and more power to the sovereign.

Rossellini's portrait of everyday life at Versailles bears a parallel with contemporary France and draws the film into sympathy with the Gaullist opposition. The television production suggests an analogy with the consumer culture of the Fifth Republic and offers vital points of contact with Guy Debord's polemic *Société du spectacle* (*Society of the Spectacle*, 1967), whose critique fed the tensions that were to explode in May 1968. Although it appeared after the film's premiere, the book illustrates some reasons why the film found favor with those opposed to the government.

Debord claims that the politics of the spectacle blinds citizens in their search for historical consciousness and isolates them in their attempt to determine their collective destiny. In particular his tract attacks the consumer culture of the 1960s:

> The first phase of the domination of the economy over social life had brought into the definition of all human realization an obvious degradation of *being* into *having.* The present phase of total occupation of social life by the accumulated results of the economy leads to a generalized sliding of *having* into *appearing,* from which all actual "having" must draw its immediate prestige and its ultimate function. At the same time all individual reality has become social, directly dependent on social force, shaped by it. It is allowed to appear only because it is *not.*[68]

The idle aristocrat of the seventeenth century is joined by the mass population of the twentieth century in passing from a political being into the realm of appearances. They are both politically disarmed by shifts in fashion and a need for luxury instilled by the society of the spectacle.

Louis's meal before his court at Versailles serves as a metaphor for the new order. The camera begins in the depths of the kitchen, where cooks and servants frantically prepare food. The adjoining room finds chefs presenting dishes to the superintendent for approval. When the view finally reaches the table, one finds that the culinary army is serving not a banquet, but a single man. The camera retreats from the monarch, revealing an assemblage of aristocrats observing the king's dinner as if it were a grand performance overflowing with significance. And so it is. The film has emptied the episode of drama and offered the spectacle of a single figure, fed by a regiment of servants and attended by an audience of princes, to convey the consolidated power of the throne, the ascendancy of the state over its subjects.

In the concluding section, the spectacle of the king embodies the organizing principle of the modern state.

The spectacle, in the tradition of the historical film, expresses the relation between the citizen and the state. The state has become personified in the king's routine, and the spectacle of the sovereign absorbs the energy of the common worker, the resources of the nation, and the attention of the elite. The state is represented by a single man, but the man himself has ceased to live except as he functions as a representation of the state. The spectacle of the ordinary experience raises personal acts onto the public stage, transforming them into political discourse and draining them of personality and intimacy. Debord notes how the society of the spectacle isolates individuals, who, rather than seeking bonds with their fellows, become transfixed by the realm of appearances:

> The spectacle within society corresponds to the concrete manufacture of alienation. . . . The spectacle is nothing more than the common language of this separation. What ties the spectators together is no more than an irreversible relation at the very center which maintains their isolation. The spectacle reunites the separate, but reunites it *as separate*.[69]

The combination of the ordinary and the spectacular in *The Rise to Power* illuminates the political significance of social practice and stimulates reflection upon the habits of contemporary life. The film presses home the idea that patterns of behavior—social gestures and daily habits—can become the very basis of power.

At the meal Louis's utter domination of his subjects is illustrated in the single note of recognition he offers his courtiers: He invites M. Lorraine to join him in feeding the dogs. Stepping forward with a flamboyant bow, the aristocrat declares, "I shall not fail." The court is immediately abuzz in response to the honor the throne has bestowed. Saint-Simon observed such tactics and marveled at the king's shrewd manipulation of his class:

> The frequent entertainments, the private drives to Versailles, and the royal journeys, provided the King with a means of distinguishing or mortifying his courtiers by nam-

ing those who were or were not to accompany him, and thus keeping everyone eager and anxious to please him. He fully realized that the substantial gifts which he had to offer were too few to have any continuous effect, and he substituted imaginary favors that appealed to men's jealous natures, small distinctions which he was able, with extraordinary ingenuity, to grant or withhold every day and almost every hour. The hopes that his courtiers built upon such flimsy favors and the importance which they attached to them were really unbelievable, and no one was ever more artful than the King in devising fresh occasions for them.[70]

The nobility, rather than joining in mutual support, were broken as a political force by the spectacular pleasures and royal favors at Versailles. Debord claims that the contemporary French citizen is likewise isolated. He contends that the apparent Gaullist majority grows not from the collective support of the people, but from their common submission to the society of the spectacle, the spectacle of which television is so much a part. In their debilitating gaze the citizens are joined and, at the same time, subdued.

The film's fetish of appearances culminates in the final episode of the royal dinner. "The king's meats," an elaborate dish of pork, is carefully prepared in the kitchen and escorted to the table by eight servants, whose heralded passage receives the bows of courtiers until the dish itself takes on the aura of the monarchy. Louis greets it with a contemptuous glance and dismisses it. The meat disappears, its previously exalted presence wholly debased. Ordinary objects are invested with enormous worth, and the king's power is hidden in the quotidian to be promoted through the excess of spectacle.

Debord was not the only commentator whose work gives *The Rise to Power* an extra critical edge. One might see in Rossellini's film an anticipation of Michel Foucault's investigation over the next decade of the relationship between power and discourse, the creation of the subject and effective social practices. Foucault writes of his project:

It is a case of studying power at the point where its intention, if it has one, is completely invested in its real and effective practices. What is needed is a study of power in its external visage, at the point where it is in direct and immediate relationship with that which we can provisionally call its object, its target, its field of application, there—that is to say—where it installs itself and produces its real effects. . . . In other words, rather than ask ourselves how the sovereign appears to us in his lofty isolation, we should try to discover how it is that subjects are gradually, progressively, really and materially constituted through a multiplicity of organisms, forces, energies, materials, desires, thoughts, etc. We should try to grasp subjection in its material instance as a constitution of subjects.[71]

Louis's ascendancy grows from his penetrating understanding that once domination by arms has been achieved, a new subject must be constituted to provide a firm foundation for new power relations. The directions to the tailor and the construction of Versaille are the underlying mechanics of a coup with no generals or armies. Louis eliminates the threat of another Fronde through the willing submission of the nobility, a submission based not on the force of arms (Mazarin's triumph) but on the debilitating pleasures, vacuous artifice, and rigid hierarchies of court life. Here, too, Rossellini's history parallels Foucault's observations:

If power were never anything but repressive, if it never did anything but to say no, do you really think one would be brought to obey it? What makes power hold good, what makes it accepted, is simply the fact that it doesn't only weigh on us as a force that says no, but that it traverses and produces things, it induces pleasures, forms knowledge, produces discourse. It needs to be considered as a productive network which runs through the whole social body, much more than as a negative instance whose function is repression.[72]

Attention to power as a social practice and the spectacle as a political tool allied the French left to the film, even though Rossellini had no intention of being their spokesman. Through his distinctive cinematic analysis of political institutions, the filmmaker portrayed fundamental social anxieties that characterized not simply the court of the Sun King, but the culture of the Fifth Republic.

The penultimate scene in the palace gardens illustrates the sovereign's transformation of living beings into powerless subjects. Saint-Simon complains that Versailles offered Louis an opportunity "to ride roughshod over nature and to use his money and ingenuity to subdue it to his will."[73] The contrast between the forest landscape of the hunt and the Versailles garden expresses the consolidation of royal power. The geometrical shrubs and manicured walkways bear no resemblance to the wild wood and the galloping deer; the courtiers no longer lounge at a picnic or casually gossip on horseback. The nobles lining the walks at Versailles, immobile, metaphorically paralyzed, have become nothing more than ornaments for the throne, subject to the royal gaze. The reification of people into objects is realized visually as the king strolls among his entourage as if among the assorted trophies of another hunt. To ponder his achievement, his rise to power, Louis announces that he wishes to be alone.

Power, Representation, and History

The closing scene of reflection bids one to think about power, representation, and history. Here Louis meditates upon the maxims of François La Rochefoucauld, and his contemplation resonates back over the entire film. The king, in his introspection, invites the spectator to join him in reflecting upon the means of his triumph. "Reasoning about history," Debord remarks, "is inseparably reasoning about power."[74] Much like the laws of fashion and etiquette at Versailles, history tailors the past and sets standards for behavior that shape a model subject. For history is a representation that constitutes social memory and grows from an episteme and its mode of discourse. As such it becomes an arena in which contending politics struggle for ascendancy.

At the conclusion Louis has become as alienated as the subjects he dominates. The final scene, shot in a single take at a medium distance, finds him by himself in a small room. We are seeing Louis alone for the first time. The king's retreat amplifies the isolation presented in the earlier scenes of the final section. In assuming a semidivine status, Louis has cut himself off from genuine human intercourse; no longer does he consult with Colbert or argue with his mother. The public significance of Louis's every act has transformed his private person into a political instrument—a condition described in *Society of the Spectacle:*

> The agent of the spectacle, put on stage as a star, is the opposite of the individual; he is the enemy of the individual in himself as obviously as in others. Passing into the spectacle as a model for identification, the agent has renounced all autonomous qualities in order to identify himself with the general law of obedience to the course of things.[75]

In determining "the course of things," Louis himself is enclosed and isolated by the realm of the spectacle.

The multiple garments generated by the politics of fashion are a metaphor for the new order. Louis deliberately takes them off and, hidden from the eyes of the court, dons a simple coat. The king must disrobe to think clearly, for the manner of the court hinders him just as it weakens the nobility. Though Louis is elevated, he is also constrained. In order to think he tries to distance himself from the political discourse he has constructed to subdue his enemies. With the disrobing the viewer's attention grows, anticipating a revelation, but the picture closes on an enigmatic note. Louis picks up a book and reads aloud.

As the king sits at his desk, the lens zooms slightly closer, evoking contemplation, but declines the accent of a closeup or the metaphorical association of a cutaway to inform the reflection with meaning. The king remains without expression, and the camera refuses to interrogate him. In keeping with the antipsychological tone of the picture, Louis does not respond to the text. Instead, the film passes the reflection on to the viewer. In watching Louis, the audience is invited to think about the political rise of the Sun King and the mechanisms of power in history.

The first maxim acknowledges the role of the great leader in history, but the film finds the individual enmeshed. For Rossellini the human position of being within history and simultaneously striving to control its direction poses a complex exchange: The human will attempts to shape social practice, while unforeseen and extrapersonal forces propel civilization with a seemingly unintended authority. Though the film bears witness to the ascendancy of a great leader, it finds men and women engulfed in the interplay between will and circumstance. Rossellini portrays even the powerful as caught within the unanticipated, labyrinthian consequences of their own creation.

The second maxim offers a method for approaching the sun and death, power and history. The sun is both the emblem of the king and the source of energy on earth—the essence of power. Death reminds one of time passing, the ever present clock dividing the living from the past—the basis of history. Rather than recommending a means for confronting these verities, the maxim obliquely affirms that they cannot be faced straight on. La Rochefoucauld counsels indirection as a method for investigation, and this is the method employed by the film's history. *The Rise to Power* explores neither the monumental military and political events of the period nor the psychology of its leading characters. These aspects of power and history are like the sun and death. Rather the film investigates the manners of the French court, probing the social landscape for political insight. This indirect method discovers in the structures of daily life the current of power. The maxim speaks of the film's approach to the representation of history.

In the closing scene Louis attempts to gain an understanding of his own political position. His meditation yields no conclusion; rather the scene suspends producer, text, and respondent over the field of intention, representation, and interpretation. The king as the creator of Versailles tries to understand his role through the text of La Rochefoucauld; Rossellini presents the maxims as a means of meditating on his history; the spectator confronts the film as a commentary on contemporary power relations. An encircling web joins all three parties: None can fully escape it; none can ever completely control it. Louis has created a political system in which he too is entangled, just as de Gaulle's network produced a homage that his enemies interpreted as a critique. History is also a part of that circle, a text in which the past serves as a wavering mirage to be grasped, contested, and lost again. In the gap between the stellar acts of great leaders and the pervading manners that channel experience, the terms of a discourse about the meaning of the past flicker in the social memory.

Like the king meditating on his maxims, the spectator con-
templates the necessity of confronting history without the means
to completely know it. History is not a truth, but a means to
knowledge, a variable method in the construction of social memory. One cannot turn from or dismiss the past; rather, history is to
be formulated, contested, and reassessed. Louis, confronting the
alienation that rises from his politics, the discourse that engen-
ders his domination, cannot face steadily the sun, the source of
life, or death, its counterpart. Final truths elude his thought; he
finds their implications only in the gestures of the quotidian, the
artifice and images that anchor power and operate the machinery
of history.

Chapter 6

Politics and History in Contemporary Hollywood: *Reds*

Montage thinking is inseparable from the general content of thinking as a whole. The structure that is reflected in the concept of Griffith montage is the structure of bourgeois society. . . . And this society, perceived only as a contrast between the haves and the haves-nots, is reflected in the consciousness of Griffith no deeper than the image of an intricate race between two parallel lines.
—SERGEI EISENSTEIN, 1944

On December 7, 1981, less than a year after Ronald Reagan assumed office, the president hosted a gala Hollywood event. The lavish Paramount Pictures release, *Reds*, had a special screening at the White House a few days after its nationwide release. Warren Beatty, the director and star, his co-star, Diane Keaton, and thirty guests joined the president for an evening at the movies. Reagan's friends had no reason to fear that the controversial film about the early days of the American Communist Party would compromise the Republican president's convictions, but the gracious host and experienced promoter had only kind words for the movie. His major reservation was, "I was hoping for a happy ending."

The unlikely embrace of a film celebrating the Bolshevik Revolution by one of the most vigilant anti-Communists ever to occupy the White House was an appropriate note upon which to begin the theatrical release of *Reds*. For the motion picture was marked by a contrast similar to that "intricate race between two parallel lines" that Eisenstein saw in Griffith.[1] *Reds* was a work whose contending elements were destined to remain at odds.

Like the president, the press gave *Reds* a warm reception. In addition to generally glowing notices, *Reds* elicited commentary from the wider intellectual community: Elizabeth Hardwick in the *New York Review of Books*, Arthur Schlesinger, Jr., in *American Heritage*, Daniel Bell in *Partisan Review*, and even William F. Buckley in the *National Review* joined in the exchange.[2] In a story on the "best films of 1981," *Variety* noted that *Reds* received more citations from American journalists than any other picture.[3] The New York Film Critics named *Reds* "best picture of 1981"; the Los Angeles Film Critics honored Beatty as "best director"; the Academy of Motion Pictures nominated the film for twelve Oscars; and in the final balloting *Reds* received awards for direction, cinematography, and best supporting actress (Maureen Stapleton).

Immediate critical success was countered by lackluster box office. The public, like their president, ultimately seemed disappointed. Though the film did well in key urban centers, it had little appeal in the suburbs and smaller communities. Paramount, whose production cost was reported to be $33.5 million before the expense of release and promotion, failed to show a profit. *Reds* was the first Warren Beatty production to be a commercial disappointment. The public's neglect has spread to the critical community. At the close of the decade, two film journals surveyed opinion on the outstanding American films of the preceding ten years. In neither case was *Reds* honored.[4]

The film itself expresses a dual character. The expensive production portrays American Communists without enough money for a decent wardrobe. The film combines unprecedented historical subjects with the worn sentiment of puppies wrapped up for Christmas. Many critics agreed with Joy Gould Boyum that "although the film's center is politics, it is not truly political."[5] *Reds* is a montage film aspiring toward Eisenstein but anchored in the Griffith tradition. Eisenstein himself spotted the problem in Griffith: the failure to achieve a thoughtful abstraction, a genuine historical synthesis out of the conflicting elements. The race between parallel lines fails to realize an integrated vision. Nonetheless, *Reds* remains a landmark in need of excavation, for both its ambitions and its shortcomings provide vivid illustrations of the state of the historical fiction film in contemporary Hollywood.

| Determination or Ambivalence: Personality, Politics, and the Production of *Reds*

"Beatty, who had been thinking about the possibility of doing a film on Reed for about ten years . . . , got so far into the material and changed his thinking so many times that he lost the clarity needed to dramatize it."
—P A U L I N E K A E L, 1 9 8 1[6]

Warren Beatty was indeed the motivating force behind *Reds*. Richard Sylbert, the production designer, remembers that Beatty first talked to him about the Reed film "after *Lilith*, around 1966." Richard Grenier pushes the initial impulse back even further, claiming that John Reed was the actor's boyhood hero.[7] From concept to premiere, the project stretched over a period of at least fifteen years. This extended history raises questions: What kept Beatty interested, and what held the production back? How did the generating idea change over time?

John Reed presented an attractive prospect for a Hollywood film. A committed journalist and a man of action living on the margins of respectable society, Reed's adventures led him into the defining political struggles of his age. Combining dash and idealism, he was a radical who forged a union between thought and action, art and politics, his professional and personal lives. Reed and his bohemian circle presented a likely site to explore the American origins of the cultural critique of the 1960s. His activities were easy to visualize as popular entertainment, even as his allegiance to Communism seemed to doom the prospect. Beatty's persona as a Hollywood filmmaker and tabloid Casanova with a fervor for liberal causes suggests that the actor's identification with "the playboy of the revolution" was more than media hyperbole. But in 1966 Beatty was more attractive to starlets than to Paramount executives, and he was hardly in a position to promote a film on a forgotten radical.

Less than two years later, however, Beatty was accepting critical accolades and reaping a box-office bonanza as the producer and star of *Bonnie and Clyde* (1967). At this point the film about Reed began to take tangible form. Beatty traveled to the Soviet Union, spoke to the director Sergei Bondarchuk, who was preparing for a film about Reed, and met a woman who claimed to have known the journalist.[8] In 1969 Beatty completed a treatment, followed by a step outline in 1971. Between 1968 and 1972, however, political activism took precedence over Beatty's filmmaking ambitions. The actor participated in Robert Kennedy's presidential campaign, and after Kennedy's assassination he worked on behalf of gun-control legislation. Three years later he became deeply involved in George McGovern's race for president. Looking back over his political activity, Beatty explained:

> Something had to be worked out in 1968 and 1972. People were dying in Vietnam, and the immediacy of that problem, and the racial problems that were underneath it, these were very immediate things. And you had the sexual revolution of the 1960s . . . and, really making movies next to the participation in the societal interaction of that was boring.[9]

Beatty began by speaking at rallies for McGovern, but soon took on the role of political strategist. Ronald Brownstein, in his book on Hollywood–Washington connections, noted that "Beatty amassed more influence inside the McGovern campaign than any Hollywood figure had ever accumulated in a presidential campaign."[10] McGovern was soundly defeated, and although there was talk in 1974 of Beatty's becoming a candidate for office, the actor shied away from a political career.

In 1972 Beatty returned to the Reed project by interviewing people who had known the radical journalist and consulting with Robert Rosenstone, a historian preparing a biography of Reed.[11] Nevertheless, Beatty did not undertake film production, perhaps for pragmatic reasons. Having produced only one hit film, he might have found it difficult to raise money; he may also have felt a need to sharpen his skills as a filmmaker. In addition, the political experience of 1968–72 aroused disillusionment rather than radical euphoria. Instead of John Reed, *Shampoo* served to express Beatty's reaction to his political activism.

With *Shampoo*, Beatty added a screenwriting credit to his experience as a producer and star. The film presents George, a hairdresser who wants to open his own shop and establish his economic independence. On Election Day in 1972, George tries to negotiate financing for his business while resolving the competing demands of his three lovers. He cares for all the women, but cannot remain loyal to any of them. In addition, he is divided between the requirements of his potential financiers, wealthy, Republican, and conventional, who want to find in George a dependable investment, and the ethos of the counterculture, embodied in George's dress, his motorcycle, his sexual "freedom." In the finale, George goes from a formal supper of Nixon supporters to a raucous, massive party of the young, whose chaotic self-indulgence seems oblivious to politics. George is unable to integrate his competing concerns. In the end, he loses everything; his personal failure is matched by Nixon's ominous reelection. Though *Shampoo* portrays the business establishment as powerful, vulgar, and corrupt, the counterculture fares no better. Self-indulgent, irresponsible, and thoughtless, the young lack the discipline necessary to challenge the establishment.

The counterculture of the 1960s was characterized by two distinct tendencies. The New Left was identified with political activism, particularly the campaign for racial justice and opposition to the Vietnam War; the hippie movement was associated with the rejection of middle-class values and the assumption of a lifestyle frequently characterized by music, drugs, and sexual freedom. The intellectual New Left emphasized social analysis, which often degenerated into doctrinaire squabbles involving a range of organizations from the Democratic Party to the Weathermen. The emotional hippie movement often avoided political struggle, believing that individuals could simply disengage from the dominant culture and pursue a personal transformation by retreating to rural communes or enclaves like the Haight–Ashbury district of San Francisco. In practice, these tendencies intermingled, and the desire "to make the personal political" was one point at which they intersected. However, the distinction is useful in understanding Beatty's choice to make *Shampoo* and delay *Reds*.

Beatty stands at a boundary between the two tendencies, linked to the hippies by residence in an art community, Hollywood, that lives by standards distinct from prevailing convention, while demonstrating through his political activism an allegiance to the ambitions of the New Left. *Shampoo* offers a critique of the counterculture that is largely aimed at the hippie tendency.

In it, Beatty lays blame for McGovern's defeat on both the corrupt business community and the disengagement and hedonism of a sector of the counterculture. As a result, George can never achieve economic independence or fulfilling personal relationships. Reed, however, represents the New Left tendency in which Beatty invested his energy between 1968 and 1972. In 1974 Beatty needed to account for the political failure of the movement, and Reed was the wrong vehicle.

After *Shampoo*, Beatty engaged a writer to develop the Reed project. In early 1976 he was introduced to the British dramatist Trevor Griffiths, and their conversations led to a contract. Griffiths' fame was based on three plays, *Occupations* (1970), *The Party* (1973), and *Comedians* (1975), which established his reputation as a playwright who delved into the problems of the left. Max Le Blond describes him as a "classic example of the dramatist engagé, passionately Marxist in his political convictions and profoundly committed in his plays to an exploration of the possibilities of and obstacles to a radical transformation of British society."[12] *Occupations*, for example, dramatized Italian factory strikes led by Communists in 1920 in which debates between Antonio Gramsci and the Soviet emissary restage controversies within the left immediately after the Bolshevik Revolution. To *Reds* Griffiths could bring political understanding, dramatic skills, and experience with a historical drama set during the period of Reed's own activism. Beatty could have chosen an established Hollywood writer, rather than a British Marxist who had never worked in film, let alone Hollywood. The bold selection signals Beatty's commitment to an innovative, political film.[13]

With the success of *Bonnie and Clyde* and *Shampoo* behind him and the assistance of Griffiths and Rosenstone, as well as his own considerable preparation, why did the filmmaker not push ahead with the Reed film? His production of *Heaven Can Wait* (1978) indicates reservations: *Shampoo* and *Reds* integrate romantic comedy with a dominant political melodrama, but *Heaven Can Wait* reverses the mix, presenting a pale evocation of Frank Capra. *Heaven Can Wait* is in fact a remake of *Here Comes Mr. Jordan*, a Hollywood film from 1941, when esteem for Capra was at its peak.

Heaven Can Wait bolstered Beatty's stock in the film industry, however. A commercial success, it was honored with nine Academy Award nominations, including best picture. Beatty had passed through his training as actor, producer, screenwriter, and, in *Heaven Can Wait*, co-director. David Thompson estimates that these three productions must have earned $100 million for Beatty alone, as well as affirming his reputation as a creative talent with remarkable commercial instincts.[14]

A decision about the Reed project was now pressing because of Beatty's cherished idea of integrating documentary testimony with the historical fiction. This concept was in jeopardy because the "old folks," as Beatty called his interview subjects, were dying. Sylbert speculates that Beatty came to realize that he had to pursue the Reed project immediately after *Heaven Can Wait* or abandon the interviews.[15]

Beatty's political instincts had been tempered by the events of the 1960s, the McGovern campaign, Griffiths' drama, and Rosenstone's history. Yet the politics of 1978 were distinct from those of ten or even six years earlier. The counterculture had failed to muster a broad coalition behind a political agenda; the promise of social transformation offered by the American left, particularly its radical contingent, had been diminished by factionalism. President Jimmy Carter, a moderate Democrat, could not draw together the rival elements of his own party, let alone the nation. As a precursor of sixties politics, Reed must have looked substantially different when Beatty finally began work on his film than he had in the heady days after the success of *Bonnie and Clyde*. Nevertheless, with the release of *Heaven Can Wait*, the production of *Reds* began in earnest. From mid-1978 through the premiere on December 4, 1981, the picture consumed Beatty's energy.

During the making of *Reds*, Beatty's uncertain vision seemed to bear out the doubts afflicting the American left. This lack of clarity manifested itself in a balancing act. Rather than adhering to a firm conception, Beatty tried to integrate the disparate contributions of his collaborators. His own movement from the political commitment of the McGovern years to the commercial acumen of *Heaven Can Wait* finds expression in the production process.

The screenplay illustrates these divisions. The basic text

was composed by the credited writers, Griffiths and Beatty. Beatty had brought his outline and ideas to Griffiths in 1976. Pleased with Griffiths' initial draft, he forwarded the manuscript to Robert Towne, co-writer on *Shampoo*, and Elaine May, co-writer on *Heaven Can Wait*, for their advice. In September 1978 he returned to Griffiths with a detailed critique. Working together in New York City, Beatty and Griffiths spent ten to twelve weeks hammering out a second draft. Political events moved to the middle ground, and the romance between Reed and the writer Louise Bryant assumed center stage. Dialogue took on a more contemporary cast, moving away from the period tone Griffiths had tried to incorporate. After completing this draft, Beatty and Griffiths parted, and the producer probably brought the manuscript back to Towne and May for further suggestions. In December Beatty went to London and worked with Griffiths for two or three days. By this point Griffiths was disillusioned, and his disagreements with Beatty became more pointed. The playwright complained that their meetings were "more like a marketing ideas session in advertising: ideas were not rooted in moral value or a sense of history or character any longer." [16] At the end of the month, Griffiths withdrew from the production.

The composition of the screenplay pitted the political dramatist, Griffiths, against the Hollywood professionals, Towne and May. As the writing progressed, Beatty relaxed his political vision in favor of his commercial instincts. The retreat from public activism toward the shelter of personal relations, a trend within the society at large, seems to have marked the evolution of the screenplay. Carolyn Porter, among others, notes that "*Reds* is haunted by the memory of the American sixties," [17] yet the film elevates romance over politics and never gains a coherent perspective on the historical relationship between Reed and the events of that decade. Rather, the fading influence of the sixties finds its analogue in the whittling away of the initial design during the scenario process. The political division and uncertainty of the seventies constrained impulses born in an earlier period.

Once the drama was established, the director could turn to the witnesses and solicit their reactions. The interviews used in the film took place between the completion of the shooting script in May and the filming of the dramatic action, which began in August 1979. In 1992 Beatty talked about the witnesses in a manner that revealed both his suspicion of history and his uncertainty about Reed's significance: "I was transfixed . . . by the disparity of points of view [among the witnesses] in what they had to say about what had happened long ago, and how like that is to my view of history, of recorded history—that it's all just a lot of varying opinions and interpretations of events."[18] The final voice of the witnesses, so important for the film's impact, waited until postproduction, when the editing would shape their role. However, the conflicts among them, discussed in more detail below, suggest the division in Beatty's grasp of his subject, his confusion of personal memory with political history.

Under Beatty's full command, the extended and exhausting shooting of *Reds* occurred between August 1979 and July 1980. Beatty followed the screenplay with little variation but gave copies only to Diane Keaton and Jack Nicholson; he gave the other performers their lines on a day-to-day basis. Beatty augmented his control by ordering an enormous number of takes, frequently asking performers for thirty or more retakes. The final shooting ratio of 40 to 1 appears to be the result of shooting the same setups again and again, rather than numerous scenes that were later cut. Giving himself plenty of options to construct performances during editing, Beatty signaled either uneasiness in his first solo as director or uncertainty about the principles molding the film.[19]

The scale of the production heightened the concern of Paramount executives already uneasy over the film's subject. Barry Diller, chairman of Paramount Pictures, reported that *Reds* was originally budgeted at $20 million, but costs grew to the reported figure of $33.5 million; some claim costs went even higher. After quarreling with Beatty, Diller flew to London at Thanksgiving and again at Christmas to investigate; he was pleased with the five hours of film he saw.[20] But Diller's concern highlights the pressure on Beatty, who wanted to produce an innovative and demanding film but needed to please a mass audience to turn a profit. There are few precedents for such success in the history of commercial cinema; *The Birth of a Nation* was exceptionally profitable, while *Intolerance* and *Citizen Kane* failed at the box office. This tension increased pressure on the production and probably accelerated the erosion of its political aims.

In the weeks before the theatrical release, Beatty supervised the advertising campaign, which expressed the tension between romance and politics. The chief advertising image presents a couple embracing (illustration 14). The picture is unusual because the figures are not clearly recognizable as Diane Keaton and Warren Beatty. Their faces are either partially or completely hidden from the camera and they are wearing ordinary, even tattered, clothes. The embrace highlights the romance, but the attire and positioning turn away from glamour. Has passion led the couple to sacrifice all in pursuit of their union? The allusion to politics arises in the lettering design and positioning of the title. "Reds" cuts diagonally across the lower right corner of the image in stenciled block letters that slip slightly off its lower edge. The lettering and slippage evoke a bureaucratic stamp, as if a customs official has hurriedly marked a passport. Authority intrudes on the privacy of the lovers, suggesting the conflict between romance and politics common to the historical fiction film. The image of the couple contends with the language of politics; nevertheless, emotion overcomes the prohibition through sheer scale. The romance is embodied as an intense embrace; politics is presented as a standardized, impersonal, and intrusive stamp. The advertising reassures the audience that in the conflict of love versus politics, romance will prevail.

Equally remarkable in the early advertising in the *New York Times* is the prominence given to the press reaction. The opening-day *Times* ad highlights reviews at the expense of the image, particularly comparisons with *Lawrence of Arabia*, *Dr. Zhivago*, and *Citizen Kane*. The ad suggests Warren Beatty's dual aspirations—the spectacle and profits of the Lean epics and the critical acclaim of Wells. The address to the elite is apparent in an advertising spread covered with tiny print; that it is too small to be read indicates that the critics are beside themselves with praise and that this groundbreaking picture is aimed not at the average movie-goer, but at the trend-setting audience. In the ad's words, the "majestic sweep" promises the spectacle, while "the great love story" makes the complementary generic claim of the historical

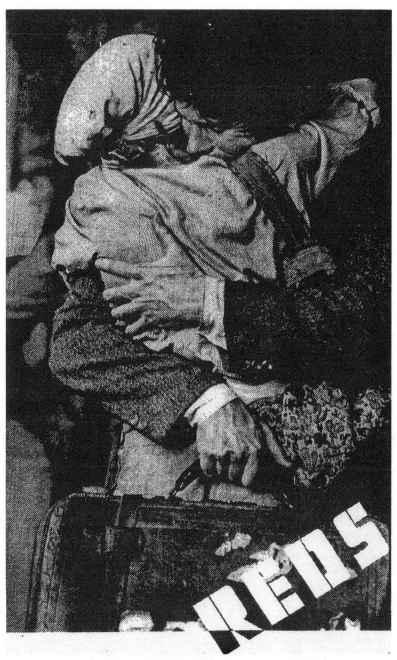

14 | *Reds* (1981), newspaper advertisement. The advertising campaign suggests the issues at stake in the film while reinforcing a widespread suspicion of both politics and history.

...uon film. Here the common ground of expectations is clearly stated. "Rueful comedy" and "historical fatalism" are darker and more provocative. Comedy offers a quality generally foreign to the pompous ambitions of the historical subject; fatalism, while typical of Hollywood's historical vision, contrasts with humor and evokes complexity and distress, the pessimistic sophistication of the European "art" cinema.

The advertising campaign succeeds in suggesting the issues at stake in the film while reinforcing a widespread suspicion of both politics and history. It also reaffirms the ambivalence marking the production. Warren Beatty realized his ambition to bring John Reed to the screen, but what, one finally asks, did Beatty make of Reed's experience? And what did that experience offer to Beatty and to the American public in 1981?

| The Politics of Romance in *Reds*

David Bordwell has noted that well over 80 percent of classical Hollywood films incorporate a romance into the established generic structure.[21] As we have seen, incorporation of the romantic couple into a historical crisis is a central element in the historical fiction film. Though *Reds* comes more than twenty years after the decline of the Hollywood studio system, much of the film, particularly its romance, remains so firmly wedded to the classical tradition that it appears to be more of a summation of that tradition than a critique.

Reds portrays the last five years in the life of John Reed, from his first meeting with Louise Bryant in Portland, Oregon, to his death at thirty-three in the Soviet Union. The film presents their relationship as a product of historical circumstances, but more fundamentally the conflicts between Jack and Louise pivot around politics as both struggle to integrate their professional goals with their personal lives. "Comrades," an early working title, conveys the sense of this struggle. Jack's and Louise's aspirations are understood not as a drive to achieve social justice by transforming political institutions, but rather as an attempt to realize a satisfactory union by transforming gender relations. The intersection of public and private life, a political issue closely associated with the sixties, becomes central to the film.

15 | *Reds* (1981), production still. Eugene O'Neill (Jack Nicholson), the great leader as artist, wooing Louise Bryant (Diane Keaton). Courtesy Museum of Modern Art/Film Stills Archive

The historical fiction film regularly positions the romantic couple in relation to the great leader. The leader represents the social and historical forces shaping the romance and typically urges the couple to subordinate their private passion to a public crusade. This rivalry between the leader and the lovers is fundamental to the meaning of the historical fiction film.

The romantic drama in *Reds* is portrayed in two distinct parts. The first part extends from the meeting of Jack and Louise to their reunion during the Bolshevik Revolution, as art and politics exercise their competing influences upon the couple. The generic conventions of romantic comedy shape the initial part, in which the lovers meet, become separated by obstacles, and finally overcome the obstacles to reunite. The second part of the film begins when Jack and Louise return to the United

States from Russia. Their success as journalists leads Jack into socialist politics and back to the Soviet Union. Here their personal commitment is juxtaposed with the social commitment to revolutionary politics. Generic elements from melodrama shape their demise as a couple. *Reds* moves from *His Girl Friday* (1940) to an amalgamation of *Way Down East* (1920) and V. I. Pudovkin's *Mother* (1926). Each part illustrates the function of the great leader in relation to the romantic couple.

Jack's arrival in Oregon as the great leader initiates the romantic triangle in *Reds*. His critique of World War I and prevailing social relations lures Louise away from her husband. He challenges her to live up to her bohemian aspirations rather than dabbling in radicalism from the haven of marriage. Louise is introduced at a gallery, where her friends and husband are shocked to discover her as the nude model for an "art" photograph. She leaves the show in the face of their muted outrage to attend a meeting of the Liberal Club at which Jack denounces the war as a catastrophe manipulated by capitalists. Journalism becomes the couple's common ground. She interviews him about international politics, and their infatuation takes hold. Soon she responds to his call and arrives in Greenwich Village.

The great leaders challenging the romantic couple are Eugene O'Neill and Emma Goldman (illustrations 15 and 16). Gene, the playwright, assumes the role of the artist and competes with Jack for Louise's affection. Emma, the anarchist, is Gene's thematic opponent as the political leader drawing Jack's attention. Throughout the film these characters express the conflict of art and politics that threatens the romance. Viewed from the perspective of romantic comedy, Gene is the rival lover threatening to separate the couple; Emma is the parent figure, whose reason objects to Jack's interest in an unworthy companion. Gene is characterized by alcohol, which incites the emotional abandon, personal expression, and cynical bitterness of the artist. Emma is associated with Chase and Sanborn, the coffee that clears the head and stimulates tireless political activism.

The Greenwich Village episode introduces the challenge to the romantic couple. Louise arrives at Jack's apartment, and hours later he returns home with Emma. Engaged in a political discussion, he has forgotten about his plan to greet Louise.

R-5527

16 | *Reds* (1981), production still. Emma Goldman (Maureen Stapleton), the great leader as political activist, is visited by John Reed (Warren Beatty) in her prison cell. Courtesy Museum of Modern Art/ Film Stills Archive

Shortly afterward, Gene comes to the aid of a woman who has appealed to Jack for a loan; Jack is too busy lecturing a workingman about capitalism. Gene's kindness in the face of Jack's distraction anticipates the former's attention to Louise. The Village sequence unfolds in a montage built around shots of Jack and Louise dancing (the romance), interspersed with conversations in which Louise fails to establish her identity in Jack's social circle because she has no work to define herself. In this regard she is challenged most forcefully—by example and in conversation— by Emma, as Gene winces in sympathy. A lovers' quarrel results, and the couple decide to leave New York.

Gene moves to the fore in Provincetown, where Jack and Louise have joined their friends in an arts community. Poetry and theatrics fail to satisfy Jack, who departs for the Democratic Convention in St. Louis. In his absence, Gene and Louise become lovers. Upon Jack's return, however, he and Louise are reconciled and marry. A countermovement toward politics arises from their conjugal home in Croton, New York. After the marriage Jack becomes increasingly involved in demonstrations against the war, and Emma reemerges as his comrade. Constantly leaving Louise in order to report on political events, Jack cannot integrate his domestic and his professional lives. As Louise repeatedly reminds him, "The taxi's waiting." The separation between work and marriage leads to mutual suspicion, and Jack's discovery of an old love poem from Gene ignites a quarrel. The "other woman" with whom Jack has been spending his time is implicitly Emma, the political leader. Enraged, Louise departs.

The romantic couple is reunited around journalism, a synthesis of art and politics. Learning of Louise's troubles as a reporter in France, Jack goes to Europe and persuades her to join him in covering events in Russia. They arrive in the midst of revolution and witness the Bolshevik seizure of power. Their romance is revived by their professional union, while the euphoria of social transformation excites a complementary personal renewal. Equally important, the couple are removed from the tensions of America and the stability of a home, and the opposition between the private and the professional, love and work, dissolves.

The first half of *Reds* appears consonant with Beatty's heroic vision of Reed as a precursor of the sixties. Maybe this is the film that would have been made in 1969 or 1972. The analogies between Reed's America and America in the late 1960s are laid out: The opposition to World War I is analogous to the crusade against the Vietnam War; the Democratic Convention of 1916 alludes to Chicago in 1968 and the complicity of the liberals Woodrow Wilson and Hubert Humphrey. Richard Corliss of *Time* saw Bella Abzug in Emma Goldman, and Diane Keaton's performance appears more like a composite of feminist struggles than a historical facsimile of Louise Bryant.[22] Greenwich Village and the arts community at Provincetown are recognizable as idealized counterculture enclaves. The opposition between art and politics embodied in Gene and Emma mirrors the divisions between the hippie movement and the New Left. Even the synthesis offered by Jack's journalism seems to echo the movement of writers like Norman Mailer and Truman Capote from fiction into engaged reporting on contemporary struggles. The Bolshevik triumph finds a parallel in McGovern's nomination. Here part one reaches its positive climax, and the achievement of the sixties turns down a darker road.

Part two of *Reds* witnesses the fall of the romantic couple as Jack abandons the marriage to take on the role of a great leader. In this section politics becomes divisive, and the synthesis represented by journalism is undermined. Jack's trial engenders melodramatic elements: his search for value in politics, his mistaking the Communist Party as a positive force, and the pathos of the romantic couple's separation. In part two Jack's misplaced ambitions are dashed and political activism destroys the romance. The factionalism and demise of the American left between 1972 and 1980 becomes the touchstone.

Upon returning from Russia, Louise describes to Max Eastman the couple's renewed commitment: "No more separation . . . we're really going to get down to living our own lives." She envisions their union as one of writing and homemaking. Their integrated careers will prevent the couple's domestic life from being sundered, and they agree to limit professional excursions. The following scenes present domestic bliss at Croton—making love, romping in the woods, setting up a Christmas tree, and writing. Gradually politics begins to intrude. Louise travels to Congress to answer questions about the Bolshevik Revolution, and Jack visits Emma in prison.

The scene with Emma helps explain Jack's move from journalism into politics. Her influence as the film's great political leader, while understated, continues to be a force. Emma has been detained as a alien agitator and sentenced to deportation; Jack brings her gifts to ease her imprisonment. Two moments highlight the scene. First, Emma's enthusiasm at seeing Jack recedes to quiet discomfort when he presents a scarf sent by Louise: The surrogate mother still finds her an unfit companion. Later she reaffirms her political will in the face of exile: "I'm not leaving the revolution, in Russia I'll be joining it." Emma's mission and her destination exert a magnetic attraction for the radical journalist.

A juxtaposition of Jack's domestic failure and literary success provides the concluding motivation for his foray into political leadership. In a comic scene inspired by a fairy-tale view of gender roles, flaming pans and a charred roast besiege Jack as he tries to cook dinner, while Louise, outside the kitchen, tells him she has turned down a reporting assignment rather than jeopardize their home life by traveling beyond New Jersey. In contrast to Reed's culinary failure is the popular success of his *Ten Days That Shook the World*, an eyewitness account of the Revolution. The enthusiasm it generates propels Jack into a leading role in the American Socialist Party.

Factionalism dooms his efforts at political leadership and exposes the petty concerns undermining his union with Louise. He breaks with his ally Louis Fraina, his faction is expelled from the Socialist Convention in Chicago, and he competes with Fraina for recognition from the Communist International. The International, however, rejects Reed's plea for support and orders the American factions to merge. The directive affirms the petty rivalry splitting the Americans and Jack's failure as a leader. More important, his limitations as a politician undermine his compact with Louise.

She witnesses the quarrels engulfing the Socialists with growing distress. Jack's insensitivity to the values of home and family are portrayed in a meeting of his faction at the Croton house. A shadowy amber light illustrates the anxiety of the meeting. The couple's dog, emblematic of their domestic union, barks, and Jack tells Louise to quiet the animal. Eddie, a member of Jack's group, is scolded for failing to contact a potential ally. Later Louise expresses her sympathy for Eddie, who missed the meeting because of a family illness. Though disappointed that socialist infighting is blinding Jack to his personal responsibilities, she travels with him to the Socialist Convention in Chicago, only to walk out when he is elected his faction's emissary to the Soviet Union. The compact to live and work together has been violated. In their final meeting at the Croton house, Louise pleads: "You're not a politician, you're a writer. . . . You're an artist. Don't go." But Jack, drawn into political activism, cannot sustain the synthesis of journalism or the stability of domestic life. He departs. In the tradition of the historical fiction film, political leadership is set at odds with the romantic couple.

Reprimanded by the Comintern, Jack retreats from leadership. *Reds* now counterposes Grigory Zinoviev and Emma Goldman to express the division within the protagonist. Zinoviev, the head of the Communist International, represents the values of the Bolsheviks and a perspective foreign to American experience. When Jack asks for passage back to the United States, Zinoviev requests that he remain: You can always return to your private concerns, the Communist insists, but this moment in history can never be retrieved. As a leader Zinoviev completely subordinates personal to political needs. Nevertheless, Jack tries to return, only to be imprisoned by counterrevolutionaries in Finland. He cannot escape from the role he has undertaken. Politics, not romance, has come to define John Reed even when he resists.

Emma expresses a different politics. Freed in a prisoner exchange, Jack visits her in Petrograd seeking news of Louise. True to her role as surrogate mother (and more influential than Zinoviev), Emma convinces him that Louise's silence in response to his telegrams is her answer. You have chosen to be a revolutionary, she claims, but Louise has not, so leave her alone. Emma complains that the Communist regime is centralizing authority and silencing dissent. She articulates a radical politics independent of the Bolsheviks and tied to Jack's American experience.

Jack's response testifies to Emma's influence. At first he drifts into melancholy, revisiting the sites he shared with Louise during his first visit to Russia. But then he reenters Communist party councils, urging support for the Industrial Workers of the World (IWW) rather than the American Federation of Labor as the proper representative of the American worker. He bases his opposition to the Party preference for the AFL upon his native understanding of American conditions. Jack's promotion of his former New York allies in the labor movement suggests the Village days under Emma's tutelage. Angry at being overruled by Zinoviev's committee, Jack resigns his post and goes to talk with her again.

By this time Emma has become thoroughly disenchanted with the Soviet regime. She rails that power has become concentrated in a few hands, dissent is being silenced, and nothing works. "The dream that we had is dying," she concludes. "I'm getting out." Jack protests that famine, oppression, and social breakdown are not the result of Communist failures, but of the international blockade and internal sabotage. The revolution has brought to power people with no experience in administration who must learn to use the machinery of government. Turning from Emma, he shakes his head in subdued regret and declares, "It's not happening the way we thought it would. It's not happening the way we wanted it to, but it's happening. If you walk out on it now, what's your whole life meant?" Reacting to his own words, Jack returns to Zinoviev, withdraws his resignation, and agrees to go to Baku as a political agitator.

The trip to Baku ends his relationship with Zinoviev and underlines the mysterious foreign nature of Bolshevism, which Jack, the American, is never able to comprehend. Shortly after his arrival, he finds Uncle Sam burning in effigy, and the sense of displacement is amplified by the Islamic setting and the simultaneous conference speeches in multiple languages. When he discovers that Zinoviev has changed his text under the guise of translation, his anger explodes. The ensuing confrontation illustrates how Jack's socialist convictions have been confounded by the Soviet experience, and lays out tensions characterizing the film.

> *Zinoviev:* Who defines this truth, you or the Party? You haven't decided what your life is dedicated to. You see yourself as an artist and at the same time as a revolutionary. As a lover of your wife and also responsible for the American Party.
>
> *Jack:* If you don't think a man can be an individual and true to the collective or speak for his own country and the International at the same time, or love his wife and still be faithful to the revolution, you don't have a self to give. You separate a man from what he loves the most, you purge what is unique in him, and when you purge what is unique in him, you purge dissent. And when you purge dissent, you kill the revolution. The revolution is dissent. You don't rewrite what I write.

An artillery shell explodes in the train, ending the conversation. The metaphorical explosion also marks Jack's final disaffection from Zinoviev. Bolshevism's authoritarian character seems to have twisted the American's politics into a grotesque and unrecognizable creed. But exotic authoritarianism aside, Zinoviev's remarks strike at the center of *Reds*. For the film does indeed present Reed as a divided character who cannot integrate Russia and America, the social and the personal, politics and romance. The American cannot realize the synthesis that he uses to challenge Zinoviev. But then, Zinoviev and Emma frequently appear to be manifestations of John Reed talking to himself, of *Reds* sorting out the meaning and consequences of Jack's politics. Furthermore, Jack's final declaration offers a pale creed: Is the revolution simply dissent, and not a radical transformation of the economic and political order? Making dissent the crux serves the narrative function of establishing a link with Emma, Zinoviev's counterpoint, but it offers a limited and shallow understanding of Reed's politics.

The blind alley Jack finds in Bolshevism concludes the portrait of the New Left developed by *Reds*. Whereas *Shampoo* criticized the self-indulgence and political disengagement of the hippie movement, *Reds* attacks the factionalism of the American left in the 1970s and its inability to put forward a viable program for change. The film's conclusion backs away from any political vision beyond the traditional liberal principles of civil dissent and individual liberties.

The concluding reels of *Reds* lay out an extended parallel narrative. Beginning with Jack's departure from the Croton home and continuing until the railroad station reunion, *Reds* intercuts Louise's attempts to reach Jack with his trials in the Soviet Union. Her journey to Europe symmetrically echoes his trip to the Continent at the end of part one. The parallel montage organized around a rescue journey adopts a cinematic device commonly associated with D. W. Griffith; it serves to amplify the melodramatic themes—miscommunication, emotional longing, and the separation of lovers—closely associated with the romance. The great leader also plays a role in Louise's quest.

Gene the artist is the parallel to Emma's politician. He resumes his leadership function when Jack leaves. When Louise visits Gene in New York, he cynically compares her crusade for socialism to the delusions of Irish Catholicism. The artist is characterized as self-absorbed, melancholy, and cruel. His wit and insight cannot mask a feeble social conscience serving to rationalize political quiescence. However, like Emma and Jack, the two fall out only to be reconciled. Louise returns to Gene, and this time he helps her reunite with Jack by securing undercover passage on a vessel that will carry her to the borders of Russia.

Emma confirms her ascendancy over Zinoviev by demonstrating flexibility and compassion. By chance she runs into Louise, who has finally arrived in Petrograd. Impressed with Louise's fortitude and devotion, Emma embraces her and admits, "I was wrong about you." Fulfilling the role of the good political leader and surrogate mother, she gives her blessing to the couple's reunion. Commitment to art and politics inhibits the capacity for romance of Gene and Emma (the historical O'Neill and Goldman were married), but they finally come to sympathize with the lovers. In contrast to Zinoviev, the American character acknowledges the claims of romance even if it cannot integrate them with competing interests.

After the various leaders have been confronted and overcome, Louise and Jack are granted their reunion. Jack's weakness and political confusion are contrasted with the single-minded passion embodied by Louise's journey. Jack asks her not to leave him, and his last wish is to go home. He dies with Louise at his bedside, but only after the romantic couple have renounced their mutual temptations and pledged themselves to each other. In conclusion, like so many melodramas, *Reds* reaffirms the romantic couple and presents the disruptive forces of art and politics as empty substitutes for conjugal bliss. "What we end up with in *Reds* then," E. Ann Kaplan notes, "is perhaps a rather sad confirmation of what Americans are brought up to believe—namely that a life devoted to politics is bound to end in disillusionment and personal destruction." [23]

Louise, the figure associated with romance, eclipses Jack, the political figure of part two. Her ascendency is repeatedly affirmed: She tells Gene off, while Jack waffles between Emma and Zinoviev; she reaches Russia, while Jack fails to fulfill his promise to return home by Christmas; she overcomes her op-

posing figure and receives Emma's blessing, while Jack con‌⸽
to be tormented by misplaced fears of Gene; she remains faithful to their love, while Jack appears to have given up. At the conclusion, her personal triumph is borne out: Louise lives and Jack dies. This victory affirms the thematic conventions of the historical fiction film, in which romance is regularly elevated over the competing forces embodied in the great leader. The parallel, competing positions in *Reds* strive for synthesis, but fail to achieve integration. The realms of the personal and the public, the private life and social engagement, romance and politics remain at odds. The liberal concept that government and its attendant politics must be subordinated to, if not expelled from, human experience remains the underlying ideology.

The rallying cry of the 1960s, to make the personal political, is tested in *Reds* and found wanting. The inflexible generic opposition of political leadership and romantic passion, so forcefully posed by Beatty, may prohibit fruitful integration. Only by questioning the conventional values associated with romantic passion can the need for social responsibility be acknowledged.

| Spectacle and the Failure of Historical Vision

It is not that representation cannot be raised with correct presentation and treatment to the structure of metaphor, simile, image. Nor is it that Griffith here altered his method, or his professional craftsmanship. But that he made no attempt at a genuinely thoughtful abstraction of phenomena—at an extraction of generalized conclusions on historical phenomena from a wide variety of historical data; that is the core of the fault.
—SERGEI EISENSTEIN, 1944[24]

Warren Beatty was undoubtedly engaged by the issues implicit in Reed's experience, but he had a tenuous grasp on how that experience developed in relation to broad historical forces. Beatty's Reed does not embody the integration of personal and social recommended by Lukacs, nor does the film respond cogently to the historical problems it posed. As Eisenstein wrote of Griffith, the core of the fault was that the filmmaker "made no attempt at a genuinely thoughtful abstraction of phenomena." The spectacle in the historical film can raise the fiction above an individual portrait to the level of an extrapersonal historical explanation. *Reds* strives for, but ultimately fails to construct, such a spectacle. As a result, the film cannot illuminate a connection between the historical movements animating Reed—the conjunction between radical art and politics, the reevaluation of marriage and gender relations, and the bohemian critique of middle-class culture— and their continuing influence upon contemporary America.

The first time we see Beatty as Reed, he is running after a gun carriage on the battlefield of the Mexican Revolution.[25] Near the conclusion, Jack again chases a gun carriage as the Red Army fights off an ambush of the train from Baku. The first time he hops onto the rolling cart; but in the second instance the film leaves his effort in progress. The American at first leaps onto the carriage of revolution but finally it eludes him. This energetic but futile quest is the defining image of the film. Unfortunately, the three hours of film time that intervene between the episodes fail to invest this analogy with complex implications.

Another image characterizing Reed is the IWW flier on the back of which Jack begins a poem at the Democratic Convention. The division between politics and art, image and language, becomes associated with the two sides of the sheet. The labor poster is linked to radical politics, whereas the poem is associated with Jack's aesthetic aspirations and his romance with Louise. Upon his return to Provincetown, she urges him to finish it. Years later, on the train to Baku, he is still carrying it around, unfinished. The poster evokes various feelings, but it does not clarify Jack's thinking, or, more important, the film's attitude toward his predicament. A juxtaposition is presented—art versus politics, poet versus revolutionary—but no synthesis to raise the elements beyond a simplistic opposition. A parallelism is posed without a new or fruitful conception of the relationship.

The chief opposition, that of the United States and Russia, expresses the conflict between the established order and revolutionary promise. Part one is dominated by a critique of the status quo in America and culminates in the successful Bolshevik uprising. Part two presents Jack's attempt to bring the revolution

17 | *Reds* (1981), production still. In the defining image of the film, John Reed (Warren Beatty) chases a Red Army gun carriage. Courtesy Museum of Modern Art/Film Stills Archive

to the United States. But the doctrinaire, foreign character of Bolshevik politics defeats the American's efforts.

Within these broadly contrary landscapes, further divisions give a more precise meaning to the spectacle of setting. Their importance is emphasized with subtitles: "Portland 1915," "Provincetown 1916," and "Croton on Hudson 1917." Various sites carry explicit associations. The sequence of Portland, Greenwich Village, Provincetown, Croton exemplifies the dialetical progression the setting occasionally realizes. Portland is linked to traditional family values—Louise's marriage and Jack's relatives. Louise goes from the artistic setting of the gallery opening to the political arena of the Liberal Club. Her husband's recriminations are countered with Jack's radicalism. The antithesis sparks Louise's departure for New York. After her initial journey through the streets, Greenwich Village is portrayed exclusively through interiors—taverns, restaurants, apartments, generally crowded with Jack's bohemian friends. The stiffness and formality of the Portland dinner party are contrasted with the casual, relaxed meals of the Village radicals. Nevertheless, the dim lighting and crowded, close camera perspectives convey the confinement of the metropolis as well as Louise's need to define herself in a space apart from Jack. In the Provincetown setting, long-shot exteriors of couples strolling the beach and wading in the surf counter New York. The white and blue costuming distinguishes the seashore from the dark earthtones of the city. Performance and song portray the ascendancy of art over politics. Croton is presented as a suburban synthesis, a physical integration of the natural and the urban. Here the emphasis is on establishing a home that can balance the political turmoil of the city and the aestheticism of the poet's retreat. The larger community of bohemian radicals is exchanged for the domestic unit of husband, wife, and dog. Though the suburban haven seems an unlikely resting place for two radicals, the move to Croton ends an expressive progression in the development of the spectacle of setting.

The remaining sites in *Reds* lack the evocative counterpoint of the film's opening sequences. The foreign landscapes present a vague and ominous sense of otherness without the textured detail of the American locales. They are more caricature than place. In the first Petrograd sequence, the diffuse backlighting, embracing silhouettes, and posing of historical figures like Lenin and Trotsky position Jack and Louise in a socialist dream space. When Jack speaks at the factory rally, the proletarians assembled appear well scrubbed and wear spanking clean work uniforms. Jack and Louise move across snow-covered panoramas that might as well be the ice flows of *Way Down East*. The weary metaphor of nature, cold and in the grip of death, threatening the lovers erases the specificity of place. Baku also functions more forcefully as a generalized symbol than a historical site. The journey to Asia allies the inhumane authority of the Party to the mystery of the Islamic East. Staring at the burning effigy of Uncle Sam, Jack seems utterly off-course. Russia is portrayed as a region whose otherness has distorted his ideals and made him a well-meaning but naive American lost in a political wilderness. The progressive counterpoint of part one slides into a simplistic contrast between the familiar and the mysterious in part two.

Reds offers a muted treatment of the spectacle of the crowd. The conventions of the historical fiction film deploy "the cast of thousands" in conflicting groups, such as armies at war, or in ceremonies of integration, such as weddings or balls. *Reds* is characterized by "ceremonies" that erupt in conflict—chiefly political meetings marked by dissension. The film goes from the Liberal Club in Portland to protest demonstrations in New York and on to Socialist Conventions, workers' rallies, and Communist Party committees, yet the crowd does not play an active role. *Reds* focuses on speeches, resignations, and arrests, but massive movements of strikers, armies, or revolutionaries are conspicuously absent. For a movie that touches on class war and proletarian uprising, the crowd is extremely polite. They listen, cheer, or march in good order. Beatty is more interested in individual than in mass action. The dynamic movement of the crowd in *The Birth of a Nation* and *October* is absent. The joy of common cause that the crowd expresses in *La Marseillaise*, the ceremonial splendor of *Senso*'s opening at the opera, and the politicized court ritual in *The Rise to Power of Louis XIV* have no equivalent in *Reds*.

The personal perspective maintained throughout the film bespeaks a certain wariness toward the masses. References to images from Eisenstein, such as a crowd, shot from an overhead perspective, rushing diagonally across the screen toward the Winter Palace, have the conspicuous status of quotations because they are so out of character with the rest of the film. A scene at the Socialist Convention in Chicago illustrates Beatty's reticence. Jack marshals his faction to take over the meeting, but his opponents call in the police to haul them out. As the camera focuses on Jack, the mass action is lost, and the walkout becomes his personal fight against the party hierarchy. In *Reds* language and interpersonal exchange carry the film; the crowd, there simply to bear witness, never assumes a forceful social presence.

Reds is emphatically a montage film. Favoring short takes, it also follows in the tradition of Griffith and Eisenstein by deploying an unrestricted dramatic field that condenses time and links spaces in elastic parallels and juxtapositions. This "montage condensation" departs from the classical Hollywood style as well as the long-take tradition that became a prominent alternative approach after 1940. The classical Hollywood style, as employed in *Reign of Terror,* uses editing to break down a scene, but generally remains within a stable and clearly identified dramatic space from one scene to the next. Montage condensation is used in the classical style, but sparingly. *Reds* is noteworthy because montage condensation dominates its design.

Griffith and Eisenstein, closely associated with the montage tradition, used editing not merely to convey dramatic information, but also as a means of thematic expression and, for Eisenstein, a means of intellectual address. *Reds* makes tentative use of this tradition, then falters. This limitation in the form of its spectacle underlies the film's inability to visualize complex social phenomena within a fundamental understanding of the historical moment.

The connection with Eisenstein and Griffith is self-conscious and readily apparent to a viewer familiar with film history. The association with Eisenstein is more obvious but less profound. Eisenstein's *October* used Reed's *Ten Days That Shook the World* as a source, and the film even adopted Reed's title for a truncated foreign-release version. *Reds* returns the favor by adapting images from *October* in the Petrograd uprising sequence. The most conspicuous example is the shot of Kerensky climbing the staircase of the Winter Palace; others include Lenin assuming the podium in Smolny and the crowd rushing across the square to attack the palace. The centrality of character in Beatty's film may be most awkwardly realized in having Jack and Louise actually follow Kerensky up the stairs, in violation of Eisenstein's concept of montage. Here Griffith, the proverbial father of Hollywood, remains the model.

Among Griffith's most celebrated and influential devices was parallel editing, particularly a parallel built around a rescue in which the hero rushes to save the beloved. From the Biograph two-reelers through *The Birth of a Nation, Intolerance,* and beyond, this cinematic device became associated not simply with Griffith, but also with the melodramatic conventions of the silent period. When Louise undertakes to save Jack from the Finnish prison, and the film alternates images of her harrowing trip with Jack suffering in his cell, the Griffith device is replicated in a fashion that returns to the worn conventions of an earlier era.

Griffith also used his parallel system to launch more conceptual linkages, such as a comparison of rich and poor in *A Corner in Wheat* (1909) or among historical periods in *Intolerance*. Beatty uses this more abstract comparative mode in sequences such as the "dance/'I write'" montage from the Greenwich Village episode. Here the director is straining toward a more conceptual design in his editing.

This conceptual quality in Griffith's montage also attracted Eisenstein. The Russian hoped to liberate the editing from the weight of dramatic continuity or character, so that Griffith's comparative device could become a dialectical means of thematic progression. Eisenstein's ambition was to employ conflicting images as a means of elaborating a montage dialectic unconstrained by dramatic convention. Setting aside individual characterization for typage and the mass hero was fundamental to Eisenstein's aim of liberating montage. *October* abandons characterization altogether.

On this count Beatty is an unyielding apostle of Griffith. However flexible the temporal and spatial relations of shots, the montage in *Reds* keeps the images firmly anchored to character. Devoted to his protagonists as the principal means of communicating with his audience, Beatty fails to develop historical analysis that can transcend personality.

The Greenwich Village sequence from early in the film holds promise. The twenty-minute episode is divided into six sections: Louise's arrival in New York, Jack's apartment, portraits of Village radicals, the "dance/'I write'" montage, Jack's trip, and the quarrel scene. "Jack's apartment" and "the quarrel scene" are the only sections with a stable dramatic space. The remaining four sections present flexible temporal and spatial sites organized around unifying themes. Three sections present Louise's arrival and introduce the members of Jack's bohemian circle. The centerpiece of the Village sequence is the "dance/'I write'" montage, which presents the conflict between the romance (embodied in Jack and Louise dancing at various parties) and Louise's attempt to define herself as a writer, and a person worthy of respect apart from her position as John Reed's lover.

As a counterpoint to the dance, Louise finds herself responding to the question of what she does by declaring, "I write." The ambiguous closure of her reply conveys the uncertainty and frustration of her struggle to define herself in Jack's shadow. The counterpoint is developed in section five, in which Jack leaves town to cover an organizing effort while Louise meets with the editor of the *Metropolitan*, who feigns interest in her writing in order to make a pass. The conflict culminates in a quarrel upon Jack's return. After their anger subsides, they agree to leave the Village and go off where they can each "write what we wanna write." The sequence presents the public spectacle of bohemian life in the Village through a swiftly drawn panorama of personalities and locales. Simultaneously the montage develops the personal conflict between Jack and Louise by focusing upon her struggle to define herself in socially viable activity. Her experience is precise enough to be historically convincing and sufficiently abstract to connect to immediate concerns over the social position of women. Montage condensation succeeds in posing thematic opposition and engineering its synthetic development.

The Bolshevik Revolution episode is designed in a similar fashion, but fails by comparison. This sequence runs for about thirteen minutes and can likewise be divided into six sections. The first three—the arrival in Petrograd, review of political conditions, and portraits of the politicians—are condensation episodes that survey the city. The pace of the montage accelerates to indicate the growing tension in the Russian capital. The next two—the cabbage dinner and the factory rally—linger in stable dramatic sites, focusing on the couple's successful negotiation of their principal conflicts. The final section, the Internationale montage, presents an extended condensation sequence in which all the issues are brought to a happy resolution. The love–work conflict turns on the division between Jack and Louise: Can they revive their romance by working together as reporters? The sequence constantly presents the couple together, as they first become a cooperative reporting team and then resume their erotic union. The resolution of their differences seems to be both circumstantial and so readily achieved as to belie the problem.

The second conflict pits the journalist's task of analyzing political struggle against the desire to commit oneself to an active role in that struggle. In the first three sections the couple gradually become informed about the turmoil of Petrograd and gain a voice as reporters. Typewriter keys are heard, and their voice-over reports describe the politicians. Jack's transition from observer to activist comes at the factory rally, where he is embraced by a crowd as a comrade rather than excluded as a journalist. In the Internationale montage, Jack and Louise join with the revolutionary crowd leafleting the city and invading the Winter Palace. The synthesis of the journalist–activist complements the working union of the couple to bring the conclusion of the first half of the film to a positive resolution.

So why does the Petrograd sequence fail as historical representation? First, because the portrait of Petrograd and the Bolshevik Revolution lacks the detail and texture necessary for historical specificity. The city has a backlot look; we are shown something more like a glossy postcard than the distinctive past. The tone comes in part from the diffuse backlighting, as when the revolutionary crowd surrounds the trolley. This romantic glow finds its corollary in the backlit silhouette shots of Jack and Louise embracing and receives its most unlikely application when the couple decorate a Christmas tree to celebrate the new order. The portrait gallery of Lenin, Trotsky, and Kerensky appropriated from Eisenstein has a stiff, waxworks quality at times appropriate for Eisenstein's typage, but jarring in contrast to the "naturalism" of Hollywood star performances. The presentation of these revolutionaries is further undermined by shots in which Beatty and Keaton appear alongside documentary-like images of historical figures. This series of portraits fails by comparison with a similar series of Village radicals. In the earlier set Beatty juxtaposes famous photographs of figures such as Walter Lippmann with posed actors about to assume screen life, such as Jack Nicholson's Eugene O'Neill. Here the contrast between fact and facsimile is acknowledged, and the audience admires the evocation and sympathetically suspends disbelief. In addition, the testimony of the witnesses helps to bridge the gulf between actual image and posing actor. The absence of either strategy invests these images of the Revolution with authenticity claims that seem transparently false. Finally, and most important, monumental historical events are simplistically equated with routine personal experiences. Inserting Jack and Louise into revolutionary sites famous from Eisenstein—following Kerensky up the stairs, hearing Lenin at Smolny, storming the Winter Palace—is like inserting a Griffith couple into a Bolshevik documentary. The complex events of the October uprising are equated with the comedy of Jack sheepishly looking to Louise for a signal that it is time to come to bed. In *Reds* the personal experience of the protagonists confines the historical treatment of the film. Beatty fails to gain a generalized, social understanding of events and prevents the film from reaching beyond the emotional sensibility of his characters to comprehend the historical circumstances in which they find themselves. Instead of a historical vision clarifying human experience, personal problems rob the work of a broader social perspective. The psychology of characterization saps the montage condensation of its ability to conceptualize historical phenomena.

The banality of the spectacle is epitomized by Louise's journey. Here the parallelism of Griffith, and Griffith at his most tiresome, establishes the form for the film's culminating experience. Louise's commitment to Jack leads her across stormy sea, over the frozen tundra, and past vigilant police patrols. All the while, Jack suffers. The editing takes the audience from one to the other, back and forth, until the predictable reunion. The montage sophistication of *Reds* gradually diminishes, from the promising complexity of the early sequences into an archaic form that predates the events of the film itself. The romantic union smothers the historical analysis and leaves the audience with the tired conventions of melodrama. The ideology of romantic passion suppresses politics and makes the couple the object of pity because historical circumstances divide them.

| The Witnesses: Memory as Historical Explanation

"Indeed there is a case for saying that Reds is the most complex and intelligent film not just about the Russian Revolution but about History that Hollywood has yet given us."
—ED BUSCOMBE, 1982[26]

"History to Hollywood is a blank cheque."
—T R E V O R G R I F F I T H S , 1 9 8 2[27]

For many, the most provocative feature of *Reds* was the occasional testimony of a group of more than twenty witnesses who had lived during the period portrayed and, in some cases, knew John Reed, Louise Bryant, and others recreated for the screen fiction. Vincent Canby in the *New York Times* described their testimony as an "extraordinary device," [28] and Arthur Schlesinger, Jr., wrote that the witnesses were "a genuine and exciting innovation," which "gives an exceptional sense of both immediacy and authenticity" to the movie.[29] Jonathan Rosenbaum in *Sight and Sound* wrote that without the witnesses, "the film and its achievement could not even begin to exist." [30] "To analyze *Reds* as history," Robert Rosenstone notes, "one must begin with its most obviously historical device, the Witnesses." [31] They provide the film's historical backbone and its most distinctive aspect.

The twenty-six witnesses appear in clusters, making approximately ninety remarks throughout the film. Sixteen voices are heard during the opening credits, and ten more speak during the closing scroll. Subsequently the testimony is offered in smaller clusters, generally two to five voices. During the montage dramatizing the American entry into World War I, ten witnesses are heard.

The witnesses establish both a visual and an aural presence. Mostly they speak to the camera in head shots before a black background; with no interviewer or prompting presented, they appear to talk spontaneously to the audience. Each appears alone, except that Dora Russell and Rebecca West often appear together. The witnesses are first introduced during the opening credits in voice-over; finally faces appear to accompany the speakers. At the close of the film a series of witnesses speak as the credits unroll.

The witnesses are concentrated in the American episodes. When *Reds* moves to Europe for the October Revolution and for the final scenes, they are nearly absent; when the witnesses do appear in these episodes, they frequently appear in solo rather than multiple voices, undermining the cluster effect. Upon Jack's release from the Finnish prison, a witness in voice-over simply reports that the Bolsheviks arranged for his release with a prisoner exchange.

Reds names thirty-two witnesses in its opening and closing credits.[32] Some witnesses do not actually appear in the film (but may be present as unidentified voices); some appear only once or twice; but the star witnesses appear three to six times. Some omissions are striking because of the figures' familiarity with the events portrayed. Andrew Dasburg, the painter, knew Reed and Bryant well. Reed introduced him to Bryant, and he became Bryant's lover. In fact she was living with Dasburg when she departed for Russia in 1920 to find Jack and corresponded with him during her journey to the Soviet Union. Few living individuals could offer more intimate personal observations on the Reed–Bryant relationship. One wonders what he told the filmmakers.[33] Dasburg's absence signals that the witnesses' testimony is not direct, comprehensive, or intact; rather, their statements have been selected and shaped by filmmakers to complement the dramatic action. They do not determine the content of the drama, but are determined by it. Even the twelve witnesses who appear once or twice fail to establish a significant presence in the film. George Jessel, for example, appears singing World War I patriotic songs, and Emmanuel Herbert, a student in Petrograd during the Revolution, offers one remark about conditions in the city at the time of Reed and Bryant's arrival.

The star witnesses, however, establish a vivid presence. They include Rebecca West, Scott Nearing, and Will Weinstone (each appears six times); Henry Miller, Dora Russell, and Hugo Gellert (who appear five times), and others such as Roger Baldwin, Tess Davis, Hamilton Fish, and Lucita Williams. Though unidentified, some of these witnesses are so engaging and colorful that they compete with characters in the fiction. Pauline Kael claimed that the wit and vitality of these "survivors from the era" overshadowed the stars of the film.[34]

Because the appearance of the witnesses precedes the first image of the fictive world, they seem a generating force. The dark surroundings, weathered faces, and untrained voices draw a sharp line between their reminiscence and the detailed panorama of the period drama (illustrations 18 and 19). The abstract nature of the setting, a completely dark, uninhabited space, makes it

18 | *Reds* (1981), production
still. Rebecca West, star witness.
Courtesy Museum of Modern
Art/Film Stills Archive

19 | *Reds* (1981), production
still. Henry Miller, star witness.
Courtesy Museum of Modern
Art/Film Stills Archive

appear as if they speak from a common position, but one that is apart from the world. They hover over and intrude upon the fictive world at will, like spirits who comment upon, but cannot change, the fate of men and women. Their collective voice animates a play between character and chorus, story and discourse, memory and history. Their voices close the film as the final credits unroll. Framing the story as they do, the witnesses resemble a Greek chorus, as noted by many commentators, probably beginning with Vincent Canby.

How does this chorus use its authority in interacting with the drama? The witnesses almost always intrude into the fiction in clusters, generally offering information from different, at times conflicting, perspectives. After the Reed–Bryant marriage, Lucita Williams comments, "I'm not sure whether she had an affair with Eugene O'Neill or not during this time. Nobody seems to know." Adele Nathan then asserts, "The report was that she and Reed and O'Neill had a *ménage à trois*." After the American entry into the world war, Scott Nearing says, "There was a lot of antiwar feeling, of course," and Dorothy Frooks retorts, "We had no one against the war. There wasn't a soul against the war." The multiple and contending perspectives seem at first to engender the modernist uncertainties attributed to films such as *Citizen Kane* (1941), *Rashomon* (1950), or *L'Année dernière à Marienbad* (*Last Year at Marienbad*, 1961). However, the tension between the witnesses is usually resolved, or at least informed, by the dramatic fiction. In each of the cases noted above, the sequencing of testimony to drama establishes a key indicator. Thus, the fiction presents Louise rejecting Gene's overtures, and then the witnesses intrude, sowing doubt as to whether her rebuff was sustained. Usually, however, the film begins with the contending report, and then resolves the uncertainty with the drama. Jack and Emma's antiwar activities follow Frooks and certify Nearing's observation. Late in the film, Hugo Gellert dismisses claims that Reed was disillusioned with the Communist Party shortly before his death. In reply, the film portrays Jack's troubles, but the conclusion leaves him undecided. The witnesses would seem to have the authority to confirm or confound the drama through documentary testimony from outside the fictive world. *Reds*, however, reverses this relationship. The drama generally resolves the ambiguity of the testimony rather than embellishing its complexity, moving the film decidedly away from the tradition of *Kane, Marienbad,* or *Rashomon,* where the image invested the verbal report with nuance and ambiguity. In spite of the framing device established by the witnesses, *Reds* gives its fiction decisive authority.

The function of the witnesses falls into two broad categories: the social spectacle and personal observation. In the first case the "old folks" describe a site such as Greenwich Village or Petrograd, report on the popular mood, such as the American reaction to Russia's withdrawal from the World War, or evoke public feeling through songs like "Over There" or "The Internationale." These panoramas often serve as transitions and establish new locales—during the move to Provincetown, for example, they evoke the setting of the artists' colony. Furthermore the oral testimony often portrays the collective mood or social perception in a broad manner that may be beyond the reach of a single image.

Witnesses also discuss the characters' motives, activities, and feelings. Tess Davis explains how Louise "operated"; Art Shields reports on Jack's "tremendous jump forward" into radical politics after the publication of *Ten Days That Shook the World.* Sometimes the speakers speculate—on whether Louise continued her affair with O'Neill for instance.

The spectacle and the personal observation are often integrated in particular clusters. In the transition from Portland to Greenwich Village, for example, a discussion of Bryant's character and a panorama of New York bohemia are intermingled. The witnesses' fusion of the social and the personal offers a vehicle for expressing an issue central to the historical fiction film— the relationship between private life and the public sphere, the integration of personal needs with political responsibilities.

This role is developed by the star witnesses, whose themes include the conflict between political action and private life. Henry Miller regularly speaks of how the dilemmas of personal life are disguised and displaced into political action, becoming a spokesperson for the ascendancy of psychology over politics. When Jack leaves Provincetown for the Democratic Convention, Miller accuses him of escaping, of "not wanting to face things of his own nature." Two prominent socialists, Scott Nearing and

Will Weinstone, emphasize Reed's struggle for social justice. "He wanted to stir up trouble for the capitalists," Nearing recalls in response to Miller, "and he also wanted to arouse the working masses to the necessity of some kind of effective united action." In this case star witnesses voice a central theme of the drama: the conflict between the romance of Jack and Louise and their work as artists, journalists, or social activists. Another counterpoint is struck by the unsympathetic, even comic witnesses, most notably the prudish Dorothy Frooks and the red-hunter Hamilton Fish. Because their views are generally repudiated by the drama, these witnesses come to represent the public mood contested by the protagonists.

The contrast between the witnesses and the drama develops an evocative tension. The nonfiction commentary expresses conflict and uncertainty in its oral spectacle and pondering of character. The fiction deploys its dramatic conflicts, but limits rather than enriches the nuances suggested by the witnesses. The give and take among the witnesses and between them and the drama is the most provocative aspect of *Reds*. The importance of the device is especially evident when the film travels to Europe and the witnesses' role is diminished. Here the movie falls into tiresome clichés, such as Louise's trek across the tundra. If the fiction had matched the witnesses' charm and resonance, *Reds* might have realized the grand ambitions of the filmmakers.

The device of the witnesses was widely praised as innovative, but reference to cinematic tradition helps to locate sources of influence in the documentary tradition, the "art" cinema, and voice-over narration.

The historical fiction film has long sought to bolster its truth claims by invoking a nonfiction authority. D. W. Griffith cited Woodrow Wilson's *History of the American People* in title cards and copied famous images, such as the surrender at Appomatox, to support the veracity of *The Birth of a Nation*. The time and place of a historical fiction were frequently introduced, in both silent and sound films, by a title scroll whose exposition seemed to carry the solemn force of an ancient chronicle. In this sense the witnesses seem to be another in the genre's long series of authenticity devices, and Beatty has explained that his original notion was to use them to replace expositional dialogue by pinning down the time, place and circumstances of the drama.[35] When Jack travels to France during the war, Will Weinstone explains, "Imagine, sixty-five million go to war; ten million die, ten million become orphans, twenty million become maimed, crippled, or wounded. You had catastrophe in Europe." The documentary authority of the device implies that although elements of the drama may be fabricated, the essential truth has been retained. The division among the witnesses paradoxically bolsters the filmmakers' claims to responsible reporting because the movie incorporates evidence that might cast doubt upon the recreation. Furthermore, it appears as if the witnesses supplied primary evidence for the drama—as if they, not the filmmakers, determined the fiction.

More explicitly, the film alludes to the documentary tradition, and particularly to such films of the preceding decade as *Le Chagrin et la pitié* (*The Sorrow and the Pity*, 1969), *Union Maids* (1976), and *The Life and Times of Rosie the Riveter* (1978), which combined contemporary interviews with participants in past events with found footage of the events themselves. *Reds* devotes a smaller percentage of screen time to the interviews, and, more important, the footage in counterpoint was shot for the production. Nevertheless, the give and take between the witnesses and the dramatic action embraces a fundamental structuring device of contemporary documentary. In the manner typical of these documentaries, the interviewer and the question are eliminated and the witness seems to speak directly and spontaneously to the camera. Association with this widely recognized nonfiction practice fortifies *Reds'* claim to authenticity.

At least since Italian neo-realism, if not since *The Battleship Potemkin* (1925), the "art" cinema has attempted to integrate the rhetoric of the documentary with the fiction film. The incorporation of the interview is prominent in Godard's work, from Patricia's interview of the novelist in *À bout de souffle* (*Breathless*, 1960) through the questioning of Mademoiselle 19 in *Masculin–Feminin* (1965) to the testimonials of Susan and Jacques in *Tout va bien* (1972) and onward. Woody Allen parodied the practice in *Take the Money and Run* (1969) and *Zelig* (1983). The conflicting testimony of the witnesses embraces, if not the modernist ambiguity of the "art" cinema, at least the process of the historian, who must sift through and weigh contrary evidence. With these devices from the "art" cinema, Beatty adds complexity to the simplistic authenticity claims typical of the historical fiction film.

The witnesses also draw on the tradition of voice-over narration. Sarah Kozloff's excellent study of voice-overs in the Hollywood film, *Invisible Storytellers*, provides a useful touchstone. Though Kozloff includes many Hollywood fictions based on fact in her filmography of roughly four hundred titles—*Juarez* (1939), *Joan of Arc* (1948), *Freud* (1962), *Julia* (1977), and *The Right Stuff* (1983)—she overlooks *Reds*. Its absence is not surprising, because many viewers would fail to see the witnesses as a third-person narrator. Understood as a group, however, they fulfill the typical functions of such a narrator: They establish a framing device for the dramatic action, offer key information, link disparate events, evoke nostalgia. In addition, *Reds* falls into the two categories of films that, Kozloff notes, most commonly use third-person narration: epics and pictures that imitate documentaries.[36] Yet the witnesses depart from that tradition in at least three ways: They appear on screen as well as in unseen voice-over, they incorporate multiple and conflicting voices, and they have a peculiar status vis-à-vis the drama. Like the typical third-person narrator, the witnesses are not "embedded" in the diegesis; they remain outside the fictive world of the characters, but the authority of their commentary is based upon the fact that they were indeed part of that world—in fact, their experience takes precedence over the fiction itself. The witnesses even give the impression that their recollections have guided and constrained the filmmakers in the construction of the fiction. In addition, the witnesses combine the "voice of God" authority of a third-person narrator with the uncertainty of a first-person narrator. Their discourse provides an unusual commentary, provoking viewers' curiosity as the drama unfolds and stimulating interest in the historical episode after they leave the theater.

In *Reds* Beatty refreshes the generic conventions of the historical fiction film by integrating contemporary documentary practice, gestures from the "art" cinema, and a complex form of narration. In this regard the film is a signal achievement.

Beatty successfully appealed against the film's initial "R" rating, arguing, in the words of David Thompson, that "his

movie reclaimed an era of American history that every school-
child should see." [37] *Reds* self-consciously promoted such claims;
however, the influence of the witnesses on the film's historical treatment has been a subject of wide disagreement. In *Sight
and Sound* Jonathan Rosenbaum explains that the witnesses' dual
character gives the historical fiction greater authenticity: The
unreliability of the testimony suggests the complexity of historical evidence, while the nonfiction reporting provides a dialectical counterpoint to the historical representation. [38] Though many
were frustrated by the speakers' anonymity, for Rosenbaum the
egalitarian absence of names allows their collective voice to embody popular wisdom. E. Ann Kaplan also emphasizes that these
reminiscences serve as a counterpoint to the fiction that underscores the constructed nature of history. [39] She identifies two
functions for the witnesses' contradictory views: the suggestion
that truth is hard to come by, and the theme of forgetting, not
merely the weakness of human memory, but also a culture's am-
nesia about its past. Ed Buscombe finds the witnesses held in a
productive but unresolved tension between the view that history
is essentially a construction and the view that it is a confused,
ultimately indecipherable jumble. [40] Though Pauline Kael found
Reds an "extremely traditional" movie, [41] Buscombe argues that,
through the witnesses, the film denies the fixed point of truth
typical of an orthodox Hollywood production and even suggests
a modernist text in its subversion of historical certainty.

I would argue that the uncertainty of the witnesses *is* generally resolved because the fiction undermines the counterpoint
or dialectic the witnesses themselves suggest. Consider the comments of the historian Robert Rosenstone, the historical consultant on the production. For him the use of the witnesses is "a
brilliant stroke," their anonymity investing them with a choral
voice that reinforces their collective authority. But he also sees
the technique as "a profoundly ahistorical one" that is "calculated
to impress and lull the audience." [42] The witnesses are ahistorical,
in this view, because their testimony fails to invite critical evaluation. Whereas the historian can weigh the quality of data, the
lack of identification keeps film viewers from doing so. Further,
Rosenstone accuses the film of equating memory with history,
thereby associating the elusive and uncertain mechanics of indi-

vidual consciousness with the more precise and reliable work of a community of scholars. The film, consciously or unconsciously, espouses the popular relativistic notion that the complexity of evidence makes one history no better than the next. Rosenstone finds that the dual nature of the witnesses allows the filmmaker to have it both ways: to play historian and to ignore, whenever convenient, standards of evidence and contradictory findings.

At the heart of these opposing critical views lies the contrast between memory and history as well as the equally important distinction between the representation of history in the cinema and the representation of history in scholarship. The witnesses themselves offer memories, not history, but in the carefully shaped chorus the filmmakers attempt to evoke history—the spectacle of 1916–20 and the personal histories of the protagonists. The filmmakers constructed their narrative history in the drama and enlisted the witnesses to bolster it. The cinema and the discipline of history offer two divergent standards for evaluating the witnesses. In the context of the cinema, they offer a fresh and engaging device at the provocative intersection of several traditions. In the context of historical scholarship, however, the film at its best excites the viewer to further investigation, but at its worst falsely convinces the viewer that the film is indeed history.

In a more particular sense, the witnesses offer, if not a historical explanation, at least a historical attitude. In this regard the framing voices are particularly important, for the opening and closing witnesses express the historical notions at work in *Reds*. The opening speakers immediately call into question their reliability. "Was it 1913 or 1917 . . . I can't remember now," the first witness begins. The note of doubt is followed by the second voice proclaiming, "Do I remember Louise Bryant? Why, of course, I couldn't forget her if I tried." After further affirmations of doubt and certainty, a string of speakers offer various opinions of Louise Bryant and John Reed. The penultimate witness of the introduction, Roger Baldwin, then declares, "All of us are victims of our time and place." The opening chorus acknowledges its own unreliability and indicates the importance of the social and political context, the historical moment, for understanding these characters. The relationship between individual acts and historical conditions is raised, and the fiction begins to offer its explanation in the context of those memories and that time.

The concluding chorus of witnesses evokes our memories of the film itself, raises questions about the influence of the past, and suggests, rather tentatively, the recurrence of historical struggles. As the closing credits appear, some voice-over remarks from earlier in the film are repeated. The chorus acknowledges Reed's death, the romance ("they were a couple"), the idealism and American character of the protagonists. But above all the witnesses point to historical influence and the prospects for historical repetition. "You know things go and come back again" is followed by Dora Russell and Rebecca West musing together, "I don't even know if they had any children. They probably didn't have any children. . . . Then you can't tell when you have children whether they will carry on your revolutionary tradition or not?" The filmmaker adopts these rambling comments and gives them a metaphorical resonance. In context the witnesses appear to be speaking of the descendants of Reed and Bryant in American culture. The final remark points optimistically to "Grand things . . . ahead. Worth living and dying for." At the conclusion of *Reds* these words evoke the counterculture of the 1960s and suggest prospects for future movements that will attempt to integrate the politics of private life with the struggle for social justice.

Coda

History represents social memory. This study finds that the historical film is fundamentally concerned with the association of the individual and the state and the relationship between personal experience and the extrapersonal forces shaping history. In essence it is a political genre. Characterization and intimate drama ground the fiction in personal acts, but the historical perspective strives to expand and generalize their significance. This tension between private and public life is expressed in the generic motifs of the romance and the spectacle.

By studying the historical film in its particularity and in its relationship to politics, history, and the cinema, one recognizes the textual complexity embodied in this often neglected genre. The filmmaker commands a series of rhetorical devices for portraying historical causation, and these extend beyond the simplistic patterns of individual acts and the superhuman leader. The historical film can offer a method of representation comparable with historiography itself.

The films discussed in this book map some of the developments within the genre and point to a range of generic conventions as they continue to evolve. Many other films and movements within the cinema invite further study. Latin American and New German cinema, for example, offer still more testimony to the central importance and the political nature of the historical fiction film.

The heritage of colonialism has been a compelling subject in the cinema of Latin America. *Lucia* (1968) and *Reed: Mexico insurgente* (*Reed: Insurgent Mexico*, 1970) present illuminating points of contact with this study. *Lucia* uses the romantic couple and the relationship between political consciousness and private passion as a pivotal device in its provocative three-part structure. Its opening episode, set in nineteenth-century Cuba, draws upon a tragic love affair, similar to the one in *Senso*. *Reed: Insurgent Mexico* strikes a vivid contrast with *Reds*. This Mexican production portrays John Reed in the period that precedes the beginning of the Beatty film, when the journalist was following the armies of Pancho Villa and reporting on the Mexican Revolution. Politics blocks out the romance, and the only object of the protagonist's passion is the revolution itself. The film draws upon the tradition of documentary and neo-realism and portrays Reed's move from detached journalist to revolutionary activist. The spectacle of combat and the incessant movement of war characterize the film in a manner that might be usefully compared to Visconti's staging of the Battle of Custoza.

Anton Kaes in *From Hitler to Heimat* and Thomas Elsaesser in *New German Cinema: A History* focus on the crucial role of the historical film in coming to terms with the heritage of National Socialism.[1] While the romantic couple remains a central figure in films such as *Die Ehe der Maria Braun* (*The Marriage of Maria Braun*, 1978) and *Deutschland bleiche Mutter* (*Germany, Pale Mother*, 1979), the family serves as an emblem of the national community that appears to supersede the position of the couple. The critique of the spectacle and the spectacle's association with the politics of the modern state link Hans Jürgen Syberberg's *Ludwig: Requiem für einen jungfräulichen König* (*Ludwig—Requiem for a Virgin King*, 1972) and *Hitler: ein Film aus Deutschland* (*Our Hitler*, 1977) to concerns explored in *The Rise to Power of Louis XIV*.

Meanwhile, the political address of historical fiction even in mainstream Hollywood cinema is borne out by such recent films as *JFK* (1991) and *Malcolm X* (1992). No study can offer the final

word on such a rich and evolving form. My intention has been
to provide a framework for a continuing discussion by illuminating the vital concerns and defining relationships of the historical
fiction film.

Notes

Chapter 1 | Analyzing the Historical Fiction Film

1. Karl Marx, *The Eighteenth Brumaire of Louis Bonaparte* (New York: International Publishers, 1977), p. 5.
2. Pierre Sorlin, *The Film in History: Restaging the Past* (Totowa, N.J.: Barnes and Noble, 1980), p. 208.
3. Siegfried Kracauer, *Theory of Film: The Redemption of Physical Reality* (New York: Oxford University Press, 1960), p. 77.
4. Thomas Elsaesser, "Film History As Social History: The Dieterle/Warner Brothers Bio-Pic," *Wide Angle* 8:2 (1986): 28.
5. D. W. Griffith, "Some Prophecies: Film and Theatre, Screenwriting, Education," in *Focus on Griffith*, ed. Harry M. Geduld (Englewood Cliffs, N.J.: Spectrum Book, Prentice-Hall, 1971), p. 34.
6. Virginia Schultz, "Interview with Roberto Rossellini, February 22–24, 1971, in Houston, Texas," *Film Culture* 52 (Spring 1971): 7.
7. "John Ford's *Young Mr. Lincoln*," a collective text by the editors of *Cahiers du Cinéma*, trans. Helen Lackner and Diana Matias, *Screen* 13, 3 (Autumn 1972).
8. Jean-Louis Comolli, "Historical Fiction: A Body Too Much," trans. Ben Brewster, *Screen* 2 (Summer 1978): 48.
9. Georg Lukacs, *The Historical Novel*, trans. Hannah Mitchell and Stanley Mitchell (Harmondsworth, England: Penguin, 1976), p. 44.

10. Comolli and his colleagues at *Cahiers du Cinéma*, along with later commentaries by Pierre Sorlin and Miriam White, spark a stimulating dialogue on historical fiction, but they do not attempt to generate a genre model for film. Marcia Landy in her chapter on "Historical Film," in *British Film Genres* (Princeton: Princeton University Press, 1992), offers a cogent exception.

11. René Welleck and Austin Warren, *Theory of Literature* (Harmondsworth, England: Penguin, 1949), p. 226.

12. Claude Lévi-Strauss, "The Structural Study of Myth," in *Structural Anthropology*, trans. Claire Jacobson and Brooke Grundfest Schoepf (London: Allen Lane, Penguin, 1968).

13. Thomas Schatz, "The Structural Influence: New Directions in Film Genre Study," *Quarterly Review of Film Studies* 3 (1977): 308–309. See also Rick Altman, "A Semantic/Syntactic Approach to Film Genre," *Cinema Journal* 3 (Spring 1984).

14. Hans Robert Jauss, "Literary History as a Challenge to Literary Theory," in *Toward an Aesthetic of Reception*, trans. Timothy Bahti, with an introduction by Paul de Man (Minneapolis: University of Minnesota Press, 1982).

15. Rick Altman, *The American Film Musical* (Bloomington: Indiana University Press, 1987), p. 108.

16. Paul Vanderwood, "Introduction: A Political Barometer," in *Juarez*, ed. Paul Vanderwood (Madison: University of Wisconsin Press, 1983).

17. Sergei Eisenstein, "Dickens, Griffith and the Film Today," in *Film Form*, ed. and trans. Jay Leyda (New York: Harcourt, Brace and World, 1949), p. 244 (emphasis in original).

18. Sergei Eisenstein, "Through Theater to Cinema," in *Film Form*, p. 16.

19. Eisenstein, "Dickens, Griffith and the Film Today," p. 239 (emphasis in original).

20. Joseph Freeman, "Biographical Films," *Theatre Arts Monthly* 12 (1941): 900.

21. David Bordwell and Kristin Thompson, *Film Art: An Introduction* (Reading, Mass.: Addison–Wesley, 1979), p. 58 (emphasis in original).

22. For a detailed study of this important work, see Kristin Thompson, *Eisenstein's Ivan the Terrible: A Neoformal Analysis* (Princeton: Princeton University Press, 1981).

Chapter 2 | The Politics of History

1. The CGT, the national labor confederation, was closely allied to the left and the Popular Front, but refrained from direct affiliation with any political party. The CGT experienced phenomenal growth during and shortly after the 1936 election, increasing membership from one to five million in a few months. See Gordon Wright, *France in Modern Times* (Chicago: Rand McNally, 1960), p. 490.

2. George Cravenne, *Paris Soir,* February 11, 1937; reprinted in "Le Tournage de *La Marseillaise,*" from *La Revue du Cinéma, Image et Son* 268 (February 1973): 24. Here and below, translations, unless otherwise attributed, are by the author.

3. The average cost of a French feature film in 1934 has been estimated to be 1.2 to 2.0 million francs by Elizabeth Grottle Strebel, in "French Social Cinema of the 1930's" (Ph.D. diss., Princeton University, 1974), p. 52.

4. Goffredo Fofi, "The Cinema of the Popular Front in France (1934–38)," *Screen Reader* 1 (1977): 202.

5. James Joll notes the contribution of the working class: See James Joll, "The Front Populaire—After Thirty Years," *Journal of Contemporary History* 1, 2 (1966): 29.

6. James Joll, "The Making of the Popular Front," in *The Decline of the Third Republic,* ed. James Joll (London: Chatto and Windus, 1959), p. 54.

7. Joll quoting Thorez, ibid., p. 62.

8. Joel Colton, *Léon Blum* (New York: Knopf, 1966), p. 275.

9. Claude Gauteur, ed., "Dossier sur *La Marseillaise,*" *La Revue du Cinéma, Image et Son* 268 (February 1973): 25.

10. Cited in R. Pithon, "La Censure des films en France et la crise politique de 1934," *Revue Historique* 258 (1977): 110; cited, in Jonathan Buchsbaum, "Left Political Filmmaking in France in the 1930's" (Ph.D. diss., New York University, 1983), p. 39, n. 27.

11. Cited in Buchsbaum, "Left Political Filmmaking in France in the 1930's," p. 227.

12. Ibid., pp. 230–231.

13. *Ciné-Liberté* 1:3; cited in Buchsbaum, "Left Political Filmmaking in France in the 1930's," p. 233.

14. *Ciné-Liberté* 3 (July–August 1936); cited in Buchsbaum, "Left Political Filmmaking in France in the 1930's," p. 269.

15. Strebel, "French Social Cinema of the 1930's," p. 201.

16. Jean Renoir, "*La Marseillaise,*" *Les Cahiers de la Jeunesse* 7 (February 15, 1938); cited in Buchsbaum, "Left Political Filmmaking in France in the 1930's," p. 309.

17. Jean Renoir quoted in Herman G. Weinberg, "Renoir Films the Voice of the People," in *Saint Cinema: Selected Writings 1929–1970* (New York: DBS Publications, 1970), p. 89.

18. The most powerful among the French ruling class were identified by the left as "200 families," whom the left accused of controlling the nation through interlocking corporate directories, positions at the Bank of France, and their own vast holdings.

19. Georges Rudé, *Interpretations of the French Revolution* (London: Historical Association, 1961), p. 3.

20. Jean Renoir, "Farthingales and Facts," *Sight and Sound* 26 (Summer 1938): n.p.

21. Rudé, *Interpretations of the French Revolution*, pp. 7–8, 10.

22. Jules Michelet, *History of the French Revolution*, vol. 4, books 7–8, trans. Keith Botsford (Wynnwood, Pa.: Livingston, 1972), pp. 13–15.

23. Ibid., p. 35.

24. Hippolyte Adolphe Taine, *The French Revolution*, vol. 2, trans. John Durant (New York: Peter Smith, 1931), p. 165.

25. Ibid., p. 184.

26. Jean Renoir, "Honneur aux Marseillais," *Regards* (February 10, 1938); reprinted in Jean Renoir, *Ecrits 1926–1971*, trans. Elizabeth Grottle Strebel (Paris: Pierre Belford, 1974) p. 253.

27. Michelet, *History of the French Revolution*, p. 53.

28. Taine, *French Revolution*, p. 181.

29. George Lefebvre, *The French Revolution, Volume 1: From Its Origins to 1793*, trans. Elizabeth Moss Evanson (New York: Columbia University Press, 1962), p. x. Note that this is the third revised edition (1957) of Lefebvre's general history of the Revolution. The first edition, written in collaboration with Raymond Guyot and Philippe Sagnac, appeared in 1930. A major revision, written by Lefebvre alone, appeared in 1951.

30. Rudé, *Interpretations of the French Revolution*, p. 20.

31. Ibid., p. 19.

32. Albert Mathiez, *The French Revolution*, trans. Catherine Alison Phillips (New York: Knopf, 1928), p. 163.

33. Lefebvre, *French Revolution*, p. 241.

34. Evelyn Ehrlich also suggests the analogy between Blum and Louis XVI in an unpublished essay, "Jean Renoir and the French Popular Front: Films and Politics, 1935–38."

35. See Colton, *Léon Blum*, pp. 193–195, for a more detailed account of the incident.

36. Renoir, "Farthingales and Facts," n.p.

37. A famous remark: The PCF leader was urging workers to support the Matignon agreement and end the strikes of May–June 1936; see *L'Humanité*, June 12–13, 1936.
38. Michelet, *History of the French Revolution*, p. 195.
39. Ibid., p. 209.
40. Rudé, *Interpretations of the French Revolution*, p. 23.
41. Taine, *French Revolution*, pp. 165–166.
42. Renoir, "La Marche de l'idee," *Cahiers du Cinéma* 23, 196 (December 1967): 13.
43. Taine, *French Revolution*, pp. 219–220.
44. Michelet, *History of the French Revolution*, p. 145.
45. Lefebvre, *French Revolution*, p. 244.
46. Roger Leenhardt, *Esprit*, March 1, 1938; reprinted in "*La Marseillaise* et la critique," *La Revue du Cinéma, Image et Son* 268 (February 1973): 55.
47. François Vinneuil, *L'Action Française*, February 11, 1938; reprinted in *La Revue du Cinéma, Image et Son* 268 (February 1973): 45.
48. Pierre Brisson, *Le Figaro:* reprinted in *La Revue du Cinéma, Image et Son* 268 (February 1973): 50–52.
49. Louis Aragon, *Ce Soir*, February 10, 1938: reprinted in *La Revue du Cinéma, Image et Son* 268 (February 1973): 40.
50. Georges Sadoul, *Regards*, February 10, 1938; reprinted in *La Revue du Cinéma, Image et Son* 268 (February 1973): 42.
51. Marcel Achard in *Marianne*, February 16, 1938, and Henri Jeanson in *La Flèche de Paris*, February 19, 1938; reprinted in "Marcel Achard, Henri Jeanson, Jean Renoir et *La Marseillaise*," *La Revue du Cinéma, Image et Son* 268 (February 1973): 64–70.
52. Harold Salemson, "A Film at War," *Hollywood Quarterly* 4 (1946): 416–419.
53. Ibid.
54. Ibid.

Chapter 3 | Hollywood History and the French Revolution

Acknowledgments: Thanks to Professor Matthew H. Bernstein of Emory University for his generous assistance and advice, particularly for access to various documents he has gathered for his research. Thanks as well to Middlebury College Faculty Development Fund for financial assistance and to Professor Robert Maniquis of U.C.L.A. and "The French Revolution: A U.C.L.A. Bicentennial Program" for inviting me to deliver the initial draft of this chapter.

1. *Variety*, February 11, 1948, page unknown.
2. Georges Sadoul, *Dictionary of Film Makers*, trans., ed., and updated by Peter Morris (Berkeley: University of California Press, 1972), p. 167.
3. Robert E. Smith, "Mann in the Dark," *Bright Lights* 2:1 (Fall 1976): 13.
4. Tino Balio, *United Artists: The Company That Changed the Film Industry* (Madison: University of Wisconsin Press, 1987), p. 26; for further details on the Eagle–Lion studio, see chap. 1, "Prelude at Eagle–Lion."
5. Matthew H. Bernstein, "Defiant Cooperation: Walter Wanger and Independent Production in Hollywood, 1934–1949" (Ph.D. diss., University of Wisconsin, Madison, 1987); see pp. 306–341 for a detailed treatment of Wanger's career at Eagle–Lion.
6. Philip Yordan, telephone interview with the author, October 14, 1989. Yordan explained that he took on the project at the request of his friend, Anthony Mann. He worked from the screenplay written by MacKenzie, but never discussed the work with the initial screenwriter, nor did he undertake any research on the historical events portrayed. Yordan saw his task as one of transforming the screenplay into an action picture that could be realized on a limited budget. After quickly completing his draft, Yordan left the production and was not consulted again. Fans of *Johnny Guitar* may be interested in the second meeting between the protagonists of *Reign of Terror*, Madelon and Charles, where the celebrated "Lie to Me" speech from *Johnny Guitar* is rehearsed.
7. Christopher Wicking and Barrie Pattison, "Interview with Anthony Mann," *Screen* 10 (July–October 1969): 36.
8. Robert Ottoson, *A Reference Guide to the American Film Noir, 1940–1958* (Metuchen, N.J.: Scarecrow Press, 1981), p. 148.
9. Alain Silver and Elizabeth Ward, *Film Noir* (Woodstock, N.Y.: Overlook Press, 1979), p. 330.
10. Among those who praise the director's achievement, Andrew Sarris, Jim Kitses, and Robin Wood fail to mention *Reign of Terror*, and Jeanine Basinger in the only extended monograph on Mann dismisses the work as a formal exercise lacking in content, "a minor film": see Jeanine Basinger, *Anthony Mann* (Boston: Twayne, 1979), pp. 74–75. Also see Andrew Sarris, *The American Cinema: Directors and Directions, 1929–1968* (New York: Dutton, 1968); Jim Kitses, *Horizons West* (Bloomington: Indiana University Press, 1969); and Robin Wood, "Anthony Mann," in *Cinema: A Critical Dictionary*, vol. 2, ed. Richard Roud (New York: Viking, 1980).

11. Walter Wanger, memo to Anthony Mann, October 1, 1948, State Historical Society of Wisconsin, Madison, Walter Wanger Papers, Box 88, File 21.

12. The studio press books for both *Reign of Terror* and *The Black Book* are available at the New York Public Library of the Performing Arts, Lincoln Center, New York City.

13. *Weekly Variety*, July 20, 1949, p. 3; ibid., July 27, 1949, p. 17.

14. *Weekly Variety*, October 26, 1949, p. 13; November 2, 1949, p. 15.

15. The other Wanger production for Eagle–Lion, *Tulsa*, reported a loss of more than $700,000: Bernstein, "Defiant Cooperation: Walter Wanger and Independent Production in Hollywood, 1934–1949," p. 402.

16. Reviews examined appeared in the *New York Times*, October 17, 1949; *New York Herald Tribune*, October 17, 1949; *Daily Variety*, July 14, 1949; *Weekly Variety*, May 18, 1949; *Newsweek*, December 5, 1949; *New Yorker*, October 5, 1949; *Los Angeles Times*, July 16, 1949; *Cue*, October 22, 1949; and *Hollywood Reporter*, July 14, 1949.

17. R. R. Palmer, *Twelve Who Ruled* (1941; Princeton: Princeton University Press, 1969), p. 373.

18. Georges Lefebvre, *The French Revolution*, vol. 2, trans. John Hall Stewart and James Friguliette (New York: Columbia University Press, 1964), p. 134.

    A likely source for MacKenzie in building his screenplay, and a text cited in the first Eagle–Lion press book, was Thomas Carlyle's *The French Revolution*. The two closing chapters of "Thermidor," Book VI of Carlyle's work, outline the central events of the film. (Book I is *The Bastille*.) See the Modern Library edition (New York: Random House, 1934).

19. Samuel F. Scott and Barry Rothaus, eds., *The Historical Dictionary of the French Revolution* (Westport, Conn.: Greenwood Press, 1985), vol. 1, p. 66.

20. Carlyle, *French Revolution*, p. 689.

21. Lefebvre, *French Revolution*, vol. 2, p. 139.

22. Paul Schrader, "Notes on Film Noir," in *Film Genre Reader*, ed. Barry Keith Grant (Austin: University of Texas Press, 1986), p. 177.

23. For a brief review of events during this period, see Gordon Wright, *France in Modern Times* (New York: Norton, 1981), pp. 415–418.

24. Frank Freidel and Alan Brinkley, *America in the Twentieth Century* (New York: Knopf, 1982), p. 359.

25. As quoted from *Weekly Variety* by Larry Ceplair and Steven En-

glund, *The Inquisition in Hollywood: Politics in the Film Community 1930–1960* (Garden City, N.Y.: Doubleday, 1980), p. 211.

26. Bernstein, "Defiant Cooperation: Walter Wanger and Independent Production in Hollywood, 1934–1949," p. 329.

27. Walter Wanger, letter to Max Youngstein, April 29, 1949, Walter Wanger Papers, Box 48, File 4.

28. Richard Maltby, *Harmless Entertainment* (Metuchen, N.J.: Scarecrow Press, 1983). See pp. 140–144 for his treatment of *Reign of Terror*.

Chapter 4 | Risorgimento History and Screen Spectacle

1. Robert Hawkins, *Variety*, September 19, 1954, n.p., in New York Public Library of the Performing Arts, Lincoln Center, New York City, Venice Film Festival file.

2. John Francis Lane, "The Hurricane Visconti," *Films and Filming*, December 1954, p. 8.

3. As reported by Gaia Servadio, *Luchino Visconti* (London: Weidenfeld and Nicolson, 1981), p. 139.

4. Don Ranvaud, "*Senso:* Masterpiece as Minefield," *Monthly Film Bulletin* 591 (April 1983): 110.

5. Arrigo Solmi, *The Making of Modern Italy* (1925; Port Washington, N.Y.: Kennikat Press, 1970), p. 121.

6. Edgar Holt, *Risorgimento: The Making of Italy* (London: Macmillan, 1970), p. 285.

7. Gianfranco Poggi, "Luchino Visconti and the Italian Cinema," *Film Quarterly* 6 (Spring 1960): 20. For a review of the controversy sparked by *Senso*'s release among Italian neo-realist critics, see Millicent Marcus, "Visconti's *Senso:* The Risorgimento According to Gramsci," in *Italian Film in the Light of Neorealism* (Princeton: Princeton University Press, 1986), chap. 7. In her informative and intelligent essay Marcus discusses the attack made on Visconti for abandoning neo-realism by Luigi Chiarini and Cesare Zavattini, as well as Guido Aristarco's defense of *Senso* as a realist work in the tradition of the nineteenth-century novel as described by Lukacs. The Italian texts are to be found in *Antologia di "Cinema nuovo," 1952–1958*, ed. Guido Aristarco (Florence: Guaraldi, 1975). Marcus also points to the influence of Gramsci and Lukacs upon the production, which I treat in greater detail in this chapter. For a more expansive treatment of *Senso*, see Leger Grindon, "The Representation of History in the Fiction Film" (Ph.D. diss., New York University, 1986), chap. 3.

8. George A. Huaco, *The Sociology of Film Art* (New York: Basic Books, 1965), pp. 185–86.

9. Jane Cianfarra, "Venice Prepares for Its Annual Film Fete," *New York Times*, August 9, 1951, in New York Public Library of the Performing Arts, Venice Film Festival file.

10. As noted by Gavin Lambert, "The Signs of Predicament," *Sight and Sound* 3 (January–March 1955): 148.

11. Norman Kogan, *A Political History of Postwar Italy* (New York: Praeger, 1966), p. 92.

12. Quoted in Huaco, *Sociology of Film Art*, p. 193.

13. As quoted by Pierre Leprohon, *The Italian Cinema*, trans. Roger Greaves and Oliver Stallybrass (New York: Praeger, 1972), p. 127.

14. In May 1946, just before the first general elections after World War II, Visconti, an aristocrat whose original name was Luchino Visconti de Modrone, published "The Reason Why I Shall Vote Communist" in *L'Unita*, the party newspaper. Visconti received financial support from the party for *La Terra Trema*, and he admired Palmiro Togliatti, the party leader, and regularly invited him to the openings of his plays and films. Togliatti, reciprocating, praised Visconti's work. See Servadio's biography, *Luchino Visconti*, particularly pp. 113–114.

15. For a translation of "Marcia Nuziale" by Gloria Monti, see Grindon, "Representation of History in the Fiction Film," app. A.

16. See correspondence between Suso Cecchi d'Amico and Grindon, ibid., app. B.

17. See d'Amico–Grindon correspondence, ibid.

18. Jacques Doniol-Valcroze and Jean Comarchi, "Luchino Visconti Interviewed," *Sight and Sound* 3–4 (Autumn 1959): 147.

19. Servadio, *Luchino Visconti*, p. 136.

20. Doniol-Valcroze and Comarchi, "Luchino Visconti Interviewed," p. 191.

21. After its Venice premiere, *Senso* had a respectable run, earning 571 million lira in Italy and placing eighth among domestic releases for the year. However, the film's costs ran to 700 million, and Lux Films was thrown into difficulties. See Ranvaud, "*Senso:* Masterpiece as Minefield," for further details. Further cuts followed the film's release in Germany and Britain, and *Senso* had to wait fourteen years, until Visconti had established an American following with *Rocco e i suei fratelli* (*Rocco and His Brothers*, 1960) and *The Leopard* (1963) before opening in New York.

22. See Grindon, "Representation of History in the Fiction Film," app. A, for the text of this scene and a note on further cuts.

23. All dialogue quoted from *Senso* follows the screenplay found in *Luchino Visconti: Two Screenplays*, trans. Judith Green (New York: Orion, 1970).
24. A. William Salomone, ed., *Italy from the Risorgimento to Fascism* (Garden City, N.Y.: Anchor Books, 1970), pp. 303–304.
25. Benedetto Croce, *A History of Europe in the Nineteenth Century*, trans. Henry Furst (London: George Allen and Unwin, 1934), p. 225.
26. Ibid., pp. 213, 219.
27. Ibid., p. 221.
28. Salomone, *Italy from the Risorgimento to Fascism*, pp. xxxvii–xxxviii.
29. Antonio Gramsci, *Selections from the Prison Notebooks*, ed. and trans. Quentin Hoare and Geoffrey Nowell Smith (New York: International Publishers, 1971), p. 90.
30. Ibid., p. 57.
31. Ibid., p. 74.
32. Denis Mack Smith, *Italy: A Modern History*, rev. ed. (Ann Arbor: University of Michigan Press, 1969), p. 39.
33. Pierre Sorlin, *The Film in History: Restaging the Past* (Totowa, N.J.: Barnes and Noble, 1980), p. 127.
34. Gramsci, *Prison Notebooks*, p. 89.
35. D'Amico–Grindon correspondence, in Grindon, "Representation of History in the Fiction Film," app. B.
36. Doniol-Valcroze and Comarchi, "Luchino Visconti Interviewed," p. 147.
37. Gramsci, *Prison Notebooks*, pp. 57–58.
38. D'Amico–Grindon correspondence, in Grindon, "Representation of History in the Fiction Film," app. B.
39. Smith, *Italy: A Modern History*, p. 492.
40. Serge Hughes, *The Fall and Rise of Modern Italy* (New York: Macmillan, 1967), p. 223.
41. Martin Clark, *Modern Italy, 1871–1982* (New York: Longman, 1984), p. 357.
42. Kogan, *Political History of Postwar Italy*, p. 68.
43. For a detailed review of the episode, see ibid., pp. 80–88.
44. Ibid., pp. 87–88.
45. Doniol-Valcroze and Comarchi, "Luchino Visconti Interviewed," p. 145.
46. Georg Lukacs, *The Historical Novel*, trans. Hannah Mitchell and Stanley Mitchell (London: Merlin Press, 1962), p. 169.
47. Georg Lukacs, "Preface," in *Studies in European Realism* (New York: Grosset and Dunlop, 1964), p. 6.
48. Gramsci, *Prison Notebooks*, p. 81.
49. Ibid., p. 98.

Chapter 5 | The Politics of the Spectacle

1. Virginia Schultz, "Interview with Roberto Rossellini, February 22–24, 1971, in Houston, Texas," *Film Culture* 52 (Spring 1971): 16.

2. Francisco Llinas and Miquel Marias, with Antonio Drove and Jose Oliver, "A Panorama of History," *Screen* 4 (Winter 1973–74): 85. The interview with Roberto Rossellini was conducted in Madrid, January 1970.

3. D. L. Hanley, A. P. Kerr, and N. H. Waites, *Contemporary France: Politics and Society since 1945* (London: Routledge and Kegan Paul, 1979), pp. 100, 109. Philip M. Williams and Martin Harrison, *Politics and Society in de Gaulle's Republic* (London: Longman, 1971), concur in linking Louis XIV and de Gaulle in a common political tradition: "From the beginning it [the Fifth Republic] functioned as a republican monarchy dominated by a man who preeminently belonged to the French tradition of *hommes providentiels.* . . . Thus, although the distinctive flavor of the Fifth Republic was inseparable from the personality and career of the man who dominated it for more than a decade, his style touched many historical chords in a nation with a greater awareness than most of its past. The 1958 constitution, as moulded by De Gaulle to his own wishes, proved an exceptionally convenient framework for a style of leadership which drew constantly on the example of earlier heroic figures" (pp. 376–377).

4. Quoted in Williams and Harrison, *Politics and Society in de Gaulle's Republic*, p. 176.

5. Hanley, Kerr, and Waites, *Contemporary France*, p. 120.

6. These statistics regarding production are noted in Schultz, "Interview with Roberto Rossellini," pp. 16–17, 22; and Jonas Mekas, "Rossellini on *The Rise of Louis XIV*," in *Movie Journal: The Rise of the New American Cinema, 1959–1971* (New York: Collier Books, Macmillan, 1972), p. 292. Peter Brunette in *Roberto Rossellini* (New York: Oxford University Press, 1987), p. 281, sets the production cost at approximately $130,000.

7. Philippe Erlanger, correspondence with the author. See Leger Grindon, "The Representation of History in the Fiction Film" (Ph.D. diss., New York University, 1986), app. E.

8. *Who's Who in France (1981–82)*, 15th ed. (Paris: Editions Jacques Lafitte), p. 541.

9. Robert Coles, "Books, Briefly Noted," *New Yorker*, October 31, 1970, p. 156.

10. Erlanger: see Grindon, "Representation of History in the Fiction Film," app. E.

11. Ibid.
12. Roberto Rossellini, quoted in "Cinema and Television: Jean Renoir and Roberto Rossellini Interviewed by André Bazin," *Sight and Sound* 28, 1 (Winter 1958–59): 27, 29.
13. David Degener, ed., *Sighting Rossellini* (Berkeley: University of California Art Museum, n.d. [ca. 1974]), n.p. This is a useful and informative text, unfortunately poorly circulated, with essays on and by Rossellini.
14. Llinas and Marias, "Panorama of History," p. 88.
15. Roberto Rossellini, "Rossellini Manifesto," trans. Judith White, *Screen* 4 (Winter 1973–74): 110–11.
16. Schultz, "Interview with Roberto Rossellini," p. 7.
17. Eric Sherman and John Dorr, "Roberto Rossellini Interviewed," *Take-One* 4 (March–April 1973): 20.
18. Jose Soltero and Toby Mussman, "Interview with Roberto Rossellini," *Medium* 2 (Winter 1967–68): 60.
19. Sherman and Dorr, "Roberto Rossellini Interviewed," p. 20.
20. Roberto Rossellini, "Man's Well-Being, Behavior, and the Spread of Knowledge," *Film Culture* 56–57 (Spring 1973): 21.
21. Jean Collet and Claude-Jean Philippe, "Roberto Rossellini: *La Prise du Pouvoir par Louis XIV*," *Cahiers du Cinéma* 183 (October 1966): 16. Translation by the author.
22. Ibid., pp. 18–19.
23. Genêt, "Letter from Paris," *New Yorker*, October 22, 1966, p. 200.
24. Mekas, "Rossellini on *The Rise of Louis XIV*," p. 292.
25. Jacques Siclier, "*La Prise du Pouvoir par Louis XIV*," *Le Monde*, October 8, 1966, p. 18. Translation by the author.
26. Jérôme Favard, "Rossellini revient au cinéma en passant par la télé," *L'Humanité*, October 8, 1966, television section, n.p. Translation by the author.
27. Incident at a press conference related by Annette Michelson in conversation with the author, winter 1983.
28. Philip Williams writes of the campaign in "The Rivals Emerge: The 1965 Presidential Election," in Philip Williams, with David Goldey and Martin Harrison, *French Politicians and Elections, 1951–1969* (London: Cambridge University Press, 1970): "In 1965 France had been at peace for three years, and Frenchmen were preoccupied with the domestic problems which had never seemed to command the great man's attention. After seven years, and at 75, their benevolent monarch was seeking re-election for seven years more. But he could not last forever, and increasingly they were worried about 'afterwards': *l'après gaullisme*. . . . Mitterand

and especially Lecanuet stressed their youth, and referred discreetly to De Gaulle's age and 'the moment of decision which must come eventually.' There were warnings that the General might not serve out his term, but might try to choose a successor unknown to his voters. His decision to stand again, and his reasons, were called an open vote of no confidence in the UNR (the political party led by De Gaulle)" (pp. 189, 191).

29. Collet and Philippe, "Roberto Rossellini: *La Prise du Pouvoir par Louis XIV*," p. 16.

30. Williams, "The Rivals Emerge," p. 191.

31. James Roy MacBean, "Rossellini's Materialist Mise-en-Scene of *La Prise du Pouvoir par Louis XIV*," in *Film and Revolution* (Bloomington: University of Indiana Press, 1975), pp. 209–229.

32. Alan Sheridan, *Michel Foucault: The Will to Power* (New York: Tavistock Publications, 1980), p. 47.

33. Foucault, Foreword to the English edition, *The Order of Things* (New York: Random House, Vintage Books, 1973), p. xi.

34. Foucault, *The Order of Things*, p. 168.

35. Michel Foucault, "History of Systems of Thought," in *Language, Counter-Memory, Practice*, edited with an introduction by Donald F. Bouchard, trans. Donald F. Bouchard and Sherry Simon (Ithaca, N.Y.: Cornell University Press, 1977), p. 200.

36. Though Foucault developed the explicit connections between political power and the episteme, or systems of knowledge, only in the next decade, the implicit relation could already be found in *Madness and Civilization* (1961) and *The Birth of the Clinic* (1963), as well as in *The Order of Things*. In an interview from 1977, quoted in "Truth and Power," in *Power/Knowledge*, ed. Colin Gordon, trans. Colin Gordon, Leo Marshall, John Meplhan, and Kate Soper (New York: Random House, Pantheon Books, 1980), Foucault comments on "the problem of the regime, the politics of the scientific statement": "It was these different regimes that I tried to identify and describe in *The Order of Things*. . . .

"But what was lacking here was this problem of the 'discursive regime' of the effects of power peculiar to the play of statements. . . . This same central problem, which at that time I had not yet properly isolated, emerges in two very different aspects at the point of junction of *Madness and Civilization* and *The Order of Things*" (pp. 112–113).

37. Foucault, "Prison Talk," in *Power/Knowledge*, p. 39.

38. The characterization of the Queen Mother deserves particular attention because this is the one point where Erlanger takes excep-

tion to the film's representation of history. Indeed, Anne seems to be used as a dramatic foil and political opponent to enable the film to express its historical perspective. This instance further emphasizes the genre's use of romance as a vehicle for interpretation.

39. Quoted in Degener, *Sighting Rossellini*, p. 24.
40. September 24, 1971, p. 1144.
41. Coles, "Books, Briefly Noted," p. 156.
42. Philippe Erlanger, *Louis XIV*, trans. Stephen Cox (New York: Praeger, 1970), p. 99.
43. Though Rossellini adopts episodes from Erlanger's book, he often accents them very differently. In the case of Queen Anne, it appears that she did not contest her son's authority but supported it. I would speculate that the film adapted the queen to the romantic conventions of the genre and used her as a dramatic vehicle for its historical interpretation. In developing the scenario, these considerations probably outweighed an accurate portrait.
44. Erlanger, *Louis XIV*, p. 109. The association between Louis XIV and de Gaulle echoes from phrases like "revolutions . . . originating at the summit," "plebiscite," and "coup d'état."
45. John B. Wolfe, *Louis XIV* (New York: Norton, 1968), p. 142.
46. Erlanger, *Louis XIV*, p. 128.
47. Pierre Goubert, *Louis XIV and Twenty Million Frenchmen*, trans. Anne Carter (New York: Random House, Vintage Books, 1972), p. 24.
48. Ibid., pp. 329–330; the title of the journal has changed, but it is generally referred to simply as *Les Annales*.
49. Fernand Braudel, "The Situation of History in 1950," in *On History*, trans. Sarah Matthews (Chicago: University of Chicago Press, 1980), pp. 11–12.
50. Fernand Braudel, "History and Sociology," ibid., pp. 74–75.
51. Ibid.
52. Brunette, *Roberto Rossellini*, p. 262.
53. Schultz, "Interview with Roberto Rossellini," p. 20.
54. Ibid.
55. Llinas and Marias, "Panorama of History," pp. 103–104.
56. Schultz, "Interview with Roberto Rossellini," p. 17.
57. André Bazin, "In Defense of Rossellini," in *What Is Cinema?* vol. 2, trans. Hugh Gray (Berkeley: University of California Press, 1971), pp. 97, 100.
58. Rossellini, quoted in Degener, *Sighting Rossellini*, p. 11.
59. Schultz, "Interview with Roberto Rossellini," p. 19.

60. Rossellini, quoted in Degener, *Sighting Rossellini*, p. 14 (emphasis in original).
61. Schultz, "Interview with Roberto Rossellini," p. 4.
62. Sherman and Dorr, "Roberto Rossellini Interviewed," p. 21.
63. Schultz, "Interview with Roberto Rossellini," p. 15.
64. Adriano Aprà and Maurizio Ponzi, "An Interview with Roberto Rossellini," *Screen* 4 (Winter 1973–74): 118–119.
65. Brunette, *Roberto Rossellini*, p. 282.
66. Rossellini acknowledges in Soltero and Mussman, "Interview with Roberto Rossellini," that "Saint-Simon was a great aid" (p. 61), and his memoir is an important source for the film's Versailles episodes.
67. Saint-Simon, *Saint-Simon at Versailles*, selected and translated from the Memoirs of M. le Duc de Saint-Simon by Lucy Norton, with a preface by Nancy Mitford (New York: Harper and Brothers, 1958), p. 261.
68. Guy Debord, *Society of the Spectacle*, trans. Black and Red (Detroit: Black and Red, 1973), n.p., paragraph 17 (emphasis in original).
69. Ibid., paragraph 29.
70. Saint-Simon, *Saint-Simon at Versailles*, p. 254.
71. Michel Foucault, "Two Lectures," in *Power/Knowledge*, p. 97.
72. Foucault, "Truth and Power," p. 119.
73. Saint-Simon, *Saint-Simon at Versailles*, p. 262.
74. Debord, *Society of the Spectacle*, paragraph 134.
75. Ibid., paragraph 61.

Chapter 6 | Politics and History in Contemporary Hollywood

1. Sergei Eisenstein, "Dickens, Griffith and the Film Today," in *Film Form* ed. and trans. Jay Leyda (New York: Harcourt, Brace and World, 1949), p. 234.
2. Elizabeth Hardwick, "A Bunch of Reds," *New York Review of Books*, March 4, 1982, pp. 9–16; Arthur Schlesinger, Jr., "History and the Imagination: *Ragtime* and *Reds*," *American Heritage* 33, 3 (1982): 42–43; Daniel Bell, "*Reds:* A Fable," *Partisan Review* 49 (1982): 445–452; William F. Buckley, "On Seeing *Reds*," *National Review*, February 5, 1982, p. 133.
3. Dennis Holly, "*Reds* Tops Critics Best Lists," *Variety*, January 27, 1982, p. 30; *Reds* was honored in thirty-one out of thirty-eight lists surveyed.
4. Kitty Bowe Hearty, "Decade's Best," *Premiere*, November 1989,

pp. 106–107; Pat McGilligan and Mark Rowland, "The Eighties," *American Film*, November 1989, pp. 23–29.

5. Joy Gould Boyum, "*Reds:* Love and Revolution," *Wall Street Journal*, December 4, 1981.

6. Pauline Kael, "Dreamers," in *Taking It All In* (New York: Holt, Rinehart and Winston, 1984), p. 278. The review essay originally appeared in the *New Yorker*, December 21, 1981.

7. "Art Directors: Richard Sylbert Interviewed by Joseph McBride," *Film Comment* (January–February 18 1982): 44; Richard Grenier, "Bolshevism for the 80s," *Commentary* 73 (March 1982): 56.

8. In the Soviet Union Sergei Bondarchuk was preparing a film about John Reed. He saw *Bonnie and Clyde* and thought that the actor playing Clyde Barrow looked remarkably like the radical journalist. Beatty was contacted, read the screenplay, but turned down the offer to play the American Communist. For reference to this event, see Aaron Latham, "Warren Beatty Seriously," *Rolling Stone*, April 1, 1982, p. 19; Mike Poole and John Wyver, *Powerplays: Trevor Griffiths in Television* (London: B.F.I. Publishing, 1984), p. 124. David Thompson reports that Beatty traveled in the Soviet Union in the late 1960s, possibly the same journey prompted by the offer to play Reed. There the actor met a Russian woman who had been Reed's lover; see David Thompson, "Looking for Mr. Beatty," *California*, January 1982, p. 73.

9. Ronald Brownstein, *The Power and the Glitter* (New York: Pantheon, 1990), p. 242.

10. Ibid., p. 243.

11. Rosenstone, a member of the history department at the California Institute of Technology, is credited as the historical consultant on *Reds*. His *Romantic Revolutionary: A Biography of John Reed* (New York: Knopf, 1975) was published in 1975, and a paperback edition accompanied the release of the film.

12. Max Le Blond, "Trevor Griffiths," in *British Dramatists since World War II, Part I: A–L of The Dictionary of Literary Biography*, vol. 13, ed. Stanley Weintraub (Detroit: Gale Research Co., 1982), p. 219.

13. Information about the Beatty–Griffiths collaboration can be found in Poole and Wyver *Powerplays*, particularly chap. 6; and in "History to Hollywood: Mick Eaton Talks to Trevor Griffiths," *Screen* 23, 2 (1982). In a letter to the author dated June 3, 1992, Griffiths confirmed key dates regarding his contribution to the project.

14. Thompson, "Looking for Mr. Beatty," p. 72.

15. "Art Directors," p. 45.

16. "History to Hollywood," p. 64.

17. Carolyn Porter, "*Reds,*" *Film Quarterly* 35 (September 1982): 44.
18. "A Question of Control: Warren Beatty Interviewed by Gavin Smith," *Film Comment* 28 (January–February 1992): 36.
19. For reports on the trials of the shooting, see Latham, "Warren Beatty Seriously," p. 20; Thompson, "Looking for Mr. Beatty," p. 75.
20. Latham, "Warren Beatty Seriously," p. 20.
21. David Bordwell, with Janet Staiger and Kristin Thompson, *The Classical Hollywood Cinema: Film Style and Mode of Production to 1960* (New York: Columbia University Press, 1985), p. 16.
22. Richard Corliss, "Go On—The Limit," *Time,* December 7, 1981, p. 67.
23. E. Ann Kaplan, "Talking *Reds,*" *Socialist Review* 12 (March–April 1982): 115.
24. Eisenstein, "Dickens, Griffith and the Film Today," p. 244.
25. Rosenstone has also described this image as "the controlling metaphor of *Reds.*" See "*Reds* as History," *Reviews in American History* 10 (1982): 310.
26. Ed Buscombe, "Making Love and Revolution," *Screen* 23, 2 (1982): 73.
27. Quoted in "History to Hollywood," p. 63.
28. Vincent Canby, "The Screen: Beatty's 'Reds' with Diane Keaton," *New York Times,* December 4, 1981.
29. Schlesinger, "*Ragtime* and *Reds,*" pp. 42–43.
30. Jonathan Rosenbaum, "Jack Reed's Christmas Puppy," *Sight and Sound* 51, (1982): 111.
31. Rosenstone, "*Reds* as History," pp. 300–301.
32. *American Film* matched the names and faces of the twenty-six witnesses whose voices and faces appear in the film: see *American Film,* March 1982, p. 8.
33. Robert Rosenstone told me in May 1991 that Beatty and his crew visited Dasburg at his home in Taos, New Mexico, the day before he died. Hardly able to talk, Dasburg made little sense, and the interview produced no usable information. Rosenstone believes that Dasburg's voice is used at some point in the film. Dasburg's obituary appeared in *New York Times,* August 14, 1979.
34. Kael, "Dreamers," p. 278.
35. "Question of Control," p. 36.
36. Sarah Kozloff, *Invisible Storytellers* (Berkeley: University of California Press, 1988), p. 73.
37. Thompson, "Looking for Mr. Beatty," p. 76.
38. Rosenbaum, "Jack Reed's Christmas Puppy," pp. 111–112.

39. E. Ann Kaplan, *"Reds:* Images of Love and Politics," *Social Policy* 12 (Spring 1982): 54.
40. Buscombe, "Making Love and Revolution," p. 73.
41. Kael, "Dreamers," p. 281.
42. Rosenstone, *"Reds* as History," p. 300.

| Coda

1. Anton Kaes, *From Hitler to Heimat* (Cambridge, Mass.: Harvard University Press, 1989); Thomas Elsaesser, *New German Cinema: A History* (New Brunswick, N.J.: Rutgers University Press, 1989).

Index